Scott Foresman

Reading

Practice Book

#1   Hoffman

Isa   S.   Barraza

Scott Foresman

Editorial Offices: Glenview, Illinois • Parsippany, New Jersey • New York, New York
Sales Offices: Parsippany, New Jersey • Duluth, Georgia • Glenview, Illinois
Coppell, Texas • Ontario, California

Teresa Anderko: pp. 187, 252, 259, 277; **Nelle Davis:** p. 279;
Waldo Dunn: pp. 8, 26, 157, 172, 247, 292; **Vickie Learner:**
p. 110; **Mapping Specialists:** pp. 111, 119; **Laurie O'Keefe:** p. 269;
Joel Snyder: pp. 12, 32, 52, 68, 112, 132, 148, 167, 192, 222, 242;
TSI Graphics: pp. 9, 39, 40, 49, 58, 63, 79, 99, 100, 113, 129,
137, 159, 199, 232, 239, 243, 289, 300; **N. Jo Tufts:** pp. 118, 142,
158, 178, 198, 262, 267, 272, 282, 297; **Jessica Wolk-Stanley:** pp. 2,
18, 48, 62, 82, 88, 92, 102, 138, 148, 167, 192, 222, 242.

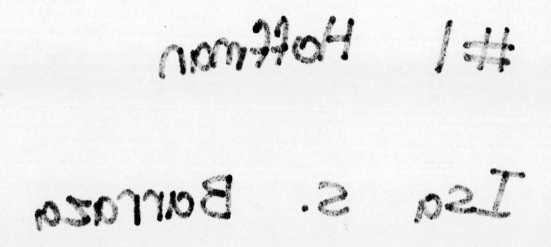

ISBN: 0-328-02249-7
ISBN: 0-328-04053-3

Copyright © Pearson Education, Inc.

All Rights Reserved. Printed in the United States of America. The
blackline masters in this publication are designed for use with
appropriate equipment to reproduce copies for classroom use only.
Scott Foresman grants permission to classroom teachers to reproduce
from these masters.

13 14 15 V011 10 09 08
18 19 20 21 22 23 24 V011 14 13 12 11

Table of Contents

Unit 4

Time and Time Again

	Comprehension	Vocabulary	Selection Test	Phonics/ Word Study	Research and Study Skills
The Yangs' First Thanksgiving	151, 153, 157	152	155–156	158	159–160
The Jr. Iditarod Race	161, 163, 167	162	165–166	168	169–170
The Night Alone	171, 173, 177	172	175–176	178	179–180
The Heart of a Runnner	181, 183, 187	182	185–186	188	189–190
The Memory Box	191, 193, 197	192	195–196	198	199–200

Unit 5

Traveling On

	Comprehension	Vocabulary	Selection Test	Phonics/ Word Study	Research and Study Skills
I Want to Vote!	201, 203, 207	202	205–206	208	209–210
The Long Path to Freedom	211, 213, 217	212	215–216	218	219–220
from Chester Cricket's Pigeon Ride	221, 223, 227	222	225–226	228	229–230
Passage to Freedom: The Sugihara Story	231, 233, 237	232	235–236	238	239–240
Paul Revere's Ride	241, 243, 247	242	245–246	248	249–250

Unit 6

Think of It!

	Comprehension	Vocabulary	Selection Test	Phonics/ Word Study	Research and Study Skills
The Baker's Neighbor	251, 253, 257	252	255–256	258	259–260
Andy's Secret Ingredient	261, 263, 267	262	265–266	268	269–270
In the Days of King Adobe	271, 273, 277	272	275–276	278	279–280
Just Telling the Truth	281, 283, 287	282	285–286	288	289–290
Is It Real?	291, 293, 297	292	295–296	298	299–300

Sequence

- **Sequence** is the order in which things happen. Keeping track of the sequence of events will help you better understand what you read.

- Words such as *then* and *after* are often clues to a sequence. Words such as *meanwhile* and *during* show that several events can happen at once.

- By arranging events in sequence, you can see how one thing leads to another.

Directions: Reread the excerpt from *Homer Price.* On the lines below, write the steps from the box in the order that Mr. Murphy follows them to build a musical mousetrap.

Steps

Make a bargain with the town mayor.
Finally, let the mice go.
Drive up and down the streets.
First, build an organ out of reeds.
Fasten the mousetrap to the car.
Then, compose a tune the mice like.
Let the mice run into the trap.
Next, drive the car to a town.
Then, start the musical mousetrap.
Drive the mice to the city limits.

How to Remove Mice with a Musical Mousetrap

1. _____

2. _____

3. _____

4. _____

5. _____

6. _____

7. _____

8. _____

9. _____

10. _____

Notes for Home: Your child read a story and identified the order in which events occurred. *Home Activity:* Choose a task that your child performs, such as making the bed, and work together to create a list of steps that are required to complete the task.

© Scott Foresman 5

Vocabulary

Directions: Choose the word from the box that best matches each clue. Write the word on the line.

_____ 1. This might keep you from sleeping.

_____ 2. You might go here if you're hungry.

_____ 3. You may not want anyone to read this.

_____ 4. You flip this to turn on a light.

_____ 5. You might do this at a science fair.

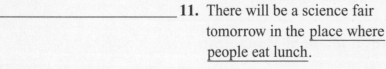

Check the Words You Know
__ cafeteria
__ demonstration
__ diary
__ racket
__ switch
__ triggered

Directions: Write the word from the box that belongs in each group.

6. sparked, began, _____

7. restaurant, diner, _____

8. explosion, noise, _____

9. journal, log, _____

10. show, display, _____

Directions: Choose the word from the box that best replaces the underlined words. Write the word on the line.

_____ 11. There will be a science fair tomorrow in the <u>place where people eat lunch</u>.

_____ 12. I will give a <u>hands-on show</u> of my new invention.

_____ 13. When you flip the <u>device that controls the flow of an electric current</u>, this turns a series of flashing lights.

_____ 14. Once these flashing lights have been <u>caused to begin</u>, the machine's sound system will give off a series of bell whistles and dog barks.

_____ 15. If this <u>loud noise</u> can't wake my brother Michael each morning, I don't know what will!

Write a News Article

Imagine you are a news reporter. On a separate sheet of paper, write an article about a demonstration you have seen. It could be a cooking show, a science fair, a karate class, and so on. Use as many vocabulary words as you can.

Notes for Home: Your child identified vocabulary words in "From the Diary of Leigh Botts." **Home Activity:** Give your child clues to words he or she knows. For example: *Heavy feet on the stairs make this.* Have your child guess the word you are describing. *(racket)*

© Scott Foresman 5

Sequence

- **Sequence** is the order in which things happen.
- Words such as *then* and *after* are often clues to a sequence. Words such as *meanwhile* and *during* show that two or more things happen at the same time.

Directions: Reread what happens in "From the Diary of Leigh Botts" when Leigh builds a burglar alarm for his lunchbox. Then answer the questions below. Think about the sequence in which things happen in the story.

I tore home with all the things I bought. First I made a sign for my door that said

KEEP OUT

MOM

THAT MEANS YOU

Then I went to work fastening one wire from the battery to the switch and from the other side of the switch to the doorbell. Then I fastened a second wire from the battery to the doorbell. It took me a while to get it right. Then I taped the battery in one corner of the lunchbox and the doorbell in another. I stood the switch up at the back of the box and taped that in place, too.

Text excerpt from DEAR MR. HENSHAW by Beverly Cleary. Text Copyright ©1983 by Beverly Cleary. By permission of Morrow Junior Books, a division of William Morrow & Company, Inc.

1. What clue words help you understand the order in which Leigh does things?

   _____

2. What does Leigh do first?

   _____

   _____

3. What does Leigh do last?

   _____

   _____

4. What does Leigh do right after fastening both wires to the doorbell?

   _____

   _____

5. What might happen if Leigh were to leave out or skip a step in building his lunchbox alarm? On a separate sheet of paper, explain your answer.

Notes for Home: Your child read a story and used story details to identify the order in which things happened. ***Home Activity:*** Invite your child to name all the important things he or she did today, in the order that they occurred.

© Scott Foresman 5

Name _____

1.	Ⓐ	Ⓑ	Ⓒ	Ⓓ
2.	Ⓕ	Ⓖ	Ⓗ	Ⓙ
3.	Ⓐ	Ⓑ	Ⓒ	Ⓓ
4.	Ⓕ	Ⓖ	Ⓗ	Ⓙ
5.	Ⓐ	Ⓑ	Ⓒ	Ⓓ
6.	Ⓕ	Ⓖ	Ⓗ	Ⓙ
7.	Ⓐ	Ⓑ	Ⓒ	Ⓓ
8.	Ⓕ	Ⓖ	Ⓗ	Ⓙ
9.	Ⓐ	Ⓑ	Ⓒ	Ⓓ
10.	Ⓕ	Ⓖ	Ⓗ	Ⓙ
11.	Ⓐ	Ⓑ	Ⓒ	Ⓓ
12.	Ⓕ	Ⓖ	Ⓗ	Ⓙ
13.	Ⓐ	Ⓑ	Ⓒ	Ⓓ
14.	Ⓕ	Ⓖ	Ⓗ	Ⓙ
15.	Ⓐ	Ⓑ	Ⓒ	Ⓓ

© Scott Foresman 5

Selection Test

Directions: Choose the best answer to each item. Mark the letter for the answer you have chosen.

Part 1: Vocabulary

Find the answer choice that means about the same as the underlined word in each sentence.

1. We met in the cafeteria.
   A. place to buy and eat meals
   B. storage area
   C. small theater or stage area
   D. entrance hall

2. The demonstration was very helpful.
   F. act of criticizing or judging something
   G. act of repairing something
   H. act of showing or explaining something
   J. act of designing something

3. For her invention, she needed a switch.
   A. the engine that makes a machine go
   B. a source of power
   C. a thin, metal wire
   D. a device to turn power on and off

4. Someone triggered the alarm.
   F. stopped
   G. repaired
   H. set off
   J. disabled

5. He opened the diary.
   A. a book of poetry or verse
   B. a book for writing down each day's thoughts or happenings
   C. a book of instructions for using something
   D. a book in which pictures or clippings are pasted

6. They were making a racket.
   F. loud noise
   G. strange sight
   H. terrible mess
   J. cage or trap

Part 2: Comprehension

Use what you know about the story to answer each item.

7. What had happened to Leigh at school before this story begins?
   A. Kids made fun of his lunchbox.
   B. Someone took his notebook.
   C. He got into trouble with the teacher.
   D. Someone took his lunch.

8. Leigh went to the hardware store to buy the things he needed to make a—
   F. new lunchbox.
   G. burglar alarm.
   H. doorbell.
   J. flashlight.

9. To make his invention, what did Leigh do first?
   A. He bought wire and a bell.
   B. He made a cardboard shelf inside his lunchbox.
   C. He went to the library for books about batteries.
   D. He connected a battery to a switch.

10. Leigh was smiling when he got to school on Monday because he—
    F. always smiled at school.
    G. was eager to show Mr. Fridley his invention.
    H. had a new lunchbox.
    J. was thinking about catching the lunch thief.

© Scott Foresman 5

GO ON

11. Why was Leigh expecting to hear his alarm go off during class on Monday morning?
    - A. Someone usually stole his food before lunchtime.
    - B. He had set the alarm to go off before lunch.
    - C. He had agreed to show his teacher how the alarm worked.
    - D. His mom had packed his lunch carefully.

12. Which of these statements from the story is a generalization?
    - F. "The kids were surprised, but nobody made fun of me."
    - G. "My little slices of salami rolled around cream cheese were gone, but I expected that."
    - H. "Boys my age always get watched when they go into stores."
    - J. "I tore home with all the things I bought."

13. At lunchtime, Leigh began to realize he had a problem just after he—
    - A. set his lunchbox on the table.
    - B. showed his invention to the principal.
    - C. set off the alarm.
    - D. opened the lunchbox lid.

14. What was the most important result of Leigh's invention?
    - F. No one stole his lunch.
    - G. Leigh felt like some sort of hero.
    - H. It made a lot of noise.
    - J. Mr. Fridley was grinning.

15. The author of this selection probably wanted to—
    - A. give information about electrical circuits.
    - B. teach a lesson about being a thief.
    - C. explain how to make a lunchbox alarm.
    - D. tell a story about a boy and how he solves his problem.

STOP

© Scott Foresman 5

Making Judgments

Directions: Read the story. Then read each question about the story. Choose the best answer to each question. Mark the letter for the answer you have chosen.

Wanted: More Vacation

So much work and too little play is not good for anybody, especially school students. That's what we have—too much work and too little play. Getting more vacation is a way to correct that problem.

I think that we students should be given much more vacation time than we get right now. Currently in our school, we're off only one week in winter, one week in spring, two months in summer, and all national holidays. It's not enough. We work hard in school, and we need time to relax. We need more time than we get now. Actually, we need a lot more time.

Students should get more vacation time because I feel we go to school too much during the year. I've only checked with my best friend Matt, but I think the whole school would agree with me on this. They all understand the importance of time away from books and homework. They would agree that more time for ballgames and television would be a good idea.

Adults who work in business get vacation, so why shouldn't kids? Yes, school is important, but so is vacation. It's something that all kids deserve. Now is the time to see that we get what we deserve.

1. The writer's opinion is that students should—
   A. vacation all year.
   B. keep the same vacation days.
   C. get more school time.
   D. have more vacation time.

2. In the third paragraph, the arguments—
   F. are wrong because the facts are wrong.
   G. contain no supporting facts.
   H. will convince everyone who reads it.
   J. are supported clearly with facts.

3. What does the author use to support his argument in the third paragraph?
   A. many details
   B. statistics
   C. his and one other person's opinion
   D. true stories

4. In the fourth paragraph, the writer gives the impression that—
   F. students have no vacation.
   G. adults never work.
   H. vacations are costly.
   J. students don't want vacations.

5. In general, the writer supports his opinion—
   A. very well.
   B. poorly.
   C. convincingly.
   D. fairly.

Notes for Home: Your child read a story and made judgments about the author's ideas. **_Home Activity:_** Read a letter to the editor in a newspaper or magazine with your child. Encourage your child to evaluate the writer's opinion and supporting arguments.

© Scott Foresman 5

Name _____

Phonics: *r*-Controlled Vowels

Directions: Read the words in the box. Say the words to yourself. Listen for the vowel sounds that the letters **ar, er, or, ur,** and **ir** represent. Some sound like **her.** Some sound like **car.** Some sound like **for.** Sort the words by sound. Write each word in the correct column.

garbage	morning	worry
portable	story	parked
first	surf	alarm

her

1. _____

2. _____

3. _____

car

4. _____

5. _____

6. _____

for

7. _____

8. _____

9. _____

Directions: Read the following "to-do" list. Each item has a word with a missing letter. Write the word on the line with the correct letter filled in.

Things to Do

_____ **10.** Go to the h_rdware store.

_____ **11.** Buy stuff for my b_rglar alarm.

_____ **12.** W_rk on my new invention.

_____ **13.** Take a sh_rt nap.

_____ **14.** Clean any d_rt from my invention.

_____ **15.** T_rn it on and test it.

Notes for Home: Your child sorted and wrote words with *r*-controlled vowels, like *first, car,* and *short.* **Home Activity:** Read some ads in newspapers and magazines to help your child recognize other words with these vowel sounds and spellings.

© Scott Foresman 5

Locate/Collect Information

You can **locate and collect information** from many different sources, such as books, magazines, newspapers, audiotapes, videotapes, CD-ROMs, and web sites on the Internet. You can also talk to people who are experts on the subject you are researching. When doing research, you need to pick the reference source that best suits the purposes of your project.

Directions: Use the following resource list from a library media center to answer the questions on the next page.

Library Media Center: Inventors/Inventions

Audiotapes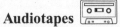
- *The Genius of Thomas Edison,* narrated by Maria Walsh. Recorded Sound Productions, 1997. (30 min.)
- *Great Inventions of the Nineteenth Century,* narrated by Joseph Smith. Educational Tapes, Inc., 1993. (30 min.)
- *Meet the Inventors: Interviews with 26 Real Kid Inventors,* narrated by Charles Osborne. Facts on Tape, 1998. (45 min.)

Videotapes
- *The Art and Science of Computers.* Documentary. Edu-films, Inc., 1994. (45 min.)
- *Computers, Computers, Computers!* Documentary. Millennium Technology Films, 1998. (60 min.)
- *The Life and Times of Thomas Alva Edison.* Documentary. Insight Productions, 1994. (58 min.)

Pictures and Print
- Smithson, Stephen. *Picture This: A Photo Collection of Great Inventions.* Chicago: AllStar Books, 1992.
- See librarian at desk for access to our photo archives of local inventors and inventions.

Internet Web Sites
- information on Alexander Graham Bell
  http://www.agbell.com/Inventions.html
- information on child inventors (under 18 years old)
  http://www.KidsInvent.org

Resource People: Inventors
- Becker, Cassandra. 43 Maple Drive, Hollistown. 555-5487.
- Danbury, Robert. 2356 Norfolk Street, Oakdale. 555-6110.
- Foxworthy, Nancy. 99200 Central Avenue, Hollistown. 555-0002.

Resource People: Experts on Specific Topics
- Lederer, David. 9 Kenosha Drive, Oakdale. 555-7360. Expert on Alexander Graham Bell.
- Prager, Benjamin, Ph.D. 1334 Rainbow Hill, Hollistown. 555-0741. Expert on Thomas Edison (published author).

© Scott Foresman 5

Name _____

1. If you were doing a report on Thomas Edison, which audiotape and videotape resources would be best to use?

_____

_____

2. What would be the best web site to use to find out about Alexander Graham Bell?

_____

3. Why are photographs useful for researching inventions? _____

_____

4. Name an inventor you could interview. _____

_____

5. Which resource person would be the best source for information about Thomas Edison?

_____

6. If you were doing a report on inventions made by children, which two resources would be best to use?

_____

_____

7. For a report on computers, which two resources would be best to use? _____

_____

8. For information about a recent invention, why might it be more useful to interview a person familiar with the invention than to use only books?

_____

_____

9. How are the two groups of resource people different from each other?

_____

_____

10. Why might you want to use different sources when researching?

_____

_____

Notes for Home: Your child chose resources to fit specific research purposes. *Home Activity:* With your child, list the resources he or she might use to do a report on the history of your family.

© Scott Foresman 5

Name _____

Character

- **Characters** are the people or animals in a story.

- You can learn about characters from the things they think, say, and do.

- You can also learn about characters from the way that other characters in the story treat them and what they say about them.

Directions: Reread "No Friends." Then complete the table. Use the examples of things that characters do and say to tell what it shows about Lucy.

	Example	What It Shows About Lucy
What Lucy Does	She leans on the window and blinks back tears.	1.
	She makes a face when asked to go to the store.	2.
What Lucy Says	"I wish we still lived in Guelph."	3.
	"There's nothing to do here."	4.
What Mrs. Bell Says	"We only got here yesterday."	5.

Notes for Home: Your child analyzed characters—the people or animals in a story. *Home Activity:* Play "Guess Who?" Think of someone you both know. Describe the way that person acts and talks, and challenge your child to guess who it is. Switch roles and play again.

© Scott Foresman 5

Name _____

Vocabulary

Directions: Choose the word from the box that best replaces the underlined word or words. Write the word on the line.

_____ 1. Billy and Carla had <u>belief without proof</u> that they would find the golden key and win the game.

_____ 2. They <u>went back over</u> their steps to make sure they had followed all the clues.

_____ 3. The last clue took them to a large stone statue in a <u>graveyard</u>.

_____ 4. Carla reached up to the statue's hand and <u>took out</u> the golden key.

_____ 5. Then Carla and Billy <u>moved quickly</u> to home base to claim their prize!

Check the Words You Know
__ alternating
__ anticipation
__ cemetery
__ darted
__ faith
__ retraced
__ scent
__ withdrew

Directions: Choose the word from the box that best matches each clue. Write the letters of the word on the blanks. The boxed letters spell something that you should have in yourself.

6. belief without proof

7. happening by turns

8. state of looking forward to something

9. a smell or odor

10. took out

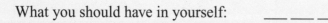

What you should have in yourself: __ __ __ __ __ __

Write a Report

Imagine you are a dog trainer. On a separate sheet of paper, write a report about a dog that you have been training. What methods do you use to get the dog to behave? How does the dog respond to your directions? Use as many vocabulary words as you can.

Notes for Home: Your child identified and used vocabulary words from "Faith and Eddie." *Home Activity:* Using a dictionary, find simple definitions for a variety of words and read them aloud to your child. See if your child can guess each word. Keep a list of "Words I Know."

Character

> • **Characters** are the people or animals in a story.
>
> • You can learn about characters from what they think, say, and do.
>
> • You can also learn about characters from the way other characters in the story treat them or talk about them.

Directions: Reread what happens in "Faith and Eddie" when Faith comes home from school one day. Then answer the questions below. Think about what you learn about the characters of Faith and Eddie.

That afternoon, Faith rushed through the door, her eyes all red and swollen. She sank to her knees and hugged me and sobbed.

"Oh, Eddie," she said. "I hate it. I just hate it."

I pressed my muzzle up into her face and licked her cheek. It tasted salty.

"The kids at school hate me," she said. "The teacher hates me. I can't understand a thing anyone says and they can't understand me, either." She sniffled. "Diego keeps making fishy faces at me."

At that she buried her face into my neck and cried.

From FAITH AND THE ELECTRIC DOGS by Patrick Jennings. Copyright © 1996 by Patrick Jennings. Reprinted by permission of Scholastic Inc.

1. What does Faith do when she gets home?

_____

2. Why does Faith think her teacher and classmates hate her?

_____

_____

3. How does Eddie react to Faith's behavior?

_____

4. What does Faith's behavior tell you about the type of person she is?

_____

_____

5. What do you learn about Eddie's character from the rest of the story? On a separate sheet of paper, write your answer and give examples to support it.

Notes for Home: Your child read a story and used story details to analyze its characters. *Home Activity:* Name a family member or friend. Talk with your child about the type of person that individual is, based on the way he or she thinks, talks, and behaves.

© Scott Foresman 5

Name _____

1.	Ⓐ	Ⓑ	Ⓒ	Ⓓ
2.	Ⓕ	Ⓖ	Ⓗ	Ⓙ
3.	Ⓐ	Ⓑ	Ⓒ	Ⓓ
4.	Ⓕ	Ⓖ	Ⓗ	Ⓙ
5.	Ⓐ	Ⓑ	Ⓒ	Ⓓ
6.	Ⓕ	Ⓖ	Ⓗ	Ⓙ
7.	Ⓐ	Ⓑ	Ⓒ	Ⓓ
8.	Ⓕ	Ⓖ	Ⓗ	Ⓙ
9.	Ⓐ	Ⓑ	Ⓒ	Ⓓ
10.	Ⓕ	Ⓖ	Ⓗ	Ⓙ
11.	Ⓐ	Ⓑ	Ⓒ	Ⓓ
12.	Ⓕ	Ⓖ	Ⓗ	Ⓙ
13.	Ⓐ	Ⓑ	Ⓒ	Ⓓ
14.	Ⓕ	Ⓖ	Ⓗ	Ⓙ
15.	Ⓐ	Ⓑ	Ⓒ	Ⓓ

© Scott Foresman 5

Selection Test

Directions: Choose the best answer to each item. Mark the letter for the answer you have chosen.

Part 1: Vocabulary

Find the answer choice that means about the same as the underlined word in each sentence.

1. She had <u>faith</u> in the plan.
   A. a position of leadership
   B. lack of confidence
   C. belief without proof
   D. strong interest

2. We <u>retraced</u> the journey.
   F. plotted on a map or chart
   G. went back over
   H. took a new route
   J. told about again

3. They walked through a <u>cemetery</u>.
   A. graveyard
   B. meadow
   C. narrow street
   D. city square

4. A mouse <u>darted</u> under the leaves.
   F. made tunnels
   G. sat silently without stirring
   H. crept quietly
   J. moved suddenly and quickly

5. His shirt had <u>alternating</u> stripes.
   A. forming a smooth wavy pattern
   B. arranged in an unexpected or disorganized manner
   C. blending together to create a single color
   D. first one and then the other, by turns

6. The children looked up in <u>anticipation</u>.
   F. state of being amazed
   G. state of looking forward to something
   H. state of being disappointed
   J. state of avoiding something

7. This plant is known for its <u>scent</u>.
   A. color
   B. size
   C. smell
   D. shape

8. She opened the drawer and <u>withdrew</u> a small package.
   F. took out
   G. discovered
   H. hid
   J. returned

Part 2: Comprehension

Use what you know about the story to answer each item.

9. Which character is the narrator of the story?
   A. Faith
   B. Hector
   C. Bernice
   D. Eddie

10. Who is Coco?
    F. a household servant
    G. Faith's tutor
    H. a family friend
    J. Faith's mother

11. In what way is Eddie an unusual dog?
    A. He comforts Faith when she is sad.
    B. He plays Fetch and Tug-of-war.
    C. He understands everything people say.
    D. He talks to Faith just as a person would.

12. From the story you can tell that Faith—
    F. loves to go on adventures.
    G. is very unhappy about living in Mexico.
    H. is trying hard to succeed in school.
    J. makes friends with almost everyone she meets.

GO ON

© Scott Foresman 5

13. Why does Eddie rush through the city without paying much attention to his old street-dog chums?

    A.   He is worried about Faith.

    B.   He no longer needs dog friends now that he has a home.

    C.   He does not like other dogs.

    D.   He no longer recognizes the dogs he once knew.

14. Which detail tells you what time of year the story takes place?

    F.   Eddie learned to play Fetch.

    G.   Faith and Eddie went outside after dinner.

    H.   Graves were still decorated from the Days of the Dead.

    J.   A crescent moon glimmered behind the wispy fog.

15. Eddie wants to help Faith. Which of his actions has an effect that is different from what he intended?

    A.   howling by the front gate until Milagros opens it

    B.   hurrying to the school and looking through the window

    C.   following his nose across a stream and a pasture

    D.   howling in the graveyard so that Faith will hear him

STOP

© Scott Foresman 5

Setting

Directions: Read the story. Then read each question about the story. Choose the best answer to each question. Mark the letter for the answer you have chosen.

A Sore Vacation

Alex looked around at the neat, clean room. He sat carefully on the edge of the chair. He was careful not to let his back touch anything. This was a nice chair. He would like to settle back into it. If he just felt better, he would like this chair. On the other hand, if he felt better, he wouldn't be here.

Everything about the room would be comfortable if only he felt better. He looked up as the doctor came into the room.

"Take off your shirt and sit down," ordered the doctor.

Alex could barely sit. His whole body was sore from the sunburn. He was glad to have his shirt off, although it hurt getting it off. He was sure the room got brighter in the glow of his red skin.

Alex tried to relax as the doctor applied lotion to his body. He jerked every time he felt the doctor's fingers. At the same time, he was glad to feel the cool, soft lotion. He wished he could just get into a bathtub full of it.

This vacation had seemed like such a good idea. The travel poster showed clear water and beautiful sand. That was just what Alex wanted.

As soon as he arrived, he was out on the beach in front of the hotel. After a long plane ride, he had been glad to relax in the sun.

"Nobody told me Mexico could be this hot," Alex said. "I should have come here for winter vacation instead of in July."

"Take my advice. Next time, try not to fall asleep in the sun," the doctor said.

1. The setting of the story is—
   A. Alex's hotel lobby.
   B. beside a pool.
   C. a doctor's office.
   D. at the beach.

2. A clue to the setting is—
   F. the hot sun.
   G. Alex's vacation.
   H. the neat, clean room.
   J. the travel poster.

3. The time of year is—
   A. summer.
   B. autumn.
   C. winter.
   D. spring.

4. The best word to describe Mexico in July is—
   F. cool.
   G. warm.
   H. chilly.
   J. hot.

5. Alex wouldn't have burned if he had—
   A. gone to the beach.
   B. sat in the shade.
   C. gone out at noontime.
   D. worn sunglasses.

© Scott Foresman 5

Notes for Home: Your child read a story and used details to answer questions about the setting.
Home Activity: Have your child look around the room and describe the setting in detail.

Phonics: Vowel Digraphs

Directions: Read each sentence. Say the underlined word to yourself. Listen for the vowel sounds that the letters **ee, ai,** and **oa** represent. Circle the word in ( ) that has the same **vowel sound** as the underlined word.

1. My dog howled, then sat to <u>wait</u> for me.   (fate/fat)

2. I rubbed my <u>cheek</u> against his warm fur.   (weak/wreck)

3. I took him for a quick walk in the wet <u>rain</u>.   (plane/plan)

4. We walked along the sand near the <u>coast</u>.   (most/moss)

5. We watched the fishing <u>boats</u> come in.   (robe/rob)

Directions: Read the postcard below. Say the underlined words to yourself. Match each underlined word with a word below that rhymes. Write the word on the correct line.

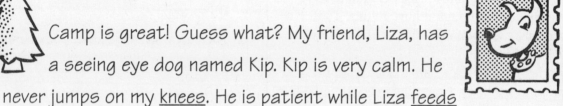

Dear Mom,

Camp is great! Guess what? My friend, Liza, has a seeing eye dog named Kip. Kip is very calm. He never jumps on my <u>knees</u>. He is patient while Liza <u>feeds</u> him. It's <u>plain</u> that he loves her. He goes <u>straight</u> to her when she calls. They swim together each day. When he shakes himself off, we all get <u>soaked</u>! I wish I had a dog like Kip.

Love,

Terri

6. ate _____   9. joked _____

7. cane _____   10. reads _____

8. ease _____

Notes for Home: Your child practiced working with words with these long vowel sounds: *long e (see), long a (rain)* and *long o (coast).* **Home Activity:** Write *see, rain,* and *coast* on separate sheets of paper. Take turns listing words that have the same vowel sounds and spellings.

© Scott Foresman 5

Dictionary/Glossary

A **dictionary** is a book of words and their meanings. A **glossary** is a short dictionary in the back of some books. It includes definitions of words used in the book. Words are listed in alphabetical order. **Guide words** appear at the top of each page and show the first and last entry word for that page.

Directions: Use this section of a dictionary page to answer the questions that follow.

---

245 fretful/frogman

fret•ful (fret′fəl), cross, discontented, or worried; ready to fret: *My baby brother is fretful because his ear hurts.* *adjective.*

fric•tion (frik′shən), **1** a rubbing of one thing against another, such as skates on ice, hand against hand, or a brush on shoes: *Matches are lighted by friction.* **2** the resistance to motion of surfaces that touch: *Oil reduces friction.* **3** a conflict of differing ideas and opinions; disagreement; clash: *Constant friction between the two nations brought them dangerously close to war.* *noun.*

Fri•day (frī′dā), the sixth day of the week; the day after Thursday. *noun.*

a hat	**i** it	**oi** oil	**ch** child	**a** in *about*
ā age	**ī** ice	**ou** out	**ng** long	**e** in *taken*
ä far	**o** hot	**u** cup	**sh** she	ə = { **i** in *pencil*
e let	**ō** open	**ù** put	**th** thin	**o** in *lemon*
ē equal	**ô** order	**ü** rule	**ŦH** then	**u** in *circus*
ėr term	**ȯ** author		**zh** measure	

fried (frīd), **1** cooked in hot fat: *fried eggs.* **2** See **fry.** *I fried the ham. The potatoes had been fried.* 1 *adjective,* 2 *verb.*

friend (frend), **1** a person who knows and likes another. **2** a person who favors and supports: *He was a generous friend of the art museum.* **3** a person who belongs to the same side or group: *Are you a friend or an enemy? noun.*

From SCOTT FORESMAN BEGINNING DICTIONARY by E.L. Thorndike and Clarence L. Barnhart. Copyright © 1997 by Scott Foresman and Company.

---

1. Using the guide words, list two other words that might appear on this page.

_____

2. According to the pronunciation key at the top right side of the page, the vowel sound in *fried* sounds like the long *i* sound in what other word?

_____

3. Which definition of *friend* is used in the following sentence?
Tyrell has been my best friend for years.

_____

_____

4. How many syllables do the words *Friday* and *friend* each have? _____

_____

5. Write a sentence using the third meaning of *friction.* _____

_____

6. Which word on the dictionary page can be used as a verb? _____

© Scott Foresman 5

Name _____

Directions: Use this section of a glossary from a textbook to answer the questions that follow.

---

eyelid/glutton

eye•lid (ī´lid´), the movable cover of skin, upper or lower, by means of which we can shut and open our eyes. *noun.*

fam•i•ly (fam´əlē), **1** a father, mother, and their children: *A new family moved to our block.* **2** all of a person's relatives: *a family reunion. noun, plural* **fam•i•lies.**

fife (fīf), a small, shrill musical instrument like a flute, played by blowing. Fifes are used with drums to make music for marching. *noun.* [*Fife* comes from German *Pfeife,* meaning "pipe."]

gar•lic (gär´lik), the bulb of a plant related to the onion, used in cooking. Its flavor is stronger than that of an onion. *noun.*

ges•ture (jes´chər), **1** a movement of the hands, arms, or any part of the body, used instead of words or with words to help express an idea or feeling: *Speakers often make gestures with their hands to stress something they are saying.* **2** to make gestures; use gestures. 1 *noun,* 2 *verb.* **ges•tures, ges•tured, ges•tur•ing.**

gla•cier (glā´shər), a large mass of ice formed from the snow on high ground and moving very slowly down a mountain or along a valley. *noun.* [*Glacier* comes from the French *glace,* which comes from the Latin *glacies,* meaning "ice."]

---

7. Which definition of *gesture* is used in the following sentence? How can you tell? *The coach gestured secretly to the player.*

_____

8. Which entry word on the glossary page has the most syllables? How many syllables does the word have?

_____

9. Which word comes from a German word? What does the German word mean?

_____

_____

10. In what ways is a glossary similar to a dictionary? How is a glossary different from a dictionary?

_____

_____

_____

_____

_____

Notes for Home: Your child used a dictionary and a glossary to find information about words. *Home Activity:* With your child, select various words from a dictionary or glossary. Discuss all the information you find about that word.

© Scott Foresman 5

Name _____

Generalizing

- **Generalizing** is making a statement that tells what several people or things have in common.
- Sometimes a clue word such as *most, all, sometimes, always,* or *never* signals that a generalization is being made.
- A valid generalization is supported by facts and logic. A faulty generalization is not.

Directions: Reread "A Special Family." Then complete the table. Tell whether each statement is a generalization. Explain your reasons for all answers.

Statement	Generalization (Yes or No?)	Reason
Joshua has a few memories of his Korean foster family.	1.	2.
Most Asians in the Levins' school have Asian parents.	3.	4.
Eric Levin is an adopted child.	5.	6.

Directions: Complete the table. Tell whether each generalization is **valid** or **faulty.** Explain your reasons for all answers.

Statement	Generalization (Valid or Faulty?)	Reason
All the Levin children have musical talent.	7.	8.
The Levins do many things together as a family.	9.	10.

Notes for Home: Your child identified generalizations. *Home Activity:* Ask your child to look around a room in your home and make a generalization about it, such as *All the walls are painted white.* Then talk about whether you agree with the generalization.

© Scott Foresman 5

Name _____

Vocabulary

Directions: Choose a word from the box that best matches each definition. Write the word on the line.

Check
the Words
You Know
___ awe
___ bitter
___ determined
___ horrified
___ panicked
___ select
___ suspicious

_____ 1. shocked; terrified

_____ 2. acted as if there was an emergency without having real cause

_____ 3. miserable; angry

_____ 4. a feeling of wonder

_____ 5. doubtful

Directions: Choose the word from the box that best completes each statement. Write the word on the line to the left.

_____ 6. The boys looked in _____ at the huge train.

_____ 7. They began to _____ their seats.

_____ 8. Each boy was _____ to find a good seat.

_____ 9. However, no one _____ in the rush to sit down.

_____ 10. None felt angry or _____ about the seats they found.

Directions: Choose the word from the box that best completes each statement. Write the word on the line to the left.

_____ 11. *Respect* is to *respectful* as *suspicion* is to _____.

_____ 12. *Terrify* is to *terrified* as *horrify* is to _____.

_____ 13. *Sleepy* is to *alert* as *happy* is to _____.

_____ 14. *Toss* is to *throw* as *choose* is to _____.

_____ 15. *Hopeful* is to *hope* as *awesome* is to _____.

Write a Description

On a separate sheet of paper, describe a real or imaginary trip by train, boat, or airplane. Include vivid sensory details to tell what you see, hear, smell, touch, or taste. Use as many vocabulary words as you can.

Notes for Home: Your child identified and used vocabulary words from "Looking for a Home." *Home Activity:* Ask your child to describe events that would cause a person to feel *awe, bitter, determined, horrified, panicked,* and *suspicious.*

© Scott Foresman 5

Generalizing

- **Generalizing** is making a statement that tells what several people or things have in common.

- Sometimes a clue word such as *most, always,* or *never* signals that a generalization is being made.

- A valid generalization is supported by facts and logic. A faulty generalization is not.

Directions: Read this passage from "Looking for a Home" that tells about the placement of orphan train riders. Then answer the questions below. Think about ways that the author makes generalizations in her writing.

Most placements were successful, and the program grew. During the first 20 years an average of 3,000 children rode the orphan trains each year. Brace continued to raise the needed money through his speeches and his writing. Railroads gave discount fares to the children, and wealthy people sometimes paid for whole trainloads of children.

Unfortunately, many children who needed homes were not allowed to go on the trains. It was always difficult to find homes for older children, and while some teenagers as old as 17 were successfully placed, 14 was usually the oldest a rider could be. It was always easiest to find homes for babies.

From ORPHAN TRAIN RIDER: ONE BOY'S TRUE STORY by Andrea Warren. Copyright ©1996 by Andrea Warren. Reprinted by permission of Houghton Mifflin Company. All rights reserved.

1. What clue words can you find in the passage that signal a generalization?

_____

2. What facts does the author offer to support her generalizations?

_____

_____

3. Explain why the sentence about Charles Loring Brace is or is not a generalization.

_____

_____

4. Explain why this generalization is valid or faulty: *Most orphans as old as 17 were easily placed.*

_____

5. What generalizations can you make about Lee and his two brothers from "Looking for Home"? Explain your thinking on a separate sheet of paper.

Notes for Home: Your child read a nonfiction article and identified generalizations that the author made. *Home Activity:* Talk with your child about members in your family. Encourage him or her to make general statements about ways that some of the members are alike.

© Scott Foresman 5

Name _____

1.	Ⓐ	Ⓑ	Ⓒ	Ⓓ
2.	Ⓕ	Ⓖ	Ⓗ	Ⓙ
3.	Ⓐ	Ⓑ	Ⓒ	Ⓓ
4.	Ⓕ	Ⓖ	Ⓗ	Ⓙ
5.	Ⓐ	Ⓑ	Ⓒ	Ⓓ
6.	Ⓕ	Ⓖ	Ⓗ	Ⓙ
7.	Ⓐ	Ⓑ	Ⓒ	Ⓓ
8.	Ⓕ	Ⓖ	Ⓗ	Ⓙ
9.	Ⓐ	Ⓑ	Ⓒ	Ⓓ
10.	Ⓕ	Ⓖ	Ⓗ	Ⓙ
11.	Ⓐ	Ⓑ	Ⓒ	Ⓓ
12.	Ⓕ	Ⓖ	Ⓗ	Ⓙ
13.	Ⓐ	Ⓑ	Ⓒ	Ⓓ
14.	Ⓕ	Ⓖ	Ⓗ	Ⓙ
15.	Ⓐ	Ⓑ	Ⓒ	Ⓓ

© Scott Foresman 5

Selection Test

Directions: Choose the best answer to each item. Mark the letter for the answer you have chosen.

Part 1: Vocabulary

Find the answer choice that means about the same as the underlined word in each sentence.

1. Eduardo <u>panicked</u> when he saw the house.
   A. felt a great and sudden fear
   B. felt a loss of confidence
   C. felt a sense of relief
   D. felt wild and silly

2. Anna wanted to <u>select</u> one.
   F. send
   G. complete
   H. choose
   J. try

3. Gillian was <u>determined</u>.
   A. sent for punishment
   B. firm; with her mind made up
   C. making the best of it
   D. very respectful

4. The sight <u>horrified</u> us.
   F. amused
   G. filled with anger
   H. made sad
   J. shocked very much

5. The stars filled him with <u>awe</u>.
   A. shame
   B. anger
   C. wonder
   D. joy

6. It was a <u>bitter</u> experience.
   F. causing pain or grief
   G. exhausting
   H. causing delight or joy
   J. surprising

7. The girl's actions made him <u>suspicious</u>.
   A. unsafe
   B. embarrassed or shy
   C. curious
   D. unwilling to trust

Part 2: Comprehension

Use what you know about the selection to answer each item.

8. Where did Lee and his brothers come from?
   F. Texas
   G. New Jersey
   H. Iowa
   J. New York

9. Children on the orphan trains were taken to other parts of the country to—
   A. make money.
   B. find new homes.
   C. go to school.
   D. make new friends.

10. Why did Lee feel a sense of dread when he got back on the train after the first children were chosen?
    F. He was afraid no one would ever choose him.
    G. He was tired of the train food.
    H. He felt sure he would be separated from his brothers.
    J. He wanted to stay in that town.

11. What happened to Lee at the Rodgerses' house?
    A. He got a haircut.
    B. He got separated from Leo.
    C. He got his own bedroom.
    D. He felt welcome in his new home.

12. Which of these events happened last?
    F. Lee spoke rudely to Ben Nailling.
    G. The Rodgerses decided to keep only Leo.
    H. A man and woman took Gerald.
    J. Lee accidentally killed some chicks.

© Scott Foresman 5

GO ON ▶

13. What was the most important difference between Lee's experience at the Naillings' and his other experiences?
   - A. The bedroom was sunny.
   - B. He was firmly disciplined.
   - C. He felt wanted.
   - D. There was lots of food.

14. Which statement is a valid generalization based on the facts in this selection?
   - F. Children on the orphan trains often fought with each other.
   - G. The oldest orphan train riders were always chosen first.
   - H. The matrons on the orphan trains treated the children kindly.
   - J. Most brothers and sisters traveling together ended up in different homes.

15. The author of this selection most likely thinks that—
   - A. orphans enjoy long train rides.
   - B. every child needs love and a good home.
   - C. the orphan trains were a useful experience for the children.
   - D. Lee Nailling was not a nice boy.

STOP

© Scott Foresman 5

Sequence

Directions: Read the passage. Then read each question about the passage. Choose the best answer to each question. Mark the letter for the answer you have chosen.

How to Adopt

Deciding to adopt a child is a big decision for any couple. It is also a big decision for those who are currently caring for the child. There are many parts involved in giving a child a happy home.

The couple wishing to adopt a child first must apply to an adoption agency. The adoption agency will take steps to find out whether it is a good idea for this couple to adopt a child.

After the couple applies, the adoption agency assigns a caseworker to investigate. The caseworker needs to know the couple's background. The caseworker also checks the couple's health and their finances.

If the agency feels that the couple will be good parents and the child will be safe and happy with them, the agency has the child live in the couple's home for 6 to 12 months. This is an important time for deciding whether or not the adoption can become legal.

If the child and the couple still want the adoption, a lawyer then prepares an adoption request. The request is given to a court. If the court approves, the adoption becomes legal and the child and parents become a family.

1. The first step in the process to adopt a child is—
   A. telling the child.
   B. finding a lawyer.
   C. applying to an agency.
   D. writing to the judge.

2. The first thing that an adoption agency does is—
   F. contact the judge.
   G. find the child.
   H. contact a lawyer.
   J. investigate the people who want to adopt a child.

3. Before a child can be adopted, he or she must—
   A. apply to the judge.
   B. get lawyer approval.
   C. live with the people who want to adopt him or her.
   D. investigate the people who want to adopt him or her.

4. After a lawyer prepares an adoption request, it is given to the—
   F. parents.
   G. court.
   H. child.
   J. adoption agency.

5. The final step in making an adoption legal is—
   A. the court's approval.
   B. the child's approval.
   C. the parents' approval.
   D. the lawyer's approval.

Notes for Home: Your child read a nonfiction article and then identified the order in which steps were presented. *Home Activity:* Review with your child the important things that have happened in his or her life so far. Have your child name the events in the order that they occurred.

© Scott Foresman 5

Phonics: Diphthongs

Directions: Read each sentence. Look at the words in ( ). Both words make sense, but only one word has a vowel sound like **cow.** Circle the correct word.

1. The (crew/crowd) was waiting for the train.

2. Someone (shouted/shushed) his name.

3. The steam drifted (about/above) him.

4. In the distance, he saw a (horse/house).

5. When he arrived, the boy (found/thought) he liked his new home.

Directions: Read the clue in ( ). Choose the letters **ou** or **ow** to complete each word. It's tricky! These letters stand for the same sound. Write the correct letters on the blanks.

6. ar _____ _____ nd   (in a circle)

7. br _____ _____ n   (the color of toast)

8. all _____ _____ ed   (let someone do something)

9. gr _____ _____ nd   (the land under our feet)

10. m _____ _____ th   (the place on a face to eat and speak)

11. fr _____ _____ n   (look unhappy)

Directions: Complete each sentence with a word that has the same vowel sound as **crowd** and **mouth.** Write the word on the line to the left.

_____   12. The train traveled _____, not north.

_____   13. It took the children _____ of the city and into the country.

_____   14. After a long journey, the train stopped in a small _____, very different from the big city.

_____   15. The conductor helped the children _____ the steps and onto the platform.

 Notes for Home: Your child practiced reading and writing words with letters *ou* and *ow* that represent the same vowel sound, such as *mouth* and *crowd*. **Home Activity:** Together, make a list of words with these spellings and this vowel sound. Make up rhymes that use pairs of these words.

© Scott Foresman 5

Poster/Announcement

An **announcement** gives specific facts about an event. Like a news article, an announcement should answer the questions: *who?, what?, when?, where?,* and *why?* A **poster** is a type of announcement printed on a large sheet of paper and posted for the public to view.

Directions: Use the information on the poster to answer the questions on the next page.

Public Notice

Centerville Foster Care Agency
1592 Boulevard West, Room 507
Centerville, NY 10129

Anyone wishing to foster or adopt a child or children should schedule an appointment with the Centerville Foster Care Agency for an interview between the hours of 9:30 A.M. and 4:45 P.M. on Friday, October 15.

- Please bring documents showing who you are, where you live, and what kind of work you do.
- You will also need to bring a <u>completed</u> foster application or adoption application form. Forms are available from Centerville Foster Care Agency at the address above, Monday through Friday, 8:30 A.M.–5:00 P.M. You can also call our offices, and an application will be mailed to your home.
- This first interview will take approximately 45 minutes. Follow-up interviews will be scheduled as needed.
- Anyone unable to interview on the date and time assigned above may call our offices to schedule an interview at 555-1214, Monday through Friday, 8:30 A.M.–5:00 P.M.

We look forward to meeting you!

© Scott Foresman 5

1. What event does this poster announce? _____
   _____
   _____

2. Where should people go if they want an interview with the Centerville Foster Care Agency?
   _____
   _____

3. On what day and at what time will the interviews be held? _____
   _____

4. What should people bring with them to the interview?
   _____
   _____

5. During what times may people call for an application to be mailed to them?
   _____

6. What should applicants do if they cannot be at the agency for an interview during the time specified in the poster?
   _____
   _____

7. If an applicant arrives at 10:30 A.M. for an interview, about what time can he or she expect the interview be done?
   _____

8. Would a person have to have more than one interview before he or she could foster or adopt a child? Explain.
   _____
   _____
   _____

9. What are two ways a person can get an application form? _____
   _____
   _____

10. What 5 "W" questions should an announcement answer?
    _____

Notes for Home: Your child answered questions about information on a poster. *Home Activity:* Find an announcement in the newspaper, such as a wedding announcement. With your child, discuss all the information the announcement provides.

© Scott Foresman 5

Cause and Effect

- A **cause** is why something happens. An **effect** is what happens.

- A cause may have more than one effect. An effect may have more than one cause.

- Sometimes a clue word such as *because* or *since* signals a cause-effect relationship. Sometimes there is no clue word, and you need to think about why something happened.

Cause → Effect

Directions: Reread "Baseball and Brothers." Then complete the table. Provide each missing cause or effect.

Cause (Why did it happen?)	Effect (What happened?)
1.	Meg says she hates baseball and thinks about giving it up.
2.	Mrs. O'Malley still plays baseball.
Mrs. O'Malley wants Meg to stop thinking about her problems, and she wants Charles to eat more peas.	3.
4.	Singing "Yankee Doodle" is very easy for Meg.
5.	Meg finds it difficult to walk away from baseball

© Scott Foresman 5

Notes for Home: Your child read a story and identified causes and effects. ***Home Activity:*** Help your child relate causes and effects by starting a sentence, such as *You eat breakfast because* _____. Ask your child to complete the sentence by giving a cause, or reason.

Vocabulary

Directions: Read the want ad. Choose the word from the box
that best completes each sentence. Write the word on the matching
numbered line to the right.

—— JOB AVAILABLE ——

We have a position open for a school **1.** _____.

Job involves keeping classrooms and **2.** _____

clean. Not easy work! The principal will be

3. _____ you regularly to prove your worth.

Do a good job and be a **4.** _____ part of our

team. Do a poor job and get **5.** _____

immediately. Call 555–1234.

1. _____

2. _____

3. _____

4. _____

5. _____

**Check
the Words
You Know**

__ challenging

__ corridors

__ custodian

__ cut

__ valuable

Directions: Choose the word from the box that best matches each clue.
Write the word in the puzzle.

Down

6. calling in question
7. long hallways
8. worth something
9. dismissed; let go

Across

10. a janitor

Write a Diary Entry

Imagine you are a school janitor. On a separate sheet of paper, write a diary
entry that tells about your day. Use as many vocabulary words as you can.

Notes for Home: Your child identified and used vocabulary words from "Meeting
Mr. Henry." *Home Activity:* Take turns using each vocabulary word in a sentence.

© Scott Foresman 5

Cause and Effect

- A **cause** is why something happens. An **effect** is what happens.

- A cause may have more than one effect. An effect may have more than one cause.

- Sometimes a clue word such as *because* or *since* signals a cause-effect relationship. Sometimes there is no clue word and you need to think about why something happens.

Directions: Reread what happens in "Meeting Mr. Henry" when Jason plays imaginary baseball with Mr. Henry. Then answer the questions below. Think about each thing that happens and why it happens.

> And then right there in the middle of Eberwoods School, old, gray-haired Mr. Henry, the school custodian, went into a full windup.
>
> And as he did, something strange happened. He didn't look so old. He looked tall and young and powerful as he kicked high and came down over his head with a smooth motion and fired the imaginary ball. I swung.
>
> "Run!" he yelled.
>
> I ran. I didn't look down the other corridor where the imaginary ball went. I lifted my feet and ran hard and hit first base with my left shoe. The base slid far down the smooth, waxed floor.
>
> Mr. Henry laughed and slapped me on the back. "Now, if you'd moved like that when you hit that ground ball, you'd still be on your team. You run like that and you'll be getting your share of hits and then some."
>
> From FINDING BUCK MCHENRY by Alfred Slote. Copyright © 1991 by Alfred Slote. Used by permission of HarperCollins Publishers.

1. What causes Mr. Henry to seem younger to Jason?

   _____

   _____

2. Why is Jason able to run faster now than he did in the game?

   _____

3. According to Mr. Henry, what is the reason Jason was cut from the team?

   _____

4. What effect does Mr. Henry's practice session have on Jason?

   _____

5. How does Jason change by the end of the story? What causes that change? On a separate sheet of paper, explain your answer.

Notes for Home: Your child used details from a story to identify causes and effects. ***Home Activity:*** Talk with your child about things that have happened to him or her or to you recently. Invite your child to explain what caused each thing to happen.

© Scott Foresman 5

Name _____

1.	Ⓐ	Ⓑ	Ⓒ	Ⓓ
2.	Ⓕ	Ⓖ	Ⓗ	Ⓙ
3.	Ⓐ	Ⓑ	Ⓒ	Ⓓ
4.	Ⓕ	Ⓖ	Ⓗ	Ⓙ
5.	Ⓐ	Ⓑ	Ⓒ	Ⓓ
6.	Ⓕ	Ⓖ	Ⓗ	Ⓙ
7.	Ⓐ	Ⓑ	Ⓒ	Ⓓ
8.	Ⓕ	Ⓖ	Ⓗ	Ⓙ
9.	Ⓐ	Ⓑ	Ⓒ	Ⓓ
10.	Ⓕ	Ⓖ	Ⓗ	Ⓙ
11.	Ⓐ	Ⓑ	Ⓒ	Ⓓ
12.	Ⓕ	Ⓖ	Ⓗ	Ⓙ
13.	Ⓐ	Ⓑ	Ⓒ	Ⓓ
14.	Ⓕ	Ⓖ	Ⓗ	Ⓙ
15.	Ⓐ	Ⓑ	Ⓒ	Ⓓ

© Scott Foresman 5

Selection Test

Directions: Choose the best answer to each item. Mark the letter for the answer you have chosen.

Part 1: Vocabulary

Find the answer choice that means about the same as the underlined word in each sentence.

1. My parents were <u>challenging</u> my answer.
   A. finding difficult to understand
   B. adding details to
   C. demanding proof of
   D. restating in different words

2. We walked quickly down the <u>corridors</u>.
   F. long hallways
   G. flights of stairs
   H. long ramps
   J. narrow streets

3. Joe's father is a <u>custodian</u>.
   A. guard
   B. coach
   C. driver
   D. janitor

4. Of the six players, only Allie was <u>cut</u> from the team.
   F. hurt
   G. dismissed
   H. named
   J. chosen

5. He knew the old book was <u>valuable</u>.
   A. popular
   B. falling apart
   C. stolen
   D. worth money

Part 2: Comprehension

Use what you know about the story to answer each item.

6. Where was Jason's team playing ball?
   F. Eberwoods School
   G. Tiger Stadium
   H. The Grandstand
   J. Sampson Park School

7. Jason offered to carry the bases into the gym because he
   A. wanted to help Mr. Henry.
   B. enjoyed talking with Mr. Henry.
   C. wanted to avoid talking with his teammates.
   D. hoped to get some batting tips.

8. Which sentence best describes Mr. Henry?
   F. He's always joking and fooling around.
   G. He doesn't like his job much.
   H. He observes people carefully.
   J. He loves baseball cards.

9. In what way were Josh Gibson, Satchel Paige, and Cool Papa Bell alike?
   A. They were all great pitchers.
   B. They all played for the Pittsburgh Crawfords.
   C. They were all known for their speed.
   D. They all played center field.

10. Jason knows about famous baseball players from the past because he—
    F. collects baseball cards.
    G. has seen them play.
    H. plays baseball.
    J. has read books about them.

GO ON

© Scott Foresman 5

11. What was Jason's problem as a baseball player, according to Mr. Henry?
    - A. He took his eye off the ball.
    - B. He didn't wait for a good pitch.
    - C. He stood watching the ball after he hit it.
    - D   He was too chubby to run fast.

12. What will Jason do when he gets to The Grandstand?
    - F. sign up for a new team
    - G. look for information about the players Mr. Henry knew
    - H. sell some of his baseball cards
    - J. find out about the newest baseball cards

13. Mr. Henry probably compares Jason with Willie Mays and Roy Campanella to—
    - A. help him gain confidence in himself.
    - B. convince him that he is bound for the major leagues.
    - C. help him understand his mistakes.
    - D. make him feel embarrassed.

14. What does Mr. Henry think about Jason?
    - F. He could be a famous player some day.
    - G. He is foolish to be so interested in baseball.
    - H. He should play a position other than catcher.
    - J. He will get to play on a team if he gets more hits.

15. What did Mr. Henry prove to Jason?
    - A. Baseball is easy to play.
    - B. He could see without looking.
    - C. Willie Mays was born to play baseball.
    - D. Keeping the school clean is more important than baseball.

© Scott Foresman 5

Name _____

Drawing Conclusions

Directions: Read the story. Then read each question about the story. Choose the best answer to each question. Mark the letter for the answer you have chosen.

The First Game

Today would be Amy's first game in the Little League. She had been awake since before the sun came up. She had dressed before breakfast. She wondered if her uniform still fit right. She brushed her teeth three times. She walked Champ twice.

At last, it was time to go to the ballpark. Amy was quiet in the car. She didn't even notice her favorite songs on the radio. She bit her nails as her mother drove her to the ballpark.

"Stop that," Mother said. "You're going to be just fine." Amy wanted to believe that. Mother was usually right. She tried to think of other things as she bent her glove back and forth.

At the park, Amy joined her teammates on their side of the field. They got together and started their team cheer. They started practicing swinging the bats. They practiced throwing the ball. They listened to their coach remind them of their plans for winning the game.

From the stands she could hear cries of, "Go Amy! Go Fireball." Fireball was a nickname her cousins had given her when she was little. She liked the nickname and was glad her team and the fans used it.

During the game, Amy didn't have time to worry. She struck out twelve batters. She got a single at her first turn at bat. Then she got a double in her next turn. By the end of the game, Amy wore a smile that no one could remove.

1. Before the beginning of the game, Amy feels—
   A. hungry.
   B. tired.
   C. nervous.
   D. confused.

2. Amy tries to think of other things because she—
   F. is bored in the car.
   G. wants to relax.
   H. doesn't like baseball.
   J. doesn't like her glove.

3. Amy's position on the team is—
   A. catcher.
   B. outfield.
   C. first base.
   D. pitcher.

4. Amy's playing is—
   F. poor.
   G. average.
   H. good.
   J. uneven.

5. After the game, Amy feels—
   A. embarrassed.
   B. happy.
   C. nervous.
   D. angry.

Notes for Home: Your child read a story and drew conclusions based on its details. *Home Activity:* Read a story together with your child. Afterward, invite your child to tell you what conclusions he or she can draw about how a character feels or why an event happened.

© Scott Foresman 5

Phonics: Common Word Patterns

Directions: Read each word below. Some words have the pattern **consonant-vowel-consonant-e** as in **game,** which forms a **long vowel** sound. Other words have the pattern **vowel-consonant-consonant-vowel** as in **number,** which has a **short vowel** sound for the first vowel. Sort the words according to their word patterns. Write each word in the correct column.

base	powder	bike	elbow	five
center	harder	lesson	home	mule

CVCe
game

1. _____

2. _____

3. _____

4. _____

5. _____

VCCV
number

6. _____

7. _____

8. _____

9. _____

10. _____

Directions: Circle all the words that have a pattern like **game.**

11. It was time for the game to start.

12. With a big swing, she made a great hit.

13. It was a race to first base.

14. She made it to first just in time.

15. I like to watch Lisa make such good plays.

Directions: Circle all the words that have a pattern like **number.**

16. One lesson we can learn from baseball is how to work as a team.

17. Mike puts all the bases in a big basket.

18. The player in center field hit a home run.

19. "Batter up!" shouted the coach.

20. There have been many great players in the history of baseball.

Notes for Home: Your child learned to recognize some common word patterns such as *CVCe (home)* and *VCCV (basket).* **Home Activity:** Look for these patterns and vowel sounds in a variety of print material such as signs, food packages, billboards, and store names.

© Scott Foresman 5

Technology: Card Catalog/Library Database

Libraries list the materials in their collections using a **card catalog** or a **computer database.** You can search for materials by author, title, or subject. Be sure to type words carefully when using a database. If you are not sure exactly what you want, you can use key words in the title, author's name, or subject to search the database. Always use the last name of an author first. Each listing will have a special **call number.** Use the call number to locate the item in the library.

Directions: Look at the starting screen for searching the library database below. Tell what number and words you should type to get information about each book or group of books.

Search Our Public Library
1 Title (exact search)
2 Title (key words)
3 Author (exact name)
4 Author (key words)
5 Subject (exact search)
6 Subject (key words)
Type a number or press return
for more choices.

1. books about the baseball player Babe Ruth _____

2. books written by the baseball player Joe DiMaggio _____

3. books about how to coach baseball _____

4. a book called *Learning How to Play Baseball* _____

_____

5. a book you heard about that you remember has the word *pitching* in the title

_____

© Scott Foresman 5

Name _____

If you search on a broad subject category, the computer may give you categories of choices. For example, the computer screen below shows that a library has 23 books or other items about the history of baseball.

Directions: Use the information on the computer screen to answer the questions that follow.

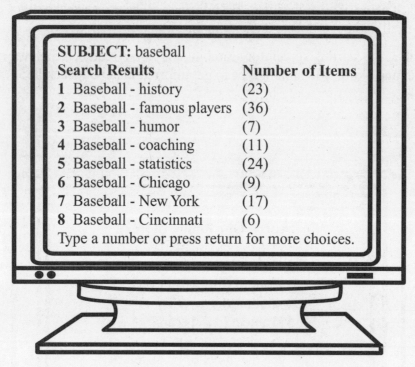

SUBJECT: baseball

Search Results	Number of Items
1 Baseball - history	(23)
2 Baseball - famous players	(36)
3 Baseball - humor	(7)
4 Baseball - coaching	(11)
5 Baseball - statistics	(24)
6 Baseball - Chicago	(9)
7 Baseball - New York	(17)
8 Baseball - Cincinnati	(6)

Type a number or press return for more choices.

6. What number should you type to find books about New York baseball teams? _____

7. What number should you type to find information about when baseball was invented? _____

8. What number should you type to find books about the baseball player Hank Aaron? _____

9. If you wanted to search for more books about baseball by Alfred Slote, the author of "Meeting Mr. Henry," would a subject search be the best way to search? Explain.

_____

_____

10. Do you think it is easier to use a library database or to look at cards in a card catalog? Explain.

_____

_____

_____

Notes for Home: Your child learned how to use an online card catalog at a library. **Home Activity:** Ask your child to make a list of five topics. At the library, work with your child to use the online catalog to find materials about these topics.

© Scott Foresman 5

Author's Purpose

- The **author's purpose** is the reason an author has for writing. The purpose is usually not stated directly in the writing. Sometimes an author has more than one purpose for writing.

- Four common purposes for writing are to persuade (convince), to inform (explain something), to entertain (amuse), or to express (describe something to help you see or feel a scene).

Directions: Reread "First Steps." Then complete the chart. For each passage given, write the author's purpose or purposes for writing. Choose from these purposes: to persuade, to inform, to express strong feeling, to entertain. You may use a purpose more than once.

Passage	Author's Purpose
I remember the very first time I walked by myself. My sister Alexis was in high school then.	1.
I was kind of scared, but I wanted to do it, so I pushed up off the arms of my wheelchair.	2.
I was so happy I'd made it that far. I looked up to heaven and said, "Thank you."	3.
Then I had to walk just a few more steps to get to the door—and I did it!	4.
She was so surprised. She burst out laughing and gave me a big hug.	5.

© Scott Foresman 5

Notes for Home: Your child learned about the purposes an author may have for writing. *Home Activity:* Read the TV listings with your child. Pick out various television programs and discuss the purpose of each one.

Name _____

Vocabulary

Directions: Read the announcement. Choose the word from the box that best completes each sentence. Write the word on the matching numbered line to the right.

■PUBLIC NOTICE■

A new apartment **1.** _____ is being built at 300 Main Street in our **2.** _____. The town **3.** _____ has ruled that any local **4.** _____ may apply for an apartment there. If you are interested and have not yet **5.** _____, please do so by December 31. Applications are available at City Hall.

1. _____
2. _____
3. _____
4. _____
5. _____

Check the Words You Know

__ applied
__ community
__ council
__ in-between
__ project
__ resident

Directions: Choose the word from the box that best matches each clue. Write the letters of the word on the blanks. The boxed letters spell something that many people in apartments pay.

6. a group of apartment buildings

7. being between

8. a group of people with power to make rules

9. people living in the same area

10. a person with a permanent home

6. __ ☐ __ __ __ __ __ __
7. __ __ - ☐ __ __ __ __ __ __
8. __ __ __ ☐ __ __ __
9. __ __ __ __ __ ☐ __ __
10. __ __ ☐ __ __ __ __

What many people in apartments pay: __ __ __ __ __

Write a Set of Rules

On a separate sheet of paper, write a set of rules you'd like to see enforced in your town. It could be rules about keeping the neighborhood clean or quiet or about keeping dogs on leashes. Use as many vocabulary words as you can.

Notes for Home: Your child identified and used vocabulary words from "Eloise Greenfield." *Home Activity:* Read an article with your child. Encourage him or her to figure out the meanings of unfamiliar words using context clues—words surrounding the unfamiliar words.

© Scott Foresman 5

Author's Purpose

- The **author's purpose** is the reason an author has for writing. Sometimes an author has more than one reason for writing. The author's purpose is usually not stated directly.

- Often an author's purpose is to persuade (convince), to inform (explain something), to entertain (amuse), or to express (describe something to help you see or feel a scene).

1. Reread "Eloise Greenfield." What is the author's purpose or purposes in telling the story?

_____

_____

Directions: Read each paragraph. For each one, identify the author's purpose.
Put an X on the line beside your choice or choices. Then explain your choice.

2. Everyone has the right to decent housing. Too many people in our community are living on the streets. Proposition 37 will solve this problem. It provides for low-income housing without new taxes. So vote *yes* on 37!

___ entertain   ___ persuade   ___ inform   ___ express

3. If you can't finish your ice cream, my dog will gladly do it for you. Last night he ate my sundae while my back was turned. Can't finish that cone? Give my dog a call. He's got a beeper.

___ entertain   ___ persuade   ___ inform   ___ express

4. I love my neighborhood. On summer evenings, a warm glow settles over the street. The old folks sit and rock on their porches. The little kids ride bikes in the street. The moms gossip on the sidewalk. It's the homiest, friendliest place you'll ever see.

___ entertain   ___ persuade   ___ inform   ___ express

5. Beginning in the 1890s, many African Americans left their homes in the South and moved to northern cities. They moved to escape poverty and discrimination. Historians call this mass movement the Great Migration.

___ entertain   ___ persuade   ___ inform   ___ express

 Notes for Home: Your child read a story and several paragraphs, and then determined each author's purpose for writing. *Home Activity:* Look through various parts of a magazine or newspaper with your child. Ask him or her to identify the purpose for writing each feature.

© Scott Foresman 5

1.	Ⓐ	Ⓑ	Ⓒ	Ⓓ
2.	Ⓕ	Ⓖ	Ⓗ	Ⓙ
3.	Ⓐ	Ⓑ	Ⓒ	Ⓓ
4.	Ⓕ	Ⓖ	Ⓗ	Ⓙ
5.	Ⓐ	Ⓑ	Ⓒ	Ⓓ
6.	Ⓕ	Ⓖ	Ⓗ	Ⓙ
7.	Ⓐ	Ⓑ	Ⓒ	Ⓓ
8.	Ⓕ	Ⓖ	Ⓗ	Ⓙ
9.	Ⓐ	Ⓑ	Ⓒ	Ⓓ
10.	Ⓕ	Ⓖ	Ⓗ	Ⓙ
11.	Ⓐ	Ⓑ	Ⓒ	Ⓓ
12.	Ⓕ	Ⓖ	Ⓗ	Ⓙ
13.	Ⓐ	Ⓑ	Ⓒ	Ⓓ
14.	Ⓕ	Ⓖ	Ⓗ	Ⓙ
15.	Ⓐ	Ⓑ	Ⓒ	Ⓓ

© Scott Foresman 5

Selection Test

Directions: Choose the best answer to each item. Mark the letter for the answer you have chosen.

Part 1: Vocabulary

Find the answer choice that means about the same as the underlined word in each sentence.

1. She <u>applied</u> for a job.
   A. wished
   B. had the skills
   C. made a request
   D. studied

2. He was the town's <u>resident</u> artist.
   F. living in a place permanently
   G. highly regarded
   H. traveling from place to place
   J. living alone

3. Mae is a member of the <u>council</u>.
   A. a club for singers
   B. a group of employees
   C. a group of people who make rules
   D. a club for checkers players

4. That summer was an <u>in-between</u> time.
   F. having a quality of sadness
   G. being or coming in the middle
   H. not interesting; boring
   J. showing strong feeling

5. They lived in a <u>project</u>.
   A. a grid formed by several streets
   B. a place where people live outdoors
   C. an unfinished building or group of buildings
   D. a group of apartment buildings built and run as a unit

6. He was a leader in the <u>community</u>.
   F. a group of people living in one place
   G. a group of people with the same last name
   H. a band or company, especially a group of performers
   J. a group of persons that has the duty to make laws

Part 2: Comprehension

Use what you know about the selection to answer each item.

7. Where was Eloise Greenfield's father when she was born?
   A. at home helping out
   B. working at Mr. Slim Gordon's store
   C. downtown playing checkers
   D. out of town

8. Langston Terrace was located in—
   F. Parmele, North Carolina.
   G. Washington, D.C.
   H. Chicago.
   J. Atlanta.

9. From her stories about school, you can tell that Eloise was a—
   A. quiet child.
   B. good student.
   C. popular girl.
   D. troublemaker.

10. Why did Eloise's parents want to move to Langston Terrace?
    F. They had friends in the neighborhood.
    G. It was named for a famous black congressman.
    H. They needed more space.
    J. The houses were very beautiful.

11. How was her home at Langston Terrace different from other places Eloise had lived?
    A. It was in the city.
    B. It had only one room.
    C. Daddy's cousin Lillie was there.
    D. Her family had a whole house to themselves.

© Scott Foresman 5

GO ON

12. Why was it difficult for families at Langston Terrace to save enough money to buy a house?
    F. Whenever they earned more money, their rents increased.
    G. They had to pay fees for the many social activities.
    H. The rents there were higher than in other parts of the city.
    J. They were too busy enjoying life to think about saving money.

13. What happened after Eloise's sister Vedie was born?
    A. Eloise went to a new school.
    B. The family moved to a three-bedroom house.
    C. Eloise celebrated her ninth birthday.
    D. The family moved to Washington.

14. The author tells about two events from when she was in grade school. She probably chose these particular events to help the reader understand—
    F. what kind of schools she went to.
    G. why she became famous.
    H. what kind of child she was.
    J. what life was like in olden times.

15. In this selection, the author's main purpose is to—
    A. explain the difficulties of being poor.
    B. share childhood memories.
    C. give information about housing in the city.
    D. entertain the reader with humor.

STOP

© Scott Foresman 5

Sequence

Directions: Read the story. Then read each question about the story. Choose the best answer to each question. Mark the letter for the answer you have chosen.

My New Home

As I think about living in Hicksville, I vividly remember the day we moved there. I hadn't known much about the town, and I didn't know anything at all about the neighborhood. Mom seemed to know I would like it. I was both scared and excited. Would I like the house? Would I make new friends?

I could hardly wait to see my new home. As soon as we got there, I raced from my parents' car and went straight into the house. It looked so much bigger than the old apartment.

"Where's my room?" I asked. Dad pointed to the long staircase.

"At the top of the stairs and to the right," Dad said.

I found my room right away because I recognized my boxes. My clothes, my music, and all my other things were in those boxes. As I began unpacking a box of school clothes, I heard a barking noise outside. I looked through my window.

I couldn't believe it. In the next yard were two dogs. I loved dogs, although I had none of my own. I went outside and looked over the backyard fence. A boy about my own age was feeding one of the dogs. The dog glanced at me and wagged its tail but kept eating. The boy came over to the fence.

"Hi," the boy said. "You must be the new neighbor."

1. The first thing the narrator does after getting to the new house is—
   A. go to the narrator's room.
   B. look out the window.
   C. leave the car.
   D. hear a dog bark.

2. In the room, the narrator first—
   F. starts to unpack.
   G. sees the window.
   H. hears dogs barking.
   J. meets the boy next door.

3. Just before looking out the window, the narrator—
   A. goes downstairs.
   B. hears the neighbors talking.
   C. hears barking.
   D. carries a box.

4. The narrator goes outside and looks over the fence because he or she—
   F. wants to meet a neighbor.
   G. is bored.
   H. hears voices.
   J. loves dogs.

5. The last thing the narrator does in the story is—
   A. return to the car.
   B. meet the neighbor.
   C. meet the dogs.
   D. unpack a box.

Notes for Home: Your child read a story, and then identified the order in which events happened. *Home Activity:* With your child, read a magazine or newspaper article that tells about an event that took place. Then have your child describe the event to you, in his or her own words, in order.

Phonics: Complex Spelling Patterns

Directions: Words that end in **-ough** or **-ought** can be tricky. They don't all sound alike. Read the sentences. Then read the words in ( ). Circle the word that has the same vowel sound as the underlined word in the sentence.

1. They saved <u>enough</u> money to buy a house.   (though/tough)

2. They <u>brought</u> their belongings with them.   (thought/bough)

3. The new neighborhood was <u>rough</u>.   (though/tough)

4. People sometimes <u>fought</u> on his block.   (brought/found)

5. The police <u>ought</u> to do something about it.   (out/thought)

6. He never got in fights, <u>although</u> others did.   (loud/dough)

Directions: Read the poster below. The phrase in ( ) is a clue to the missing word. Choose the word from the box with the same vowel sound as the word in ( ). Make sure the words make sense in the sentence. Write the word on the line.

Hey everyone! We _____ (sounds like *fought*) you could use a party!

We _____ (sounds like *fought*) lots of food at the store.

Even _____ (sounds like *dough*) you have a lot of work to do, come join us!

It's a _____ (sounds like *tough*) job, but someone has to have fun!

though	thought	rough	bought

7. _____   9. _____

8. _____   10. _____

Notes for Home: Your child matched vowel sounds for words that end in *-ough* and *-ought* such as *though* and *thought*. **Home Activity:** Make up several short sentences that include words ending in *-ough* or *-ought*. Say the sentences aloud and have your child write them.

© Scott Foresman 5

Manual

A **manual** is a written set of directions that helps readers understand or use something. It usually comes in the form of a booklet or a book.

Directions: Use the pages from a manual for a refrigerator to answer the questions that follow.

Know Your Refrigerator

Table of Contents

Temperature Controls

There are two types of controls for your refrigerator. The fresh food control uses numbers. The freezer control uses letters. When installing, set the fresh food control at 5 and the freezer control at C as shown in the diagrams.

The fresh food control maintains the temperatures throughout the refrigerator. Setting the control to OFF will stop the cooling in both the fresh food area and the freezer area, but this will not shut off the power to the refrigerator.

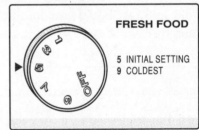

FRESH FOOD
5 INITIAL SETTING
9 COLDEST

The freezer control moves a damper that changes the amount of cold air that moves from the freezer to the fresh food compartment.

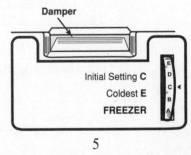

Damper

Initial Setting **C**
Coldest **E**
FREEZER

5

© Scott Foresman 5

Name _____

1. What is the purpose of this manual? _____

_____

2. When might you use this manual? Give an example. _____

_____

_____

3. The table of contents is listed in alphabetical order. Why might this be helpful?

_____

_____

_____

4. On which page would you find information to clean the drawers? _____

5. What kinds of information would you expect to find on page 4? _____

_____

_____

6. What are the two types of temperature controls? _____

_____

7. At what settings should you put the two temperature controls when you are installing the refrigerator?

_____

_____

8. What is the coldest setting for each temperature control? _____

_____

9. Why are diagrams like the ones shown helpful in a manual?

_____

_____

10. If you were using this manual to help install a new refrigerator, why is it important to follow the directions for installation exactly as they are written?

_____

_____

_____

Notes for Home: Your child answered questions about a refrigerator manual. *Home Activity:* Together with your child, read part of a manual you have at home, such as a manual for operating your TV. Talk about the different kinds of information that the manual gives.

© Scott Foresman 5

Steps in a Process

- The actions you take to make something or to reach a goal are the **steps in a process.**

- When you read, look for clues that help you follow the steps. Clues may be numbers, illustrations, or words such as *first, next, then,* and *last.*

- If there are no clues, think of what you already know about how the process might be done.

Directions: Reread "First-Aid ABCs." Then complete the flowchart by listing in order the steps you should take if you suspect that someone is choking.

Step 1:

↓

Step 2:

↓

Step 3:

↓

Step 4:

↓

Step 5:

↓

Step 6: Repeat until the food or object comes out of the person's mouth.

Notes for Home: Your child read an article and showed the order of the steps for the Heimlich maneuver. *Home Activity:* Have your child describe the steps of the Heimlich maneuver in order. Then take turns acting out the Heimlich maneuver, without using any thrusting force.

© Scott Foresman 5

Name _____

The Diver and the Dolphins

Vocabulary

Directions: Choose the word from the box that best completes each
statement. Write the word on the line to the left.

_____   1. *Bus* is to *travel* as *telephone* is to _____.

_____   2. *Desert* is to *camels* as *ocean* is to _____.

_____   3. *Enemy* is to *argue* as *friend* is to _____.

_____   4. *Medal* is to *honored* as *bandage* is
                               to _____.

_____   5. *Separation* is to *separate* as *desperation*
                               is to _____.

Check the Words You Know
__ communicate
__ cooperate
__ desperate
__ dolphins
__ doomed
__ hovered
__ injured

Directions: Choose the word from the box that best matches each clue.
Write the word in the puzzle.

Down

6. stayed near
7. sea mammals

Across

8. headed for a terrible fate
9. work together
10. hurt

Write a Persuasive Paragraph

Think of a problem that an ocean creature has, such as polluted waters, lack of
food, or safe resting places. On a separate sheet of paper, write a paragraph that
persuades readers to help this ocean creature. Use as many vocabulary words as
you can.

Notes for Home: Your child identified and used vocabulary words from "The Diver and the
Dolphins." *Home Activity:* Using a dictionary, find simple definitions for words and read
them aloud to your child. See if your child can guess each word.

52 Vocabulary

© Scott Foresman 5

Name _____

Steps in a Process

- The actions you take to make something or to reach a goal are the **steps in a process.**

- When you read, look for clues that help you follow the steps. Clues may be numbers, illustrations, or words such as *first, next, then,* and *last.*

- If there are no clues, think of what you already know about how the process might be done.

Directions: Reread what happens in "The Diver and the Dolphins" when Wayne frees the baby dolphin. Then answer the questions below. Think about the order of the steps.

> I gently held the baby on the sea floor, then cut the trailing fishing line free until all that was left was the part embedded under the baby's tender skin. Getting it out with as little pain for the baby as possible was going to be the hard part.
>
> Then, bit by bit, I started pulling the embedded line loose so I could cut it with my knife. As I pulled it up, more blood flowed out.
>
> I looked around for sharks, not wanting to get in the way if the parent dolphins needed to protect their baby from attack.
>
> Seeing no sharks, I gently continued to pull some line free.... Finally, all the line was cut free except for a short piece attached to the hook.
>
> From DOLPHIN ADVENTURE by Wayne Grover. Copyright 1990 by Wayne Grover. By permission of Greenwillow Books, a division of William Morrow & Company, Inc.

1. What process is being described?

_____

2. Write all the steps Wayne took to get the line free. Number the steps in correct order.

_____

_____

3. What clue words does the writer use to indicate the order of the steps?

_____

4. Did Wayne work quickly or slowly? How do you know?

_____

_____

5. On a separate sheet of paper, write all the steps Wayne took to get the hook out of the dolphin's flesh. Number the steps in the correct order.

Notes for Home: Your child read a story and described the steps in a process. *Home Activity:* Work with your child to describe the steps in a simple process, such as making a sandwich or getting ready for school.

© Scott Foresman 5

Name _____

1.	Ⓐ	Ⓑ	Ⓒ	Ⓓ
2.	Ⓕ	Ⓖ	Ⓗ	Ⓙ
3.	Ⓐ	Ⓑ	Ⓒ	Ⓓ
4.	Ⓕ	Ⓖ	Ⓗ	Ⓙ
5.	Ⓐ	Ⓑ	Ⓒ	Ⓓ
6.	Ⓕ	Ⓖ	Ⓗ	Ⓙ
7.	Ⓐ	Ⓑ	Ⓒ	Ⓓ
8.	Ⓕ	Ⓖ	Ⓗ	Ⓙ
9.	Ⓐ	Ⓑ	Ⓒ	Ⓓ
10.	Ⓕ	Ⓖ	Ⓗ	Ⓙ
11.	Ⓐ	Ⓑ	Ⓒ	Ⓓ
12.	Ⓕ	Ⓖ	Ⓗ	Ⓙ
13.	Ⓐ	Ⓑ	Ⓒ	Ⓓ
14.	Ⓕ	Ⓖ	Ⓗ	Ⓙ
15.	Ⓐ	Ⓑ	Ⓒ	Ⓓ

© Scott Foresman 5

Name _____

The Diver and the Dolphins

Selection Test

Directions: Choose the best answer to each item. Mark the letter for the answer you have chosen.

Part 1: Vocabulary

Find the answer choice that means about the same as the underlined word in each sentence.

1. He was <u>desperate</u>.
   - A. ready to try anything
   - B. totally out of control
   - C. very sad
   - D. greatly pleased

2. The dogs <u>hovered</u> as we ate.
   - F. stayed in or near one place
   - G. moved about in a secret way
   - H. paid no attention
   - J. gave long, sad cries

3. They were trying to <u>communicate</u>.
   - A. blend in with others
   - B. show sorrow for another's suffering
   - C. help someone in need
   - D. send and receive information

4. We watched the <u>dolphins</u>.
   - F. kinds of seals
   - G. fish that live in lakes
   - H. kinds of sharks
   - J. mammals that live in the sea

5. The king was <u>doomed</u>.
   - A. weakened in spirit
   - B. certain to have an unhappy end
   - C. very excited
   - D. having the most power

6. The children were learning to <u>cooperate</u>.
   - F. speak clearly
   - G. try hard to win
   - H. work together with others
   - J. find the way home

7. The horse was <u>injured</u>.
   - A. hurt
   - B. exhausted
   - C. filled with anger
   - D. tied down

Part 2: Comprehension

Use what you know about the selection to answer each item.

8. What noise were the dolphins making as they approached Wayne Grover?
   - F. splashing
   - G. clicking
   - H. crying
   - J. swishing

9. The baby dolphin's wound was caused by —
   - A. a diver's knife.
   - B. sharks.
   - C. a fish hook.
   - D. a boat.

10. What did Wayne Grover do first in the process of helping the baby dolphin?
    - F. He went to the surface to breathe.
    - G. He cut the fishing line.
    - H. He tried to loosen the hook with his finger.
    - J. He used his knife on the hook.

11. Grover stroked the baby dolphin to—
    - A. find the wound.
    - B. help it breathe.
    - C. calm it.
    - D. stop the bleeding.

© Scott Foresman 5

GO ON

12. Why was Grover especially fearful of sharks while he worked to help the baby dolphin?

    F.   Sharks are attracted to blood.

    G.   Sharks often attack divers who stay in one place.

    H.   Sharks often hunt for young dolphins.

    J.   Sharks follow the sounds that dolphins make.

13. What was the last step Grover took before he let the baby dolphin go?

    A.   He slipped the knife into the wound.

    B   He took the hook out of the muscle.

    C.   He held the dolphin down with his leg.

    D.   He pressed hard on the wound to stop the flow of blood.

14. You can tell from reading this selection that the author—

    F.   learned how to speak with dolphins.

    G.   was frightened by this experience.

    H.   was very moved by this experience.

    J.   gained a new respect for sharks.

15. Which action by the father dolphin best supports the idea that the dolphin parents were asking Wayne Grover to help their baby?

    A.   The father shot away when Grover reached out to touch him.

    B.   After bringing the baby to Grover, the father lifted Grover's arm.

    C.   The father raced off to attack a large bull shark.

    D.   The father returned quickly when the mother clicked.

STOP

© Scott Foresman 5

Cause and Effect

REVIEW

Directions: Read the story. Then read each question about the story. Choose the best answer to each question. Mark the letter for the answer you have chosen.

Fun with Fins

"Let's go scuba diving, Nick!" Luis said on the phone.

"Great idea!" I answered. "I'll check with my parents and get back to you this afternoon."

My parents knew I was a good diver, so they gave me permission right away.

I called Luis back, and we made plans to dive at Crescent Reef in a week. Crescent Reef was one of our favorite spots.

Since I had not been scuba diving in a while, I spent the week rereading my safety manual. I studied the rules carefully. I reviewed how to use the breathing equipment and how to fasten the weight belt. I read about how long it is safe to stay in the deep water. I felt a lot more confident as a result.

On the day of the dive, Luis picked me up early. I loaded my diving equipment. Then I went back for the extras. Luis laughed when he saw my pack. On the four-hour drive to get to the reef, though, he was glad I had packed food and water bottles. On the four-hour drive back, he was glad I'd brought the extra dry towels too.

Thanks to my planning, the dive was a great success. We had the best time! I can't wait to do it again.

1. Nick asked his parents if he could go scuba diving because—
   A. he needed to get their permission first.
   B. he thought it was a great idea.
   C. Luis told him to ask.
   D. diving was his favorite sport.

2. One effect of Nick's not having dived for a while was that—
   F. he asked permission first.
   G. he packed a lot of food.
   H. he reread his safety manual to review the diving rules.
   J. he felt confident.

3. Rereading his safety manual caused Nick to—
   A. feel more confident.
   B. study the rules harder.
   C. pack more food.
   D. be a better friend.

4. Why did Nick pack food, water, and extra dry towels?
   F. Luis always forgot to pack.
   G. They had to drive four hours each way.
   H. They were leaving early.
   J. His parents told him to do it.

5. Why was Nick and Luis's diving trip a great success?
   A. Luis is a good friend.
   B. The weather was good.
   C. Nick planned the trip carefully.
   D. Nick wanted to go again.

Notes for Home: Your child read a story and identified causes and effects. *Home Activity:* Invite your child to explain the causes (why something happens) and effects (what happens) of playing a sport such as baseball or soccer.

© Scott Foresman 5

Phonics: Consonant Sounds for *c* and *g*

Directions: Read the sentences below. Two words in each sentence have the letter **c.** One word has a **hard-c** sound as in **care.** The other word has a **soft-c** sound as in **face.** Circle the words with the **hard-c** sound. Underline the words with the **soft-c** sound.

1. I decided to try to call the dolphin.

2. My voice seemed to encourage the dolphin.

3. In fact, the dolphin surfaced immediately.

4. I carefully placed my hand on its skin.

5. The dolphin soon became peaceful.

Directions: Read the sentences below. Two words in each sentence have the letter **g.** One word has a **hard-g** sound as in **get.** The other word has the **soft-g** sound as in **giant.** Circle the word with the **hard-g.** Underline the word with the **soft-g.**

6. A large dolphin was snagged in the net.

7. It began to thrash its huge tail.

8. The situation grew dangerous.

9. One gentle tug released it.

10. I imagined the dolphin gave me a smile.

Directions: Find the word in each sentence that has both a **hard** and a **soft consonant sound.** Write the word on the line.

_____ 11. Dolphins can be very engaging and gentle creatures.

_____ 12. They speak their own language using signals.

_____ 13. I'm convinced they like me to come dive near them.

_____ 14. I see them circling around me in the water.

_____ 15. I encourage their playful behavior.

Notes for Home: Your child identified words with hard-*c* sounds *(care)*, soft-*c* sounds *(face)*, hard-*g* sounds *(get)*, and soft-*g* sounds *(giant)*. **Home Activity:** Read a book about sea animals with your child. Have your child to find and pronounce words with these letters and sounds.

© Scott Foresman 5

Chart/Table

A **chart** organizes information in a visual way. It may include words, numbers, or both. A **table** is a type of chart that organizes information in rows and columns.

Directions: Use the table to answer the questions that follow.

Type of Whale	Scientific name	Where It Lives	Length
Dall porpoise	*Phocoenoides dalli*	Pacific Ocean	up to 6 feet (1.8 meters)
pilot whale	*Globicephala melaena*	Atlantic Ocean	up to 20 feet (6 meters)
white-sided dolphin	*Lagenorhynchus albirostris*	North Atlantic Ocean	up to 9 feet (2.7 meters)
killer whale	*Orcinus orca*	all oceans	up to 30 feet (9 meters)
bottle-nosed dolphin	*Tursiops truncatus*	all oceans	up to 9 feet (2.7 meters)
common porpoise	*Phocoena phocoena*	all oceans	up to 6 feet (1.8 meters)
common dolphin	*Delphinus delphis*	all oceans	up to 8 feet (2.4 meters)

1. What is the scientific name for the bottle-nosed dolphin? _____

_____

2. Where does the pilot whale live? _____

3. How long may a killer whale be? _____

4. What kind of dolphin has the scientific name *Phocoena phocoena?* _____

_____

© Scott Foresman 5

Name _____

5. Which type of whale may be the longest in length? _____

_____

6. Which types of dolphins may be the shortest in length? _____

_____

7. Which type of dolphin is found only in the Pacific Ocean? _____

_____

8. Which types of dolphins may be found in all oceans? _____

_____

_____

9. How much longer may a common dolphin be than a common porpoise? _____

_____

10. Where can the white-sided dolphin be found? _____

_____

11. Which dolphin has the scientific name *Lagenorhynchus albirostris?* _____

_____

12. Is every pilot whale 20 feet long? Explain. _____

_____

_____

_____

13. Which types of dolphins are found in only one ocean? _____

_____

14. Are most full-grown dolphins longer or shorter than most fifth graders? Explain.

_____

_____

_____

15. Are tables useful for comparing information? Explain. _____

_____

_____

Notes for Home: Your child analyzed information in a table. *Home Activity:* Work with your child to create a table with information about different family members. Columns on the chart might list information such as each person's name, age, color of hair, color of eyes, and height.

© Scott Foresman 5

Graphic Sources

- A **graphic source** is something that shows information visually. Pictures, charts, graphs, and maps are graphic sources.

- Graphic sources can help you better understand what you read because they provide a lot of information that can be seen quickly.

Directions: Reread "Hurricane Seasons." Then use the bar graph and the text to answer the questions below.

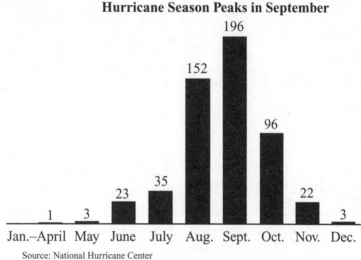

Hurricane Season Peaks in September

Source: National Hurricane Center

1. Read the labels on the bar graph and text. What does the bar graph show?

_____

_____

2. How do you know to which years the bar graph refers?

_____

_____

3. The text says that more than 80% of the hurricanes occur from August through October. How does the bar graph help show this information?

_____

_____

4. Would you use the text or the bar graph to compare different months?

_____

5. Which month has the second highest number of hurricanes? _____

Notes for Home: Your child read a short text and studied a related bar graph. ***Home Activity:*** Together with your child, read a weather report and study a weather map from a newspaper. Discuss what information each reveals and how the map can help you understand the text.

© Scott Foresman 5

Vocabulary

Directions: Read the following weather bulletin. Choose the word from the box that best completes each sentence. Write the word on the matching numbered line to the right.

WEATHER BULLETIN

Our weather radar has managed to

1. _____ a dangerous **2.** _____ that is

blowing over the Atlantic Ocean. We

3. _____ that the **4.** _____ winds will

hit our area around noon tomorrow.

Since they could do heavy **5.** _____,

all residents are advised to board up

their windows.

1. _____

2. _____

3. _____

4. _____

5. _____

Check the Words You Know

__ damage

__ ecology

__ hurricane

__ identify

__ mightiest

__ predict

__ pressure

__ recovered

Directions: Choose the word from the box that best matches each clue. Write the word in the puzzle.

Down

6. the force per unit of area
7. relationship between living things and the environment
8. tell before an event happens
10. harm or injury

Across

9. got back something lost

Write a Weather Report

Imagine you witnessed a storm. On a separate sheet of paper, report what happened. Use as many vocabulary words as you can.

Notes for Home: Your child identified and used new vocabulary words from "The Fury of a Hurricane" **Home Activity:** Imagine you and your child are weather reporters. Use as many vocabulary words as possible to describe a terrible storm.

© Scott Foresman 5

Graphic Sources

- A **graphic source** shows information, such as a picture, graph, or map, visually.

- As you read, compare the written words to the graphic sources for a better understanding of the main ideas.

Directions: Study the following maps from "The Fury of a Hurricane." Then use the maps to answer the questions below.

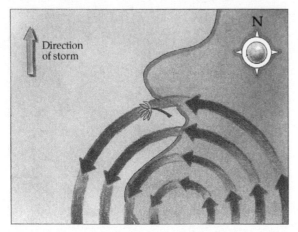 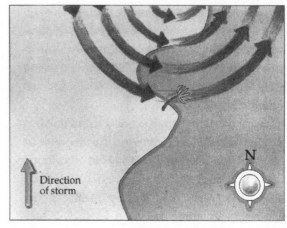

If hurricane winds first blow from the east, they will blow from the west after the eye has passed.

From HURRICANES: EARTH'S MIGHTIEST STORMS by Patricia Lauber. Copyright © 1996 by Patricia Lauber. Reprinted by permission of Scholastic Inc.

Directions: Refer to the graphics to answer the questions below.

1. According to the compass and the arrow, in which direction is the storm moving?

_____

2. What do the maps show?

_____

_____

_____

3. How does the caption help you interpret the maps?

_____

4. How do the maps help you understand what the text is saying about wind direction?

_____

5. Choose another graphic source from "The Fury of a Hurricane." On a separate piece of paper, tell how the graphic source helps you understand the information in the text.

 Notes for Home: Your child analyzed two maps and a caption. *Home Activity:* Use newspapers to discuss with your child what is shown in a different graphic source, such as a schedule or a bar graph.

© Scott Foresman 5

Name _____

1.	(A)	(B)	(C)	(D)
2.	(F)	(G)	(H)	(J)
3.	(A)	(B)	(C)	(D)
4.	(F)	(G)	(H)	(J)
5.	(A)	(B)	(C)	(D)
6.	(F)	(G)	(H)	(J)
7.	(A)	(B)	(C)	(D)
8.	(F)	(G)	(H)	(J)
9.	(A)	(B)	(C)	(D)
10.	(F)	(G)	(H)	(J)
11.	(A)	(B)	(C)	(D)
12.	(F)	(G)	(H)	(J)
13.	(A)	(B)	(C)	(D)
14.	(F)	(G)	(H)	(J)
15.	(A)	(B)	(C)	(D)

© Scott Foresman 5

Selection Test

Directions: Choose the best answer to each item. Mark the letter for the answer you have chosen.

Part 1: Vocabulary

Find the answer choice that means about the same as the underlined word in each sentence.

1. These are the <u>mightiest</u> storms.
   A. most frightening
   B. longest lasting
   C. most interesting
   D. most powerful

2. The <u>ecology</u> of the area has changed.
   F. population growth
   G. physical features such as rocks
   H. kinds of houses
   J. relation between living things and their environment

3. They ran to take shelter from the <u>hurricane</u>.
   A. a storm with violent winds that begins over tropical waters
   B. a seasonal wind that brings rain from April to October
   C. a cloud shaped like a funnel
   D. a storm with heavy snow

4. People in the area soon <u>recovered</u>.
   F. got help or support
   G. became smaller
   H. got back to normal
   J. were hit again

5. The storm did not cause much <u>damage</u>.
   A. loss of courage
   B. harm or injury
   C. change in how people live
   D. feeling that nothing good can happen

6. Did you <u>predict</u> that this would happen?
   F. tell ahead of time
   G. make up one's mind
   H. feel afraid
   J. take for granted

7. The weather report shows an area of low <u>pressure</u> to the west.
   A. amount of water in the air
   B. wind speed
   C. weight of the atmosphere on the earth's surface
   D. calm area in the center of a storm

8. We wanted to <u>identify</u> each tree.
   F. find a use for
   G. give a name to
   H. look at carefully
   J. protect the life of

Part 2: Comprehension

Use what you know about the selection to answer each item.

9. Beginning in 1979, hurricanes for the first time were named after—
   A. men.
   B. women.
   C. animals.
   D. cities.

10. As a hurricane forms, the warm air—
    F. becomes colder.
    G. sinks into the water.
    H. goes up.
    J. becomes very dry.

11. On each side of a hurricane, the—
    A. warm air sinks.
    B. winds blow in different directions.
    C. rain turns to snow.
    D. water turns different colors.

GO ON

© Scott Foresman 5

12. During Hurricane Andrew, the greatest damage was caused by—
  F. clouds.
  G. rain.
  H. thunder.
  J. wind.

13. When Hurricane Andrew hit Florida, help was slow to arrive because—
  A. the army was not prepared.
  B. too many people were using telephones at once.
  C. people did not realize how great the damage was.
  D. members of the government refused to spend money.

14. Which conclusion does this selection best support?
  F. Hurricanes and human activities have changed Florida's environment.
  G. Areas hit by hurricanes generally recover quickly.
  H. People should be doing more to stop hurricanes.
  J. Hurricanes have ruined most of Florida.

15. The author's main purpose in writing this selection is to—
  A. entertain with an exciting story.
  B. describe the towns of Homestead and Florida City.
  C. express strong opinions about hurricanes.
  D. give information about hurricanes.

STOP

© Scott Foresman 5

Author's Purpose and Text Structure

Directions: Read the passage. Then read each question about the passage. Choose the best answer to each question. Mark the letter for the answer you have chosen.

Fighting the Floodwaters

The city of New Orleans has always had a problem with flooding. The city's location is part of the reason. New Orleans lies between two great bodies of water, the Mississippi River on the south and Lake Pontchartrain on the north. When the Mississippi River rises from heavy rainfall to the north, the extra water naturally tries to spread out into the city. There is danger to the city from the river during heavy rains. Hurricanes traveling along the Gulf Coast also bring a threat of flooding in the city.

Another reason New Orleans often has water problems is that the city itself is like a saucer in a way. Its edges are higher than its middle. The middle dips below sea level. When a hurricane hits or when the river floods, there is always a chance that the city will fill with water.

The Orleans Levee Board was created to address the problem of flooding. The Levee Board taxes citizens and uses the money to build high banks along the river called *levees* and floodwalls.

Over the years, millions of dollars have been spent on hurricane and flood protection. Today the city is safeguarded by a complex system of levees, floodwalls, and floodgates. The longest of the levees and floodwalls are along the Mississippi River and Lake Pontchartrain.

1. This text is—
   A. fiction.
   B. nonfiction.
   C. poetry.
   D. drama.

2. This passage—
   F. describes a terrible flood.
   G. argues that levees are useful.
   H. provides flood statistics.
   J. describes a way to solve a flooding problem.

3. The organization of this text is best described as—
   A. cause and effect.
   B. problem and solution.
   C. comparison and contrast.
   D. sequence of events.

4. This passage is—
   F. funny.
   G. emotional.
   H. informative.
   J. persuasive.

5. What do you think is the author's purpose for writing?
   A. to entertain
   B. to express
   C. to persuade
   D. to inform

Notes for Home: Your child read a passage and identified the author's purpose and the organization of the text. *Home Activity:* Work with your child to analyze a newspaper article. Study the way the article is organized and evaluate the author's purpose.

© Scott Foresman 5

Phonics: Silent Consonants

Directions: **Silent consonants** are letters you don't hear when you say a word. Read the groups of words below. Say each word to yourself. Circle the word that has the silent consonant. Underline the consonant that is silent.

1. kitten
   kite
   knocked
   keep

2. wrist
   ring
   rack
   rust

3. gate
   ghost
   gale
   gone

4. icing
   icicle
   igloo
   island

5. wrong
   won
   rang
   wind

6. baseball
   bomb
   burger
   basket

7. corridor
   careful
   charter
   column

8. forget
   forest
   foreign
   forgive

9. knife
   kissing
   kept
   kilometer

Directions: Read the weather report. Find six words with silent consonants. Write each word on the line.

WEATHER BULLETIN

A large storm will hit our area sometime today. Radar signs show us that it will bring strong winds and heavy downpours. If you live near the coast, take cover. Listen for the warning whistle. We know it will be hard, but stay off the roads. Watch out for fallen tree limbs. Fasten all your shutters and doors and stay inside.

10. _____
11. _____
12. _____
13. _____
14. _____
15. _____

Notes for Home: Your child identified words with silent consonants, such as the *g* in *design*. ***Home Activity:*** Read or listen to a local weather report with your child. Ask your child to point out any words with silent consonants.

© Scott Foresman 5

Parts of a Book

Parts of a book include its cover, title page, copyright page, table of contents, chapter titles, captions, section heads, other text features, glossary, and index.

Directions: Use the parts of a book shown below to answer the questions on the next page.

Natural Disasters Since 1900
by Ronald O'Day

Chronicle Publication Society
New York, NY

Title Page

Copyright © 1985 Ronald O'Day

All rights reserved. No part of this book may be reproduced in any form without written permission of the publisher. Permission requests should be addressed to Chronicle Publishing Society, 100 Main Street, New York, NY, 10000.

O'Day, Ronald.
　Natural Disasters Since 1900/by Ronald O'Day.
　Includes index.
　ISBN 1-33000-219-6
　1. Earthquakes, Volcanoes, Floods, Storms.

Copyright Page

Table of Contents

Table of Contents

Index

Index

Name _____

1. What is the title of this book? _____

2. Who wrote this book? _____

3. When was the book published? _____

4. If you were seeking information about the Johnstown flood of 1889, would this book be helpful to you? Explain.

   _____

   _____

5. If you were seeking information about the California earthquake of 1989, would this book be helpful? Why or why not?

   _____

   _____

6. How many chapters are there in this book? _____

7. What is the main topic of Chapter 3? _____

8. In which chapter would you learn about tornadoes? _____

9. In which chapter would you learn about causes of an earthquake? _____

10. On which page or pages are sandstorms discussed? _____

11. On which page or pages are blizzards discussed? _____

12. What is the meaning of the index entry **"Rivers,** see **Floods"?** _____

    _____

    _____

13. Which part of a book will help you decide how up-to-date its information is? Explain.

    _____

    _____

    _____

14. If you were seeking information on the volcanic eruption of Mt. St. Helens in Washington on May 18, 1980, would this book be helpful to you? Explain.

    _____

    _____

15. Which chapter might explain what the term *disaster* means? _____

Notes for Home: Your child used the parts of a book (the title page, copyright page, table of contents, and index) to find information. ***Home Activity:*** Choose a book. Have your child identify and talk about the different parts of the book.

© Scott Foresman 5

Fact and Opinion

- A **fact** is something that can be proved true or false. Statements of fact can be proved by checking reference books, observing, measuring, and so on.

- An **opinion** tells a person's ideas or feelings. It cannot be proved true or false, but it can be supported or explained.

Directions: Reread "A Volunteer's Help." Then complete the table. Read each statement about Ellen's flood volunteer work, and answer the questions at the top of each column.

Statements	Does it state a fact or an opinion?	If an opinion, are there any clue words? If a fact, how could you try to prove it?
Ellen and her friends gathered 15 cartons of food and toys.	1.	2.
I felt really sad.	3.	4.
I thought there should be something we could do to help.	5.	6.
Lots of kids brought stuff in.	7.	8.
I felt good about it.	9.	10.

Notes for Home: Your child read a story and identified statements of fact and opinion. *Home Activity:* Read a movie or TV review with your child. Together, decide which statements are statements of fact and which are statements of opinion.

© Scott Foresman 5

Vocabulary

Directions: Match each word on the left with its definition on the right. Write the letter of the definition next to the word.

_____ 1. advised   **a.** things sent and received

_____ 2. deliveries   **b.** not lucky

_____ 3. donate   **c.** arranged

_____ 4. organized   **d.** told how to do

_____ 5. unfortunate   **e.** give money or help

Check the Words You Know

__ advised
__ deliveries
__ donate
__ organized
__ unfortunate

Directions: Choose the word from the box that best completes each statement. Write the word on the line to the left.

_____ **6.** *Pony* is to *ponies* as *delivery* is to _____.

_____ **7.** *Happy* is to *sad* as *lucky* is to _____.

_____ **8.** *Invent* is to *create* as *give* is to _____.

_____ **9.** *Acted* is to *performed* as *counseled* is to _____.

_____ **10.** *Long* is to *short* as *jumbled* is to _____.

Directions: Choose the word from the box that best completes each sentence. Write the word on the line.

_____ **11.** Keitha and Matt _____ their time at the local food bank.

_____ **12.** Last month the food bank _____ a drive to collect canned goods from the community.

_____ **13.** Keitha and Matt designed flyers that _____ people on what kinds of goods were most needed and when donations could be dropped off at the food bank.

_____ **14.** The food bank also provides meals to any _____ person who needs it.

_____ **15.** Since Matt is old enough to drive, he makes _____ of hot meals to people who can't leave their homes.

Write a News Story

On a separate sheet of paper, write a news story about someone who did a good deed. Use as many vocabulary words as you can.

Notes for Home: Your child identified and used vocabulary words from "Dwaina Brooks." *Home Activity:* Discuss with your child ways people can help out others. Use the vocabulary words, such as: *You can <u>donate</u> your time to visiting someone in a nursing home.*

© Scott Foresman 5

Fact and Opinion

- A **fact** is a statement that can be proved true or false. Even if it is false, it is still a statement of fact.

- An **opinion** is someone's ideas or feelings. Opinions cannot be proved true or false.

Directions: Reread this passage from "Dwaina Brooks" about Dwaina's accomplishments and goals. Then answer the questions below.

In a little more than two years, Dwaina Brooks, now in sixth grade, has organized several thousand meals for unfortunate people in the Dallas area. She and her mother and the classmates who sometimes still join in have perfected the art of helping others and having fun at the same time. They do it by doing something they already love to do: cooking and putting meals together.

Dwaina hopes to become a doctor and open her own clinic someday, but she thinks it's crazy to wait till then to start caring for others. "Kids should get going," she says. "There aren't enough jobs out there, especially for people without diplomas. Not even at McDonald's. We should try to help. If we don't act, there will be more and more homeless people. . . ."

From IT'S OUR WORLD TOO! by Phillip Hoose. Copyright ©1993 by Phillip Hoose. By permission of Little, Brown and Company.

1. Is the first sentence a statement of fact or a statement of opinion? Explain.

_____

2. List two ways you could verify the statement made in the opening sentence.

_____

_____

3. Reread the quote from Dwaina. Is she stating facts or is she stating her opinion when she says, "Kids should get going."

_____

_____

4. How might you prove that there are not enough jobs for people without diplomas?

_____

_____

5. On a separate sheet of paper, write two statements of fact and two statements of opinion from the rest of the article.

 Notes for Home: Your child read a nonfiction article and identified statements of fact and opinion. *Home Activity:* Work with your child to recognize statements of fact and opinion in a television or movie review.

© Scott Foresman 5

Name _____

1.	(A)	(B)	(C)	(D)
2.	(F)	(G)	(H)	(J)
3.	(A)	(B)	(C)	(D)
4.	(F)	(G)	(H)	(J)
5.	(A)	(B)	(C)	(D)
6.	(F)	(G)	(H)	(J)
7.	(A)	(B)	(C)	(D)
8.	(F)	(G)	(H)	(J)
9.	(A)	(B)	(C)	(D)
10.	(F)	(G)	(H)	(J)
11.	(A)	(B)	(C)	(D)
12.	(F)	(G)	(H)	(J)
13.	(A)	(B)	(C)	(D)
14.	(F)	(G)	(H)	(J)
15.	(A)	(B)	(C)	(D)

© Scott Foresman 5

Selection Test

Directions: Choose the best answer to each item. Mark the letter for the answer you have chosen.

Part 1: Vocabulary

Find the answer choice that means about the same as the underlined word in each sentence.

1. Leon agreed to <u>donate</u> his old bike.
   A. fix up
   B. give to a cause
   C. rent out
   D. set the value of

2. Alice made <u>deliveries</u> for her uncle.
   F. acts of carrying and giving out things
   G. requests or orders
   H. acts of collecting and organizing things
   J. reasons for doing something

3. The librarian <u>advised</u> me.
   A. refused to help
   B. gave an order to
   C. offered suggestions to
   D. tried to prevent

4. They <u>organized</u> the clothing.
   F. used again
   G. cleaned and repaired
   H. looked at carefully
   J. put together in order

5. He was an <u>unfortunate</u> man.
   A. not lucky
   B. not powerful
   C. not happy
   D. not interesting

Part 2: Comprehension

Use what you know about the selection to answer each item.

6. What grade was Dwaina in when she started making meals for the homeless?
   F. third
   G. fourth
   H. fifth
   J. sixth

7. Dwaina got the idea of making meals for the homeless when she—
   A. saw homeless people on the street.
   B. talked to a homeless man on the telephone.
   C. visited a homeless shelter.
   D. discussed the homeless with her class at school.

8. Which of these events happened first?
   F. A baker gave Dwaina twenty free boxes.
   G. Dwaina took 105 meals to the homeless center.
   H. Crystal and Stephanie helped make sandwiches.
   J. Two men helped carry the boxes into the homeless center.

9. Which word best describes Dwaina?
   A. nosy
   B. quiet
   C. wealthy
   D. caring

10. Dwaina and her mother decided to buy day-old bread instead of fresh bread because it—
    F. saved money.
    G. tasted better.
    H. lasted longer.
    J. was sold nearby.

GO ON

© Scott Foresman 5

11. Which sentence states an opinion?
    A. Dwaina gave her lunch money to a homeless shelter.
    B. They spent three days shopping and preparing.
    C. Kids should pitch in to help the homeless.
    D. Dwaina and her classmates made more than 300 meals in one night.

12. Which statement is a valid generalization based on the facts in this selection?
    F. Most people who help the homeless were once homeless themselves.
    G. Many homeless people once had lives that were going along okay.
    H. Most homeless people need only one good meal.
    J. Many children are looking for ways to help homeless people.

13. Which sentence states a fact?
    A. We should all take care of other people.
    B. Dwaina Brooks will be a great doctor.
    C. Dwaina Brooks is the most generous girl in her school.
    D. There are hundreds of homeless people in Dallas.

14. What can you tell about the author of this selection?
    F. He is a lot like Dwaina.
    G. He is related to Dwaina.
    H. He has helped Dwaina.
    J. He admires Dwaina.

15. Which title below best fits this story?
    A. "Kids Can Make a Difference"
    B. "How to Make Hundreds of Sandwiches"
    C. "Coming Home on Fridays"
    D. "Life in a Homeless Shelter"

STOP

© Scott Foresman 5

Steps in a Process

REVIEW

Directions: Read the passage. Then read each question about the passage. Choose the best answer to each question. Mark the letter for the answer you have chosen.

Working for the Homeless

Thursdays are one day of the week when Becky and her mother work together. They work as volunteers at a local soup kitchen. They cook and serve food to anyone who comes in.

There is a regular routine Becky, her mother, and the other volunteers always follow. They feed from 50 to 125 people every week, and they need to be well organized.

The first thing Becky does when she arrives is wash her hands. Then she puts on an apron. Then she goes to work on getting things ready for the next day. Next she scrubs and chops vegetables for the next day's meal. She puts the vegetables into several large pots on the stove.

Next it's time to work on the Thursday evening meal. Every Thursday the meal is chili. Chili is very popular at the soup kitchen. As each person files by a low counter, Becky dishes up a bowl of chili. She likes seeing the smiles as the smell of hot chili fills the room.

After everyone has been served, Becky helps clean up the kitchen. She washes the table tops and then wipes the trays.

At the end of the night, Becky is tired. She and her mother talk about the experience on the way home.

"Working in the soup kitchen is not always what people would call fun," Becky says, "but I really love doing it."

1. This article describes the process of—
   A. chopping vegetables.
   B. working in a soup kitchen.
   C. fighting homelessness.
   D. dishing up chili.

2. First, Becky—
   F. scrubs vegetables.
   G. washes counters.
   H. puts on her apron.
   J. washes her hands.

3. Right before she serves dinner, Becky always—
   A. cleans the kitchen.
   B. helps prepare the next day's meal.
   C. puts on her apron.
   D. washes her hands.

4. Last, Becky—
   F. helps clean up the kitchen.
   G. dishes up bowls of chili.
   H. puts on her apron.
   J. scrubs and chops vegetables.

5. What would happen if Becky forgot to put pots on the stove?
   A. She would be punished.
   B. The food would get burned.
   C. Dinner for the next day would not get cooked.
   D. The chili might taste spicy.

© Scott Foresman 5

Notes for Home: Your child read a story and identified steps in a process. *Home Activity:* Invite your child to list the steps necessary to brush his or her teeth.

Dwaina Brooks

Word Study: Compound Words

Directions: Compound words are words formed from two other words, such as **something** and **bookshelf.** Combine a word from the left box with a word from the right box to form a compound word that makes sense. Write both words and the resulting compound word on the lines below.

mail	pop
bread	night
fore	basket
with	up
any	out

head	ball
body	stairs
out	doors
corn	stick
gown	box

Left Box	**Right Box**	**Compound Word**
1. _____	+ _____	= _____
2. _____	+ _____	= _____
3. _____	+ _____	= _____
4. _____	+ _____	= _____
5. _____	+ _____	= _____
6. _____	+ _____	= _____
7. _____	+ _____	= _____
8. _____	+ _____	= _____
9. _____	+ _____	= _____
10. _____	+ _____	= _____

Directions: Read each sentence. Part of a compound word is missing. Choose the word that best completes the compound word and makes sense in the sentence. Write the whole compound word on the line to the left.

_____ **11.** I was out_____ on my front porch.

_____ **12.** Since it was summer_____, it was very hot.

_____ **13.** I heard some_____ call out my name.

_____ **14.** The sound came from _____where behind me.

_____ **15.** It was my best friend Sue, who wanted me to play base_____ with her.

Notes for Home: Your child formed compound words, such as *something.* ***Home Activity:*** Experiment with common words children see around the house. Have your child put two words together to try to make a compound word. Check each word in a dictionary.

© Scott Foresman 5

Newspaper

A **newspaper** is a daily or weekly publication containing news, advertisements, features, editorials, and other useful information, such as TV listings. You can scan headlines to help you find articles you would like to read.

Directions: Scan the headlines from different parts of a newspaper. Then answer the questions that follow.

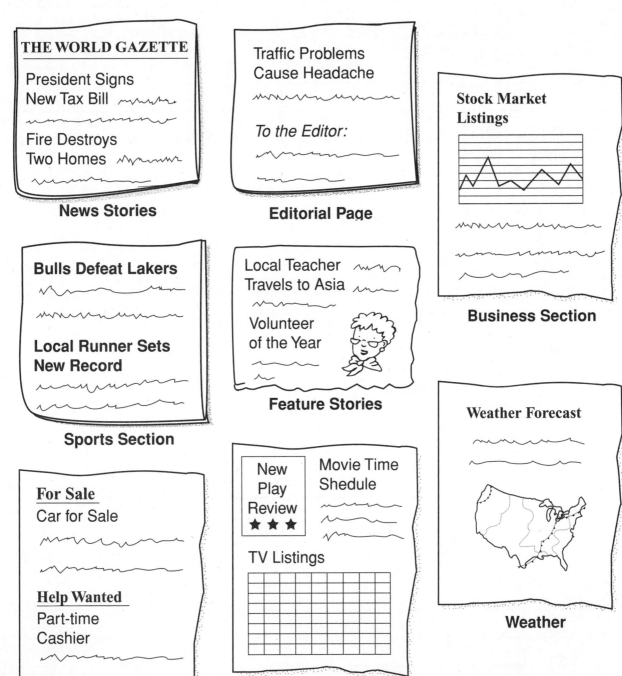

THE WORLD GAZETTE

President Signs
New Tax Bill

Fire Destroys
Two Homes

News Stories

Traffic Problems
Cause Headache

To the Editor:

Editorial Page

**Stock Market
Listings**

Business Section

Bulls Defeat Lakers

**Local Runner Sets
New Record**

Sports Section

Local Teacher
Travels to Asia

Volunteer
of the Year

Feature Stories

Weather Forecast

Weather

For Sale
Car for Sale

Help Wanted
Part-time
Cashier

Classified Ads

New
Play
Review
★ ★ ★

Movie Time
Shedule

TV Listings

Entertainment Section

© Scott Foresman 5

Name _____

Dwaina Brooks

1. Which part of the newspaper reports news about the U.S. President? What is the headline for an article on the President?

   _____

2. Which part of the paper has an article expressing the editor's opinion? What is the headline of that article?

   _____

3. Where would you look to find the latest stock market results? Give an example of another kind of article you might find in this section.

   _____

   _____

4. In which section would you find predictions about the high and low temperatures for the upcoming week?

   _____

5. Which part of the paper has an article on someone who volunteers time to help others? What is the headline for this article?

   _____

6. In which section would you look to find a job? What job is available? _____

   _____

7. In which section might you find information on an international peace treaty?

   _____

8. Which section includes a review of a new play? _____

9. Which section includes letters written to the editor? _____

10. When might a newspaper be a more useful resource than a nonfiction book? Explain.

   _____

   _____

   _____

   _____

   _____

   _____

   _____

Notes for Home: Your child answered questions using information found in a newspaper. *Home Activity:* Look through your local newspaper with your child and find the different sections, such as News Stories, Editorial Page, Sports Section, and Entertainment.

80 **Research and Study Skills: Newspaper**

© Scott Foresman 5

Author's Viewpoint

- **Author's viewpoint** is the way an author thinks about the subject of his or her writing.

- To learn an author's viewpoint, think about the author's opinion and choice of words. Sometimes you can figure out an author's viewpoint even when it is not stated directly.

- Unbalanced, or biased, writing happens when an author presents only one viewpoint. Balanced writing presents both sides of an issue equally.

Directions: Reread "Action Against Pollution." Then complete the table.
Identify key words or phrases that reveal the viewpoint of the two authors. Then tell the authors' viewpoint.

Statement	What It Reveals
Young people realize that actions speak louder than words.	1.
. . . they're taking responsibility through a wide variety of actions that will help make the world a better place.	2.
When kids returned to class, they decided to do something about the problem.	3.
Thanks to their hard work and determination, it now has more than 2,500 chapters in 20 countries around the world.	4.
Authors' Viewpoint 5.	

Notes for Home: Your child read an article and identified the authors' viewpoint. **Home Activity:** Together with your child, read a column from the editorial page of a newspaper. Help your child figure out the author's viewpoint.

© Scott Foresman 5

Vocabulary

Directions: Write the word from the box that belongs in each group.

1. leaked, drained, _____

2. amazing, unbelievable, _____

3. edge, border, _____

4. thought, considered, _____

5. amounts, numbers, _____

Check the Words You Know

__ brim
__ miraculous
__ pondered
__ prospered
__ quantities
__ seeped

Directions: Choose the word from the box that best matches each clue. Write the word in the puzzle.

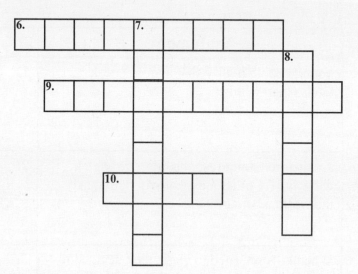

Across

6. It's what the rich person did.
9. Eggs by the dozen are these.
10. A cup can be filled to here.

Down

7. It's what the careful planner did.
8. It's what the leaky bag did.

Write a Description

Imagine a beautiful lake or pond and the animals and plants that live there. On a separate sheet of paper, describe the place. Use as many vocabulary words as you can.

Notes for Home: Your child identified and used new vocabulary words from *Everglades*. *Home Activity:* Think of words your child knows. Give your child clues about each word. For example: *It's something that rings and is used for talking to others. (telephone)*

© Scott Foresman 5

Author's Viewpoint

- An **author's viewpoint** is the way an author thinks about the subject of his or her writing. You can learn an author's viewpoint by looking at the words used and the opinions expressed.

- Balanced writing presents both sides of an issue. Unbalanced, or biased, writing presents one side more than another.

Directions: Reread what happens in *Everglades* as the storyteller completes his story. Then answer the questions below. Think about how the author reveals her viewpoint in the article.

> *Another child looked around. "And where did the mammals and snails and one-celled plants and animals go?"*
>
> They vanished when the engineers dug canals in the Everglades and drained the fresh water into the sea to make land. Farmers tilled the land; business people built towns and roads upon it. Pesticides and fertilizers flowed into the river waters and poisoned the one-celled animals and plants. The snails died, the fish died, the mammals and birds died.
>
> *"But this is a sad story," said a fifth child.*

Text Copyright ©1995 by Jean Craighead George. Used by permission of HarperCollins Publishers.

1. How do you think the author feels about the destruction of the Everglades?

_____

2. What words does the author use that convey this viewpoint?

_____

_____

3. Is the description of what happened to the creatures balanced or unbalanced? Explain.

_____

_____

4. State, in your own words, the viewpoint the author has about what happened to the creatures.

_____

_____

5. On a separate sheet of paper, identify the author's viewpoint as expressed in the article as a whole. Support your answer with examples.

Notes for Home: Your child read a passage, described the author's viewpoint, and identified whether the writing shows a bias. *Home Activity:* Work with your child to read a letter to the editor and identify the author's viewpoint and bias.

Name _____

1.	Ⓐ	Ⓑ	Ⓒ	Ⓓ
2.	Ⓕ	Ⓖ	Ⓗ	Ⓙ
3.	Ⓐ	Ⓑ	Ⓒ	Ⓓ
4.	Ⓕ	Ⓖ	Ⓗ	Ⓙ
5.	Ⓐ	Ⓑ	Ⓒ	Ⓓ
6.	Ⓕ	Ⓖ	Ⓗ	Ⓙ
7.	Ⓐ	Ⓑ	Ⓒ	Ⓓ
8.	Ⓕ	Ⓖ	Ⓗ	Ⓙ
9.	Ⓐ	Ⓑ	Ⓒ	Ⓓ
10.	Ⓕ	Ⓖ	Ⓗ	Ⓙ
11.	Ⓐ	Ⓑ	Ⓒ	Ⓓ
12.	Ⓕ	Ⓖ	Ⓗ	Ⓙ
13.	Ⓐ	Ⓑ	Ⓒ	Ⓓ
14.	Ⓕ	Ⓖ	Ⓗ	Ⓙ
15.	Ⓐ	Ⓑ	Ⓒ	Ⓓ

© Scott Foresman 5

Selection Test

Directions: Choose the best answer to each item. Mark the letter for the answer you have chosen.

Part 1: Vocabulary

Find the answer choice that means about the same as the underlined word in each sentence.

1. Dinah sat quietly and <u>pondered</u>.
   - A.   thought carefully
   - B.   worried
   - C.   stared at closely
   - D.   became sad

2. It was a <u>miraculous</u> day.
   - F.   long and tiring
   - G.   marvelous; wonderful
   - H.   full of jokes and teasing
   - J.   upsetting; disturbing

3. Water spilled over the <u>brim</u>.
   - A.   a stone wall
   - B.   a cover
   - C.   a large pile
   - D.   an edge

4. Water <u>seeped</u> into the basement.
   - F.   ran through pipes
   - G.   flowed quickly
   - H.   fell steadily
   - J.   leaked slowly

5. There were <u>quantities</u> of small fish.
   - A.   small clusters
   - B.   something hidden
   - C.   large numbers
   - D.   something dark

6. The wildlife <u>prospered</u>.
   - F.   became fewer in number
   - G.   spread out in different directions
   - H.   grew or developed well
   - J.   became too crowded

Part 2: Comprehension

Use what you know about the selection to answer each item.

7. What is the Everglades?
   - A.   a round, deep lake
   - B.   a shallow, warm river
   - C.   a long, thin piece of land
   - D.   an ocean bay

8. Limestone is made from—
   - F.   water.
   - G.   tiny one-celled animals.
   - H.   seashells.
   - J.   grass and trees.

9. Alligators can live in saw grass because of—
   - A.   their leathery skin.
   - B.   the abundance of birds.
   - C.   their sharp teeth.
   - D.   the blowing winds.

10. Which of these came to the Everglades first?
    - F.   Spanish conquistadors
    - G.   panthers
    - H.   Calusa people
    - J.   orchid hunters

11. Which sentence states an opinion?
    - A.   Hunters shot tens of thousands of egrets.
    - B.   *Seminole* means "runaway."
    - C.   Alligators were hunted for their hides.
    - D.   This is a sad story.

© Scott Foresman   5

GO ON

12. What can you tell about the author of this selection?
    F.   She has a great love for the beauty of the natural world.
    G.   She would like to build a new home in the Everglades.
    H.   She sees no future for the creatures of the Everglades.
    J.   She thinks storytellers should tell happy stories, not sad ones.

13. Which sentence best describes this selection?
    A.   It is mostly make-believe, but some of it is based on facts.
    B.   It is mostly based on facts, but the author's choice of words expresses her point of view.
    C.   It is mostly based on old legends.
    D.   It is mostly opinions, with some facts to support the opinions.

14. Which of these human acts does the author think was harmful to the Everglades?
    F.   draining water from the Everglades to make land
    G.   catching fish in the Everglades
    H.   making tools out of seashells found in the Everglades
    J.   poling a dugout canoe through the Everglades

15. The author would most likely agree with which of these statements?
    A.   Some of the plants and animals of the Everglades should probably be restored, but only the ones people like.
    B.   People should continue to make money from the rich resources in the Everglades.
    C.   The wonders of nature in the Everglades can return only if people change their ways.
    D.   The Everglades was never a good environment for fishing.

STOP

© Scott Foresman 5

Cause and Effect

REVIEW

Directions: Read the passage. Then read each question about the passage. Choose the best answer to each question. Mark the letter for the answer you have chosen.

Here Today—Gone Tomorrow?

Remember the dinosaurs? They are now extinct. They disappeared about 63 million years ago. Nobody knows exactly why. Remember the dodo? Remember the moa? Remember the passenger pigeon? The dodo, moa, and passenger pigeon are species of birds that are now extinct. They all disappeared within the last 200 years. Some of the mammals that have also become extinct in the last 200 years include a form of zebra called a quagga and a sea mammal called Steller's sea cow.

Over millions of years, many species have died out because natural conditions changed. However, the process of extinction may not be over. Many plants and animals *today* are in danger of becoming extinct. There are several reasons for this more recent pattern of extinction. Pollution, highway construction, overhunting, and wetland drainage all contribute to the extinction of plant and animal species. These reasons are all caused by humans.

Since the 1800s, the process of extinction has speeded up. This is a result of more people as well as more business and industry. Humans have changed the world more in the past 200 years than in all the previous centuries of human history. These changes are so rapid that many plants and animals cannot adapt. As a result of the changes, the plants and animals die out.

1. What has caused species to die out over millions of years?
   A. too much pollution
   B. too many people
   C. changing natural conditions
   D. growth of industry

2. What is the effect stated in the second paragraph?
   F. Many of today's plant and animal species are endangered.
   G. Wetlands are drained.
   H. Water is polluted.
   J. Highways are built.

3. The process of extinction has speeded up because of—
   A. more people on the earth.
   B. slowed industrial growth.
   C. clean air and water.
   D. animals' ability to adapt.

4. What is the effect of environmental changes that are too rapid?
   F. People now have more time for entertainment.
   G. Plants and animals adapt easily with changes.
   H. Plants and animals cannot adapt.
   J. Habitats stay the same.

5. What happens if plants and animals cannot adapt?
   A. They reproduce.
   B. They die out.
   C. They thrive.
   D. They get lost.

Notes for Home: Your child read a nonfiction article and identified causes and effects. **Home Activity:** Work with your child to identify causes and effects. Use "Because" statements such as *I hurt my arm because I tripped over the rock.*

© Scott Foresman 5

Name _____

Word Study: Base Words

Directions: Many words are formed by adding letters at the beginning or end of a word. The word you start with is called the **base word.** Read each sentence. Find the base word in the underlined word. Write the base word on the line.

_____   1. The water <u>sparkled</u> in the bright sun.

_____   2. Flowers once <u>bloomed</u> everywhere.

_____   3. The waters were <u>spilling</u> over with fish.

_____   4. Wild birds <u>gracefully</u> flew above the marshy waters.

_____   5. The sounds of insects <u>filled</u> the air.

_____   6. Some animals have all but <u>disappeared</u>.

_____   7. Other kinds of wildlife remain <u>unharmed.</u>

_____   8. Many people would like to <u>undo</u> the damage.

_____   9. Some <u>workers</u> help care for injured birds.

_____ 10. The Everglades today are <u>unlike</u> the Everglades of long ago.

Directions: Combine each base word and ending to make a new word. You might need to add or take away letters to spell the word correctly. Write the word on the line.

11. leather   +   -y   =   _____

12. sun   +   -y   =   _____

13. cut   +   -ing =   _____

14. quick   +   -ly   =   _____

15. glitter   +   -ed   =   _____

 Notes for Home: Your child identified base words in longer words, such as *appear* in *disappeared,* and used base words to form longer words. **Home Activity:** Read a magazine article with your child. Look for words made of base words and endings.

© Scott Foresman 5

Name _____

Everglades

Thesaurus

A **thesaurus** is a kind of dictionary in which synonyms (words that have the same or similar meanings), antonyms (words that have opposite meanings), and other related words are classified under headings. You can use a thesaurus to help you find new and interesting words when writing.

Directions: Use the thesaurus entry to answer the questions that follow.

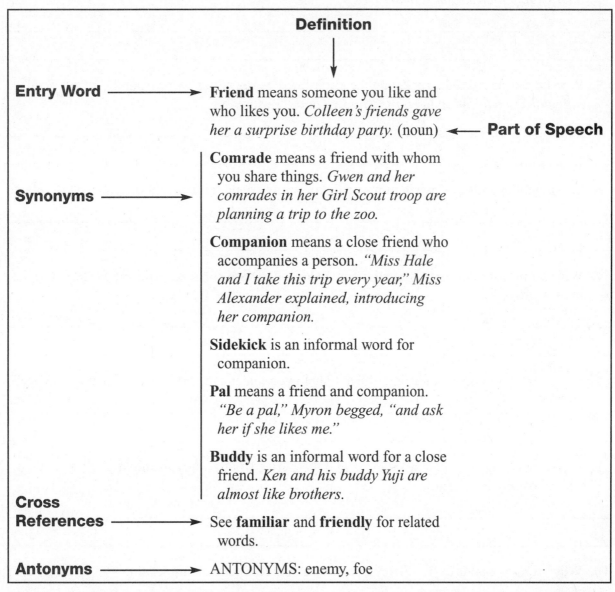

From EVERYDAY SPELLING by James Breers, Ronald L. Cramer, W. Dorsey Hammond. © 1998 Addison-Wesley Educational Publishers Inc.

© Scott Foresman 5

Research and Study Skills: Thesaurus 89

Name _____

1. What entry word is shown? _____

2. Name the part of speech of the entry word. _____

3. What synonyms are given for the entry word? _____

_____

4. Rewrite this sentence using one of the synonyms from the entry: *My friend Marta and I went on a swamp tour in New Orleans.*

_____

_____

5. Rewrite this sentence by replacing the underlined words with a word from the entry: *The alligator is no friend to the birds who live in the swamp.*

_____

_____

6. Would you use *sidekick* when introducing a visiting friend to your school principal? Explain.

_____

_____

7. What would you do if you wanted to find additional words that have meanings similar to the entry word?

_____

_____

8. How does knowing the meaning of *friend* help you understand how to use *foe* in a sentence?

_____

_____

9. If you looked up the entry word *large* in a thesaurus, what synonyms might you find? What antonyms might you find?

_____

_____

10. Why might a thesaurus be a helpful reference source when you are writing a report for class?

_____

_____

Notes for Home: Your child answered questions about a thesaurus entry. **Home Activity:** If a thesaurus is available, challenge your child to look up five words and tell what information is shown. If not available, work together to write five thesaurus entries.

© Scott Foresman 5

Drawing Conclusions

- When you form opinions based on facts and details, you are **drawing conclusions.**

- To draw a conclusion, use logic and clues from what you've read, as well as your own knowledge and experience.

- To check your conclusion, ask yourself if it makes sense. Are there other possible conclusions?

Directions: Reread "Granny's Missing Food." Then complete the table. Write a conclusion for each piece of evidence given. Write evidence that supports each conclusion drawn.

Evidence	Conclusions
Chicken, fruit, and cookies are missing from Granny's house.	1.
2.	The woman is the narrator's grandmother.
Clooz has only one business card.	3.
4.	The dog did not steal Granny's food.
Clooz and the narrator trade funny looks when Granny points to the newspapers she got from the checkout line at the supermarket.	5.

Notes for Home: Your child read a story and used story details, as well as logic, to draw conclusions. ***Home Activity:*** Offer clues about what you did today. Ask your child to draw conclusions about your activities.

© Scott Foresman 5

Vocabulary

Directions: Choose the word from the box that best matches each definition.
Write the word on the line.

_____ 1. a long, flat, raised surface in a store, restaurant, or a bank

_____ 2. precious gem, brilliant blue in color

_____ 3. ring, bracelet, necklace, or other ornament to be worn

_____ 4. smear of dirt or grease

_____ 5. points out; shows; suggests

Check the Words You Know

__ counter

__ indicates

__ jewelry

__ sapphire

__ smudge

Directions: Choose the word from the box that best completes each sentence.
Write the word on the matching numbered line to the right.

> I wanted to buy the perfect gift for my older sister's graduation. I went to the local **6.** _____ store to look at some necklaces. The sales clerk behind the large **7.** _____ where the jewelry was displayed was very helpful. While looking for a gift, I saw the most beautiful blue stone in a gold necklace. The sales clerk told me that the stone was a **8.** _____. The clerk told me the color and cut of the stone **9.** _____ that it is an excellent piece of jewelry. The necklace was so beautiful that I put my face close to the display case and made a big **10.** _____ on the glass. That was embarrassing! The necklace was too expensive, but I did find a very nice pair of earrings for my sister.

6. _____

7. _____

8. _____

9. _____

10. _____

Write a Story

Imagine that a robbery has taken place at a local jewelry store, and you are the detective in charge. On a separate sheet of paper, write a story about searching the crime scene for clues. What do you find? Use as many vocabulary words as you can.

Notes for Home: Your child identified and used new words from the story "Missing Links."
Home Activity: Act out a radio drama with your child about a jewelry robbery. Use the vocabulary words in your dialogue.

© Scott Foresman 5

Drawing Conclusions

- When you form opinions based on facts and details, you are **drawing conclusions.**

- To draw a conclusion, use logic and clues from what you've read, as well as your own knowledge and experience. To check your conclusion, ask yourself if it makes sense. Are there other possible conclusions?

Directions: Reread what happens in "Missing Links" when Amanda and Sherlock inspect the smashed jewelry case. Then answer the questions below. Use story details to help you draw conclusions.

The case that Amanda had been looking into just a few minutes before was now smashed and almost empty. All the cuff links, the tie pins, and the beautiful ring were gone.

"What happened?" Amanda asked the salesman excitedly.

"I don't know, I don't know. I must have been putting some ladies' jewelry away in the next counter . . . there was so much confusion . . .

I just didn't see . . . but I haven't been near the case. I know you're not supposed to touch anything. The police will probably want to check for fingerprints."

Sherlock, apparently, was already doing just that. He had his magnifying glass out and was peering intently into the shattered display case.

From FLUTE REVENGE PLUS TWO MORE MYSTERIES by Andrew Bromberg. Copyright © 1982 by William Morrow and Company, Inc. By permission of Greenwillow Books, a division of William Morrow & Company, Inc.

1. What has happened to the items from the jewelry case?

_____

2. What conclusion can you draw about the salesman from the way that he speaks?

_____

3. Why does the salesman say you're not supposed to touch anything?

_____

_____

4. Why does Sherlock study the case through his magnifying glass?

_____

_____

5. What conclusions can you draw about Amanda and Sherlock from the whole story? On a separate sheet of paper, write your conclusions. Support them with evidence from the story.

Notes for Home: Your child used story details to draw conclusions. *Home Activity:* Work with your child to draw conclusions about a movie you've seen or a book you've read together. Talk about why something happened or how the characters might feel in a certain situation.

© Scott Foresman 5

Name _____

1.	Ⓐ	Ⓑ	Ⓒ	Ⓓ
2.	Ⓕ	Ⓖ	Ⓗ	Ⓙ
3.	Ⓐ	Ⓑ	Ⓒ	Ⓓ
4.	Ⓕ	Ⓖ	Ⓗ	Ⓙ
5.	Ⓐ	Ⓑ	Ⓒ	Ⓓ
6.	Ⓕ	Ⓖ	Ⓗ	Ⓙ
7.	Ⓐ	Ⓑ	Ⓒ	Ⓓ
8.	Ⓕ	Ⓖ	Ⓗ	Ⓙ
9.	Ⓐ	Ⓑ	Ⓒ	Ⓓ
10.	Ⓕ	Ⓖ	Ⓗ	Ⓙ
11.	Ⓐ	Ⓑ	Ⓒ	Ⓓ
12.	Ⓕ	Ⓖ	Ⓗ	Ⓙ
13.	Ⓐ	Ⓑ	Ⓒ	Ⓓ
14.	Ⓕ	Ⓖ	Ⓗ	Ⓙ
15.	Ⓐ	Ⓑ	Ⓒ	Ⓓ

© Scott Foresman 5

Selection Test

Directions: Choose the best answer to each item. Mark the letter for the answer you have chosen.

Part 1: Vocabulary

Find the answer choice that means about the same as the underlined word in each sentence.

1. Miko put the box on the <u>counter</u>.
   - A. small container with a cover
   - B. large, square floor
   - C. display table or cabinet in a store
   - D. room where things are stored

2. Someone stole her <u>jewelry</u> case.
   - F. flat pouch for carrying paper money
   - G. belief or plan
   - H. rings, bracelets, or other ornaments to be worn
   - J. collection of coins

3. The clock <u>indicates</u> that it is two o'clock.
   - A. shows
   - B. pretends
   - C. discovers
   - D. hides

4. A <u>sapphire</u> ring was missing.
   - F. hard gray or pink rock
   - G. clear blue precious stone
   - H. gold band
   - J. deep red gem

5. He had a <u>smudge</u> on his chin.
   - A. short beard
   - B. healed cut
   - C. small dimple
   - D. dirty mark

Part 2: Comprehension

Use what you know about the story to answer each item.

6. Amanda and Sherlock went to the department store to—
   - F. play computer games.
   - G. look at men's jewelry.
   - H. solve a mystery.
   - J. buy a tie for their dad.

7. What happened while Sherlock and Amanda were in the department store?
   - A. A fire broke out in the store.
   - B. The sprinklers went off.
   - C. Amanda stole a sapphire ring.
   - D. The manager announced a big sale.

8. The salespeople were racing back and forth because they were trying to—
   - F. put out the fire.
   - G. keep the customers happy.
   - H. protect their merchandise.
   - J. catch a thief.

9. The sprinklers probably stopped suddenly because—
   - A. the store ran out of water.
   - B. they were not working properly.
   - C. someone turned them off.
   - D. someone opened the emergency exit.

10. Why was Sherlock studying the salesman's tie with his magnifying glass?
    - F. He was looking for clues.
    - G. He forgot his glasses at home.
    - H. Amanda suggested he should.
    - J. The spot was impossible to see otherwise.

© Scott Foresman 5

GO ON

11. Amanda and Sherlock could not stay until the police arrived because they—
   A.   would be in the way.
   B.   would be late getting home.
   C.   might become suspects.
   D.   didn't know anything about solving mysteries.

12. The stolen jewelry was most likely hidden in—
   F.   a loaf of bread.
   G.   the baker's hat.
   H.   the sprinklers.
   J.   Sherlock's eclair.

13. You can tell that the baker is not very smart because he—
   A.   could not bake a loaf of bread properly.
   B.   didn't charge enough for the bread.
   C.   didn't try to keep his bread dry.
   D.   was wearing the stolen ring.

14. Which fact best supports the idea that Sherlock might make a good detective someday?
   F.   He carries a magnifying glass with him wherever he goes.
   G.   He has the same first name as the famous detective, Sherlock Holmes.
   H.   He notices clues that help solve the mystery.
   J.   He and his sister Amanda work well together.

15. The title of this story probably refers to the missing cuff links and to—
   A.   loaves of bread.
   B.   Sherlock and Amanda.
   C.   the thieves.
   D.   the clues needed to solve the mystery.

STOP

© Scott Foresman 5

Predicting

Directions: Read the story. Then read each question about the story. Choose the best answer to each question. Mark the letter for the answer you have chosen.

Thrills and Chills

Suddenly, the lion moved! He stretched his neck, shook himself, yawned, and jumped from his pedestal. He then looked at the two girls and took a step toward them.

"Run for it!" Jill screamed.

Instead of moving, Tracy stared. "This is a mystery," she whispered. "How did that lion move?"

"I don't know. I just want to get out of here," Jill said, trembling.

The lion looked from Jill to Tracy, then turned away. He stalked away down the avenue, head high, looking straight ahead. As they watched, fascinated, he disappeared from sight.

Tracy and Jill stared at one another, then went to look at the empty pedestal. "Look!" cried Tracy. "There's a note here." She picked it up and read it aloud.

> **You have just witnessed an amazing sight.**
> **Tell all your friends to come to the museum for tomorrow night's grand opening of Laser Lights!**

"So that's how he moved," said Tracy.

"What do you mean?" asked Jill.

"That was no lion! That was a laser show demonstration to promote a new museum exhibit."

The two girls heard a sound high above them. They turned and looked. A museum staff person was standing in a special projection booth. He waved and called out, "Hope to see you tomorrow night."

1. After reading the first paragraph, you would probably predict that—
   A. the girls are going to attack the lion.
   B. the lion is going to attack the girls.
   C. the girls will stand still.
   D. the girls will feed the lion.

2. What do you think about Tracy after she speaks for the first time?
   F. Tracy loves lions.
   G. Tracy is dreaming.
   H. Tracy is more surprised than scared.
   J. Tracy is more scared than Jill.

3. What clue word or words in the note would probably cause you to change your initial prediction?
   A. witnessed
   B. amazing
   C. laser lights
   D. friends

4. After listening to Tracy's explanation, Jill will likely feel—
   F. scared.
   G. relieved.
   H. angry.
   J. sad.

5. What do you predict Jill and Tracy will do next?
   A. They will agree never to go to the museum again.
   B. They will go searching for the lion.
   C. They will complain to museum security.
   D. They will go to the Laser Lights opening.

 Notes for Home: Your child read a story and predicted events in the story. **Home Activity:** As you watch a movie with your child, make predictions about the characters and events. Make new predictions as needed as you continue watching.

© Scott Foresman 5

Word Study: Prefixes

Directions: Letters added to the beginnings of words are called **prefixes.**
Prefixes can change the meaning of the base word. Add the prefixes to each
word below to make a new word. Write each new word on the line.

1. re   +   heat   =   _____

2. pre   +   occupied   =   _____

3. un   +   believable =   _____

4. pre   +   school   =   _____

5. re   +   turn   =   _____

6. un   +   changed   =   _____

7. pre   +   paid   =   _____

8. re   +   view   =   _____

Directions: Read the detective's report. Circle the words that contain the
prefixes *un-, re-,* and *pre-*. Write the prefix and the base word on the line
connected by a + sign. For example, **prepaid,** you would write **pre + paid.**

Detective's Report: Case No. 57

Submitted by Lydia Lookout, P. I.

   I was hired to investigate the disappearance of peanuts from
the local grocery store. Bob, the owner of the small
neighborhood store, was very unhappy about the missing
peanuts. He had suspected one or two people as thieves but
Bob felt that it would be unfair to prejudge his loyal
customers. Bob was unable to solve the mystery, so he hired
me to solve the case. I told Bob that I couldn't replace the
missing peanuts, but I could find the thief. After two days on
the case, I was still uncertain about the disappearing peanuts. I
decided to stay overnight in the store to catch the thieves in
action. Sometime after midnight, I heard a noise and turned on
the lights. The store was filled with happy squirrels eating
peanuts. The next day Bob called a roofer to repair the hole
where the squirrels had entered the store.

9. _____

10. _____

11. _____

12. _____

13. _____

14. _____

15. _____

Notes for Home: Your child formed new words by adding the prefixes *un-, re-,* and *pre-*.
Home Activity: Read a newspaper story with your child. Help your child find words that have
these prefixes. Have your child write each word and circle its prefix.

© Scott Foresman 5

Technology: Telephone Directory

A **telephone directory** is a book that lists entries that give the names, phone numbers, and addresses for individual people and businesses. The **white pages** list entries for individual people and businesses in alphabetical order. The **yellow pages** list entries and ads for businesses. Entries are grouped by category or type of business, such as *jewelry*. You can find this same information using a computer and the Internet. You can search online to find phone numbers for people and businesses in other cities, states, and even countries.

Directions: The computer screen shows you how to search a directory of online white pages. Use the computer screen to answer the questions that follow.

1. What entries will you get if you type "Gomez" in the box for Last Name, "Boston" in the box for City, and "MA" in the box for State?

_____

_____

2. Would typing "Pamela" in the box for First Name and "USA" in the box for Country give you good search results? Explain.

_____

_____

3. You know Nan Worth lives in Florida. Tell how to find her phone number and address.

_____

_____

4. What should you do if you need help using this online telephone directory?

_____

© Scott Foresman 5

Name _____

Directions: The computer screen shows you how to search a directory of online yellow pages. Use the computer screen to answer the questions that follow.

Enter a business category or name.
Then click Find!
[   ]

City [   ]
State (required) [   ]

Find!   If you need help, click here.

5. What will you get if you enter the category "hotel" and "CA" for California?

_____

6. If you want information on Joe's Flower Shop in Dallas, Texas, what should you enter?

_____

_____

7. If you want to find a jewelry store in Albuquerque, New Mexico, what should you enter?

_____

_____

8. If you enter "bookstore" in the category box, will this produce good search results? Explain.

_____

_____

9. Do you have to type something in all three boxes? Explain. _____

_____

_____

10. Can you use an online telephone directory if you don't know how to spell someone's last name? Explain.

_____

_____

_____

Notes for Home: Your child answered questions about using an online telephone directory. *Home Activity:* Use your telephone books. Ask your child to find one person and a type of business to practice using both the white and yellow pages.

© Scott Foresman 5

Name _____

Character

> • **Characters** are the people or animals in a stories.
>
> • You learn about characters from their words, actions, and the way other characters act toward them.

Directions: Reread "Jerome's Dream." Then complete the table. Give examples of things that characters think, say, and do to show what Jerome is like.

What the Characters Think, Do, and Say	Examples
What Jerome Thinks	1.
	2.
What Jerome Says	3.
What Jerome Does	4.
What Liza Says	5.

Notes for Home: Your child read a story and analyzed its main character. *Home Activity:* Think of a relative or neighbor. Describe things that the person frequently thinks, does, or says. Have your child guess who the person is, based on your clues. Switch roles and repeat the activity.

© Scott Foresman 5

Vocabulary

Directions: Choose the word from the box that best completes each sentence.
Write the word on the line to the left.

_____ 1. Many _____ took part in the school games.

_____ 2. The principal raised her hands and _____ for the games to begin.

_____ 3. Some students _____ down nearby mountain slopes.

_____ 4. Others were good at _____ basketballs indoors.

_____ 5. All over school, people's _____ was about the games.

Check the Words You Know
__ conversation
__ dribbling
__ gestured
__ interpreter
__ skied
__ volunteers

Directions: Choose the word from the box that best matches each clue. Write
the word in the puzzle.

Down

6. people who offer their services
7. informal talk
8. signaled by hand
9. glided on skies

Across

10. one who translates

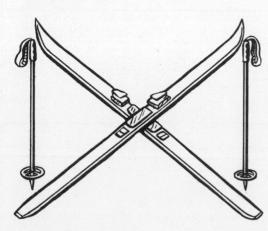

Write a Broadcast

Imagine you are a sportscaster. On a separate sheet of paper, write a broadcast
that describes a real or imaginary sports competition. Describe the action as if it
were happening right now in front of your eyes. Use as many vocabulary words
as you can.

Notes for Home: Your child identified vocabulary words in *Going with the Flow*. **Home
Activity:** Work with your child to write a sports article about a favorite sport or athlete, using
as many vocabulary words as you can.

© Scott Foresman 5

Name _____

Character

- **Characters** are the people or animals in stories.
- You learn about them from their words, actions, and the way other characters act toward them.

Directions: Reread what happens in *Going with the Flow* when Mark attends his new class for the first time. Think about what you've read, and then answer the questions below.

"Hi, Mark. How are you?" Mrs. LaVoie signed and mouthed the words silently to me across the room.

The whole fifth grade was watching us.

"This is dumb!" I signed back.

"They've never met a deaf kid before," she replied. "They..."

I didn't wait for her to finish. I had to get out of there. I raced down the center aisle, nearly tripped over the leg of some big, long-haired guy with a smirk on his face, and ran out the door.

Mrs. LaVoie found me in the gym under one of the bleachers. She put a hand on my arm.

From GOING WITH THE FLOW by Claire H. Blatchford. Copyright Text 1998 by Claire H. Blatchford, illustrations 1998 by Janice Lee Porter. Used by permission of Carolrhoda Books, Inc. All rights reserved.

1. What do the other students do when Mark signs with Mrs. LaVoie?

_____

_____

2. How does Mark feel about being in his new class? How do you know?

_____

_____

3. Why does Mark leave the room?

_____

_____

4. How does Mrs. LaVoie treat Mark?

_____

_____

5. How does Mark change by the end of the story? Write your answer on a separate sheet of paper. Give examples from the story to support your answers.

Notes for Home: Your child read a story and used story details to analyze a character. *Home Activity:* Watch a TV show or movie with your child, and then have your child describe his or her favorite character in the story.

© Scott Foresman 5

Name _____

1.	Ⓐ	Ⓑ	Ⓒ	Ⓓ
2.	Ⓕ	Ⓖ	Ⓗ	Ⓙ
3.	Ⓐ	Ⓑ	Ⓒ	Ⓓ
4.	Ⓕ	Ⓖ	Ⓗ	Ⓙ
5.	Ⓐ	Ⓑ	Ⓒ	Ⓓ
6.	Ⓕ	Ⓖ	Ⓗ	Ⓙ
7.	Ⓐ	Ⓑ	Ⓒ	Ⓓ
8.	Ⓕ	Ⓖ	Ⓗ	Ⓙ
9.	Ⓐ	Ⓑ	Ⓒ	Ⓓ
10.	Ⓕ	Ⓖ	Ⓗ	Ⓙ
11.	Ⓐ	Ⓑ	Ⓒ	Ⓓ
12.	Ⓕ	Ⓖ	Ⓗ	Ⓙ
13.	Ⓐ	Ⓑ	Ⓒ	Ⓓ
14.	Ⓕ	Ⓖ	Ⓗ	Ⓙ
15.	Ⓐ	Ⓑ	Ⓒ	Ⓓ

© Scott Foresman 5

Selection Test

Directions: Choose the best answer to each item. Mark the letter for the answer you have chosen.

Part 1: Vocabulary

Find the answer choice that means about the same as the underlined word in each sentence.

1. I didn't understand that <u>conversation</u>.
   A. a friendly talk
   B. a long book
   C. a math test
   D. a movie

2. A group of <u>volunteers</u> met at the town hall.
   F. people who have been elected to represent others
   G. teachers
   H. people who offer to work or help for free
   J. government workers

3. Nell works as an <u>interpreter</u>.
   A. person who helps others learn to study better
   B. person who translates one language into another
   C. writer for a newspaper
   D. coach who teaches others how to play a sport

4. Mike <u>gestured</u> excitedly.
   F. called out in a loud voice
   G. argued against something
   H. jumped up and down
   J. made hand movements

5. The girl <u>skied</u> very well.
   A. picked out skis
   B. explained how to ski
   C. waxed the skis
   D. glided on skis

6. All the players need to practice their <u>dribbling</u>.
   F. moving a ball by bouncing
   G. communicating without words
   H. throwing a ball into a basket
   J. passing a ball from one player to another

Part 2: Comprehension

Use what you know about the story to answer each item.

7. Who follows Mark into his classroom on the first day at his new school?
   A. his mother
   B. his fifth-grade teacher
   C. his interpreter
   D. the principal

8. Just after he rushes out of the classroom, Mark—
   F. takes a bus home.
   G. goes to eat in the cafeteria.
   H. hides in the gym.
   J. calls his friend Jamie.

9. After his first day at school, Mark feels—
   A. confident that he will succeed.
   B. ignored by his classmates.
   C. sure that he will make friends.
   D. sorry for himself.

10. Mark wants to move back to Vermont mainly because he wants to—
    F. play basketball.
    G. be with other deaf people.
    H. ski in races against Jamie.
    J. go to a better school.

© Scott Foresman 5

GO ON

11. You can tell that his father thinks Mark should—
   A. give the new school a chance before he gives up.
   B. forget the friends he had in Vermont.
   C. pretend he is not deaf so he will be accepted by others.
   D. move back to Vermont.

12. What is the first sign that Keith is a kind person?
   F. He smirks at Mark on Mark's first day in class.
   G. He laughs when Mark asks if his name is Teeth.
   H. He offers to take notes for Mark.
   J. He asks Mark to play basketball.

13. Keith trips Mark during the basketball game because he—
   A. knows that Mark is a better player than he is.
   B. is slower than Mark and cannot get out of his way.
   C. is trying to get Mark to give up and leave the basketball team.
   D. thinks Mark is playing without respect for him and the other players.

14. What makes the biggest difference in Mark's life?
   F. He joins the basketball team.
   G. Some of the boys laugh at him.
   H. Mrs. LaVoie helps him.
   J. He gets angry while playing basketball.

15. As a result of playing basketball with Keith, Mark learns to—
   A. try to fit in by working with others.
   B. look after himself first.
   C. realize that being deaf is not a problem.
   D. accept that he will always be left out.

STOP

© Scott Foresman 5

Drawing Conclusions and Predicting

Directions: Read the story. Then read each question about the story. Choose the best answer to each question. Mark the letter for the answer you have chosen.

Seeing the Problem

It was Tony's first day in his new school. As the newest student, Tony was seated in the back of the classroom.

Tony's new teacher, Mr. Brown, said they would start the day with a spelling lesson. Tony knew that the spelling book was blue, and he got it out of his book bag. Mr. Brown called on Tony. He asked Tony to read the spelling words which were written on the board.

Tony looked at the board. He squinted his eyes. He leaned his head forward and stared for a minute. When he didn't say anything, one or two children giggled.

Mr. Brown asked Tony if he would like to sit in the front of the room. Tony agreed. He picked up his book bag and spelling book and moved to a new seat at the very front of the class.

Mr. Brown then asked Tony once more to read the spelling words on the board. Tony squinted again and finally said, "I'm sorry, but I can't."

After class, Mr. Brown asked Tony to stay a few minutes. Tony hoped he hadn't done anything wrong on his first day.

Mr. Brown said, "Tony, I'd like you to visit the school doctor. She can give you an eye test."

1. Tony squints because he—
   A. dislikes being in the back of the classroom.
   B. has trouble seeing.
   C. can't hear the teacher.
   D. is in pain.

2. Tony doesn't read the words because he—
   F. dislikes Mr. Brown.
   G. dislikes reading.
   H. is embarrassed.
   J. can't see them clearly.

3. Mr. Brown changes Tony's seat to the front so that—
   A. he can talk to Tony.
   B. Tony is with his friends.
   C. Tony is closer to the chalkboard.
   D. Tony won't misbehave.

4. The eye doctor will probably tell Tony that he—
   F. needs glasses.
   G. is fine.
   H. should switch classes.
   J. should sit up front.

5. You could find out if your prediction is right by—
   A. rereading the passage.
   B. asking a friend.
   C. making another prediction.
   D. reading the rest of the story.

© Scott Foresman 5

Notes for Home: Your child drew conclusions and made predictions based on story details. *Home Activity:* As you read with your child, pause often to let your child predict what will happen next. After reading, have your child draw conclusions about the characters and events.

Drawing Conclusions and Predicting 107

Word Study: Regular Plurals

Directions: To form the plural of most nouns, add **-s**. For nouns that end in **x, s, ss, ch,** or **sh,** add **-es.** For nouns that end in **consonant** and **y,** change the **y** to **i** and add **-es.** Write the plural form for each noun below.

1. player _____
2. bleacher _____
3. basketball _____
4. box _____
5. lunch _____
6. turkey _____

7. enemy _____
8. glasses _____
9. teacher _____
10. photograph _____
11. signal _____
12. victory _____

Directions: Read the sports article. Make each word in ( ) plural. Write the plural word on the line. You might need to change the spelling of a word to make it plural.

We Are the Champions!

(Sign) for the game had been posted for (month). When the night finally arrived, you could see in the players' (eye) that something special was going to happen. (Word) can't do justice to how the team played that night. Their (hand) were everywhere, shooting, dribbling, stealing. The star made great (pass) and shot from all corners of the court. No (speech) were given that day, but the final score spoke for itself. We will all have great (memory) of this game for a long time to come.

13. _____
14. _____
15. _____
16. _____
17. _____
18. _____
19. _____
20. _____

Notes for Home: Your child practiced forming plural nouns, such as *steps* and *boxes*. **Home Activity:** Read the labels on game boxes and food packages with your child. Help your child notice plural words. Look to see whether *-s* or *-es* were added.

© Scott Foresman 5

Name _____

Evaluate Information/Draw Conclusions

Directions: Read the article below and the advertisement on the next page.
Then answer the questions that follow the advertisement.

Ready? Get Set . . . Move!

Moving to a new home can be very challenging. It's not just all the packing and unpacking. If you're planning a move in the near future, here are some tips that will help you get where you're going.

Set Your Dates

It may sound obvious, but before you move, you must know exactly *when* you're moving. Whether you're leaving a house or an apartment, timing is everything. So check exactly when you're leaving your old home and arriving at your new home.

Notify All Services

Before you exit your old home, notify all important services. This includes utility companies, such as gas, electric, and telephone, and the bank. Most importantly, notify the U.S. post office of your change of address. The post office will forward your mail for up to six months. After that, letters may be returned.

Notify People

At least one month before you move, make a list of everyone you want to have your new address. This includes family, friends, neighbors, co-workers, doctors, dentists, and any other people with whom you communicate on a regular basis. The post office will supply you with cards that you can send to each person with your new address. If you already know your new telephone number, include that on the card as well.

Pack It Up

Perhaps the hardest part of any move is physically moving items from home to home. Plan ahead, and be sure to have plenty of boxes, tape, and other packing materials. Pack carefully. Mark your boxes to indicate the contents. Keep a list of what gets packed in each box and its condition. Double check to make sure you've left nothing behind.

Get Settled

Remember how you had to notify all your old services to discontinue? Well, now you've got the opposite task. Once in your new home, be sure all your new services have been activated. Is your telephone working? Do you have gas and electricity? Have you opened new bank accounts? Of course, in time you'll realize things you've forgotten. But the more that gets done immediately, the easier it will be to cope later!

Moving Day Checklist

Have I notified. . .

___ family
___ friends
___ neighbors
___ co-workers
___ doctors
___ dentists

___ U.S. government (tax forms)
___ U.S. post office
___ bank
___ telephone company
___ gas/electric company
___ landlord

___ magazine subscriptions
___ newspaper subscriptions
___ clubs/organizations
___ others
___ _____
___ _____

© Scott Foresman 5

MOVING? WE CAN HELP!

Whether moving across the street or across the country, you need the services of a reliable mover. **Transport Movers** are the finest professional movers in the country.

- We are trustworthy, efficient, and economical.
- Other movers often break items in transport, but we almost never do. (And if we do, we'll reimburse you the full value of the item.)
- We require no more than three days' notice to be at your doorstep on the day you move.
- To find out more about **Transport Movers**, just call this toll free number: 1-800-555-MOVE.

Transport Movers
Moving Across America

1. What is the topic of the article in the pamphlet shown on the previous page?

_____

2. What are the five main points in the article? _____

_____

_____

_____

3. How reliable do you think the information is in the article? Explain.

_____

_____

4. What opinions are presented in the advertisement from Transport Movers?

_____

_____

5. Do you feel the information in the advertisement is as reliable as the information in the article? Explain.

_____

_____

Notes for Home: Your child read an article and an advertisement, evaluated their information, and then drew conclusions about them. *Home Activity:* Read a newspaper or magazine article and advertisement with your child. Talk about the main ideas presented.

© Scott Foresman 5

Graphic Sources

- A **graphic source,** such as a picture, graph, or map shows information visually.

- Before you read, look for graphic sources of information that could give you an idea of what the article or story is about.

- As you read, compare the written words to the graphic source for a better understanding of the main ideas.

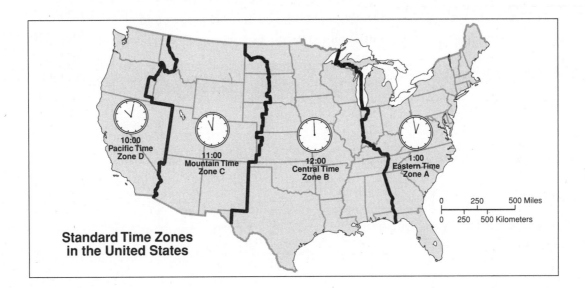

Standard Time Zones in the United States

Directions: Reread "Train Time." Use the text and map to answer each question.

1. What does the map show?

_____

2. What information does the map give that the article does not?

_____

3. How do you know that the map shows the United States after 1883, not before?

_____

4. How does the map help show the main idea in a different way than the text does?

_____

_____

5. If it were 3:00 Pacific Time, what time would it be Eastern Time? _____

Notes for Home: Your child read an article and got information from a related map. *Home Activity:* Together with your child, look at a map of your city, state, or country. Have your child describe locations of certain places, or the distances between two places on the map.

© Scott Foresman 5

Vocabulary

Directions: Choose the word from the box that best completes each sentence.
Write the word on the line.

_____   1. Last night's heavy _____ caused
                                    massive mud slides in our town.

_____   2. The _____ for buses, trains, and postal
                                    service were all ruined.

_____   3. The mud slides caused local roads and
                                    trails to become even more _____ and
                                    difficult to use.

_____   4. People who came to help did a _____ job.

_____   5. The mayor gave an award to the _____
                                    for their brave work.

Check the Words You Know
__ dispatched
__ downpour
__ heroic
__ locomotives
__ rescuers
__ rugged
__ schedules

Directions: Choose the word from the box that best matches each clue. Write
the letters of the word on the blanks. The boxed letters spell something you can
take on trains.

6. train engines   6. ___ ___ ___ ___ ___ [ ] ___ ___ ___

7. rough and uneven   7. [ ] ___ ___ ___ ___ ___

8. very brave   8. ___ ___ ___ [ ] ___ ___

9. heavy rainfall   9. ___ ___ ___ ___ [ ] ___ ___ ___

10. sent off   10. ___ ___ [ ] ___ ___ ___ ___ ___ ___ ___

Something you take on trains: ___ ___ ___ ___ ___

Write a Journal Entry

On a separate sheet of paper, write a journal entry about an imaginary train trip
that runs into trouble. Describe the problem and how it was solved. Use as many
vocabulary words as you can.

Notes for Home: Your child identified and used new vocabulary words from *Kate Shelley:
Bound for Legend*. **Home Activity:** Make up a story with your child of a daring rescue, using
the vocabulary words. When finished, share your story with others.

© Scott Foresman 5

Graphic Sources

- A **graphic source,** such as a picture, graph, or map, shows information visually.

- Before you read, look for graphic sources of information that could give you an idea of what the article or story is about.

Directions: Look at the map of the vicinity of Kate Shelley's home from *Kate Shelley: Bound for Legend.* Then answer the questions below.

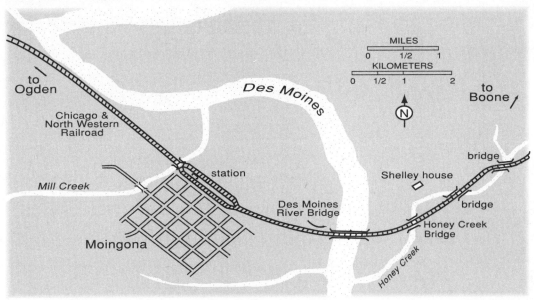

From KATE SHELLEY: BOUND FOR LEGEND by Robert D. San Souci, paintings by Max Ginsburg.
Paintings copyright © 1995 by Max Ginsburg. Used by permission of Dial Books for Young Readers, a division of Penguin Putnam Inc.

1. In which direction does a train travel from Moingona to the Honey Creek Bridge?

_____

2. Is the Shelley house closer to the Honey Creek Bridge or to the station at Moingona?

_____

3. If you traveled by train from Ogden to Boone, what bridges and stations would you travel past along the way?

_____

_____

4. Which bridge is closest to the Moingona station?

_____

5. How does the map help you better understand the story? Explain your answer on a separate sheet of paper.

Notes for Home: Your child answered questions about a map. ***Home Activity:*** Look at a map with your child. Talk about the information you can find by reading the map, such as distances between two locations.

© Scott Foresman 5

1.	Ⓐ	Ⓑ	Ⓒ	Ⓓ
2.	Ⓕ	Ⓖ	Ⓗ	Ⓙ
3.	Ⓐ	Ⓑ	Ⓒ	Ⓓ
4.	Ⓕ	Ⓖ	Ⓗ	Ⓙ
5.	Ⓐ	Ⓑ	Ⓒ	Ⓓ
6.	Ⓕ	Ⓖ	Ⓗ	Ⓙ
7.	Ⓐ	Ⓑ	Ⓒ	Ⓓ
8.	Ⓕ	Ⓖ	Ⓗ	Ⓙ
9.	Ⓐ	Ⓑ	Ⓒ	Ⓓ
10.	Ⓕ	Ⓖ	Ⓗ	Ⓙ
11.	Ⓐ	Ⓑ	Ⓒ	Ⓓ
12.	Ⓕ	Ⓖ	Ⓗ	Ⓙ
13.	Ⓐ	Ⓑ	Ⓒ	Ⓓ
14.	Ⓕ	Ⓖ	Ⓗ	Ⓙ
15.	Ⓐ	Ⓑ	Ⓒ	Ⓓ

© Scott Foresman 5

Name _____

Selection Test

Directions: Choose the best answer to each item. Mark the letter for the answer you have chosen.

Part 1: Vocabulary

Find the answer choice that means about the same as the underlined word in each sentence.

1. The newspaper included a report about the underlined downpour.
   A. heavy rainfall
   B. ruined plan
   C. huge fountain
   D. falling prices

2. Please pick up some schedules.
   F. books about historic events
   G. lists of addresses and phone numbers
   H. times of arrival and departure
   J. guides to interesting places

3. That museum has some old locomotives.
   A. uniforms of railroad engineers
   B. engines used to push or pull trains
   C. oil lanterns
   D. letters and diaries

4. The rescuers looked into the cave.
   F. scientists
   G. people trying to save others
   H. artists
   J. people traveling to new places

5. We hiked across the rugged land.
   A. damp and muddy
   B. green and grassy
   C. dry and dusty
   D. rough and uneven

6. The mayor dispatched the rescue team.
   F. said good things about
   G. sent out
   H. gave instructions to
   J. welcomed

7. The girl told us about her heroic acts.
   A. unusual
   B. against the law
   C. unknown
   D. very brave

Part 2: Comprehension

Use what you know about the selection to answer each question.

8. How did fifteen-year-old Kate Shelley spend most of her time?
   F. She attended school with her younger brothers and sisters.
   G. She helped her father on the railroad.
   H. She swam in the nearby stream and played with her friends.
   J. She ran the family farm.

9. Which of these events happened first?
   A. Kate heard a pusher engine fall into Honey Creek.
   B. Kate moved the farm animals to higher ground.
   C. Kate decided to try to stop the midnight train bound for Chicago.
   D. Kate helped her mother bring in the laundry.

© Scott Foresman 5

GO ON

10. When Kate decided that she had to go through the storm to the train station, her mother was—
    F. worried that she would be hurt.
    G. eager for Kate to face the danger.
    H. furious at Kate for disobeying her.
    J. confident that Kate would be safe.

11. According to the map in this selection, a train heading in a westerly direction as it passed the Shelley house was going toward—
    A. Boone.
    B. Ogden.
    C. Chicago.
    D. Ohio.

12. What was Kate's most terrifying moment while crossing the Des Moines River Bridge?
    F. realizing that the ties were two feet apart
    G. seeing the spot where her brother had died
    H. seeing the lights of the railway station in the distance
    J. seeing a huge tree rushing toward the bridge

13. Which sentence states an opinion?
    A. "She turned and headed for the Des Moines River Bridge."
    B. "As it headed for the fallen trestle, the engineer kept sounding the whistle."
    C. "The girl is crazy."
    D. "But the structure proved solid, and the storm was quieting at last."

14. Traveling east from Moingona, a train would first come to the—
    F. Des Moines River Bridge.
    G. Shelley House.
    H. Honey Creek Bridge.
    J. town of Boone.

15. Of all the honors Kate received, which did she think was the best?
    A. a medal from the state of Iowa
    B. whistles from trains that passed by
    C. a lifetime pass on the railroad
    D. greetings from passengers on the trains

© Scott Foresman 5

STOP

Atlas/Map

An **atlas** is a book of maps. A **map** is a drawing of a place. A **map key** shows what the symbols on a map mean. A **compass** shows the directions north, south, east, and west.

Directions: Use the map below to answer the questions on the next page.

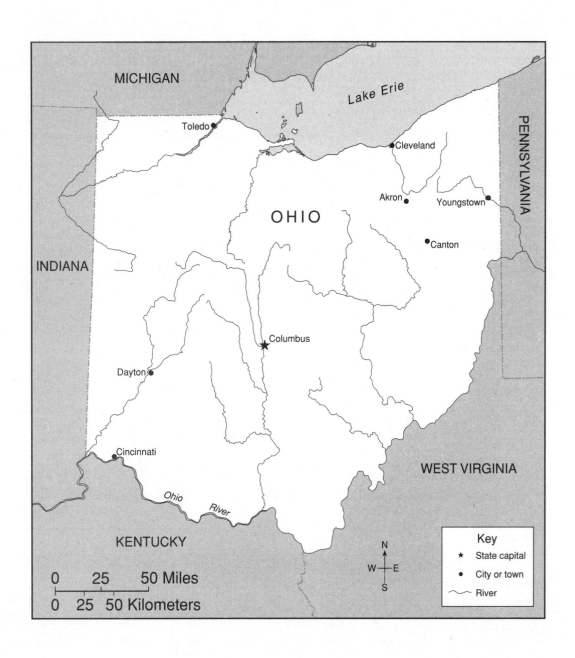

© Scott Foresman 5

Name _____ **Kate Shelley: Bound for Legend**

1. What five states border Ohio? _____

_____

2. Which state is on Ohio's western border? _____

3. If you measured that the distance between two cities was two inches on the map, how many actual miles is this distance? How do you know?

_____

_____

4. Approximately how many miles is it from Columbus to Dayton? _____

5. Approximately how many miles is it from Toledo to Dayton? _____

6. What body of water is located north of Cleveland? _____

7. What body of water runs along Ohio's southern border? _____

8. Which city in Ohio is the state capital? How do you know? _____

_____

9. If you flew from Toledo to Cincinnati, what other city would you fly over? _____

10. If you traveled west from Youngstown, what city would you come to first? _____

11. If you went from Cincinnati to Cleveland, in which direction would you be traveling?

_____

12. Is the distance between Toledo and Columbus greater or less than the distance between Toledo and Akron?

_____

_____

13. Why is it important for a map to have a compass? _____

_____

14. Why is it important for a map to have a map key? _____

_____

15. Describe a situation where you might use a map. _____

_____

_____

© Scott Foresman 5

Notes for Home: Your child read a map and answered questions about it. *Home Activity:* Look at any map you have at home. Have your child point out information on it, such as the location of places or the direction and distance from one place to another.

Plot

- The important events that happen in a story make up the **plot.**

- A plot has several parts. **Conflict** is the story's main problem. During the **rising action** one event follows another. Each event adds interest or suspense to the conflict. The **climax** is the high point when the main character faces the problem directly. The **outcome** is the ending of the story.

Directions: Reread "Anything You Set Your Mind To." Then complete the plot map by identifying each important part of the story.

Climax: When is Terry's problem finally solved?

4. _____

_____

_____

Rising Action: What does Terry do to try to solve his problem?

2. _____

_____

3. _____

Outcome: How does the story end?

5. _____

_____

_____

_____

_____

_____

_____

Conflict: What problem does Terry have?

1. _____

_____

_____

Notes for Home: Your child identified the main events in the plot of a story. **Home Activity:** Read a story with your child. Have your child identify the different plot elements described above.

© Scott Foresman 5

Vocabulary

Directions: Choose the word from the box that best matches each clue.
Write the word on the line.

_____ 1. Healthy foods do this to you.

_____ 2. You might play in this.

_____ 3. You might win this.

_____ 4. It's someone to defeat.

_____ 5. A hurt finger might become this.

**Check
the Words
You Know**

__ championship
__ opponent
__ strengthen
__ swollen
__ trophy

Directions: Write the word from the box that belongs in each group.

6. enemy, foe, _____

7. award, medal, _____

8. enlarged, puffy, _____

9. contest, competition, _____

10. toughen, harden, _____

Directions: Choose the word from the box that best completes each sentence.
Write the word on the line.

_____ 11. The big _____ wrestling match would be held this Saturday
night.

_____ 12. My _____ was bigger than me, but I was faster.

_____ 13. I had worked hard to _____ my upper body muscles.

_____ 14. Although my wrist is a little _____, I believe I can win the
match.

_____ 15. I already know where I want to display the _____ in my
room.

Write a Pep Talk

Imagine you are a sports coach. On a separate sheet of paper, write a pep talk to
give to your players. Your pep talk should help make the team eager to win. Use
as many vocabulary words as you can.

 Notes for Home: Your child identified and used vocabulary words from "The Marble
Champ." *Home Activity:* Choose items in the room where you and your child are sitting.
Describe each item. See if your child can guess what it is, based on the clues you offer.

© Scott Foresman 5

Selection Test

Directions: Choose the best answer to each item. Mark the letter for the answer you have chosen.

Part 1: Vocabulary

Find the answer choice that means about the same as the underlined word in each sentence.

1. Maria watched her opponent.
   A. person who helps a player
   B. person who judges a game
   C. person who writes about sports
   D. person one plays against in a game

2. The championship is on Saturday.
   F. game to decide the first-place winner
   G. important test
   H. party held to honor a special person
   J. practice time

3. Sarah put the trophy on her dresser.
   A. book signed by the author
   B. award in the form of a figure or cup
   C. marble of three different colors
   D. woven string worn around the neck

4. I need to strengthen my legs.
   F. wash
   G. stretch
   H. make stronger
   J. cool off

5. My hand was swollen.
   A. cut
   B. larger than normal
   C. broken
   D. covered with spots

Part 2: Comprehension

Use what you know about the story to answer each item.

6. The beginning of this story is mostly about—
   F. what Lupe has done in the past.
   G. how Lupe plans to become the marble champ.
   H. where Lupe Medrano comes from.
   J. when Lupe learned to ride a bike.

7. Lupe's main problem in this story is that she—
   A. doesn't get along with her family.
   B. never gets enough attention for her achievements.
   C. is doing poorly in school.
   D. wants to be good at sports, but she isn't.

8. The first time Lupe tries to play marbles, what is her main problem?
   F. The marbles keep breaking.
   G. Her thumb is too weak.
   H. Her aim is not accurate.
   J. Her brother takes his marbles back.

9. Which word best describes Lupe?
   A. lazy
   B. determined
   C. complaining
   D. nervous

© Scott Foresman 5

GO ON

10. How do the members of Lupe's family react to her plans to become the marble champ?
    F. They tell her to focus on schoolwork and give up on other activities.
    G. They are positive that she will win.
    H. They are surprised, but they support her.
    J. They pay no attention to her.

11. Lupe's hardest match is against—
    A. Rachel, her first opponent.
    B. Yolanda, her second opponent.
    C. the girl in the baseball cap.
    D. Alfonso, a boy from her neighborhood.

12. During the rising action in this story, Lupe is—
    F. practicing.
    G. beating the girls' champion.
    H. beating the boys' champion.
    J. receiving a trophy.

13. Why was Lupe's decision to play marbles a sensible one?
    A. She picked a sport that nobody else could play well.
    B. She picked a sport that fit her abilities.
    C. She picked a sport in which winning is a matter of luck rather than skill.
    D. She picked a sport that would make her stronger and healthier.

14. The author's main purpose in this selection is to—
    F. tell an amusing story about Lupe.
    G. explain how to play marbles.
    H. persuade kids to play marbles.
    J. describe the awards that Lupe has won before.

15. What does Lupe's treatment of the girls she defeats suggest about her?
    A. She wishes she had never won.
    B. She is a good sport.
    C. She wants to embarrass them.
    D. She is a mean person.

STOP

© Scott Foresman 5

Theme

Directions: Read the story. Then read each question about the story. Choose the best answer to each question. Mark the letter for the answer you have chosen.

A Runner's Shortcut

Kevin really wanted to win the city runners' marathon. First prize was a hundred dollars in cash. Kevin needed the money badly. He had persuaded his brother to loan him money for a new stereo, and it was time to pay him back. His brother had already asked him twice about getting his money back.

Keven hadn't been running on a regular basis lately, but he really wanted a chance at the hundred dollars. He decided he would enter the race.

When the race began, Kevin ran hard. But he just couldn't keep up with the leaders. After two hours, his legs hurt and he was panting. He was also very far behind. He could see the hundred dollars slipping away, and he could hear his brother yelling at him about paying back the loan.

Then Kevin had a new thought. He decided to cheat. He remembered that the Number 10 bus came along the same route as the race. He left the running path and caught the bus. It drove him near the finish line where Kevin got off the bus and ran the rest of the race. He arrived feeling fresh and hardly out of breath. The judges awarded Kevin the cash prize.

Later, however, many people complained. They said they saw Kevin get on and off the bus. The judges had no choice but to take the prize away from Kevin. He felt embarrassed. He was sorry he had cheated and knew that no prize was worth his good name.

1. Kevin wanted to win the race because—
   A. he was a good runner.
   B. he was proud.
   C. he had won before.
   D. he needed money.

2. When Kevin saw he was behind, he decided to—
   F. ride the bus.
   G. quit the race.
   H. run faster.
   J. rest for a while.

3. In the end, Kevin—
   A. won the prize.
   B. lost the prize.
   C. split the prize with someone else.
   D. gave away the prize.

4. One theme of the story is that—
   F. cheaters sometimes win.
   G. cheaters never lose.
   H. cheating doesn't pay.
   J. cheating is okay.

5. Another theme of the story is that cheaters—
   A. should hide better.
   B. shouldn't need money.
   C. may end up embarrassed and sorry.
   D. may win big money.

Notes for Home: Your child read a story and identified its underlying meaning, or theme. *Home Activity:* Watch a TV show or movie with your child. Later, discuss what the characters learned from their experiences, and what the story can teach you about real life.

© Scott Foresman 5

Name _____

Word Study: Contractions

Directions: A **contraction** is a word made by putting two words together. An **apostrophe** (') replaces the letter or letters that are left out. Combine each word pair to form a contraction. Write the contraction on the line.

1. I will _____

2. that is _____

3. was not _____

4. he is _____

5. should not _____

6. she will _____

7. is not _____

8. will not _____

9. we have _____

10. let us _____

11. that is _____

12. we would _____

Directions: Read the letter. Circle each contraction. Write the two words that make up each contraction on the line.

Dear Kelly,

I met this girl in school who's teaching me to play chess. It's a really interesting game. I didn't want to learn at first. The tricky part is remembering what each chess piece can do. I wasn't very good in the beginning, but she's been really patient. I'm getting the hang of it and, with practice, I'll get better. Maybe you'll play chess with me when I visit!

Your friend,
Malcolm

13. _____

14. _____

15. _____

16. _____

17. _____

18. _____

19. _____

20. _____

Notes for Home: Your child formed contractions such as *I'd (I had)* and *haven't (have not)*. **Home Activity:** Watch a favorite television show with your child and listen for contractions in the dialogue or narration. See who can be the first to say the two words that the contraction represents.

© Scott Foresman 5

Technology: Diagram/Scale Drawing

The Internet is a great place to find information. To find your topic, use a search engine to look for web pages. The computer screen for a search engine might look like this:

Search the Web

Search Tip: Type in more than one word and put AND in between them. Enter your words, then click Find.

Find!

If you need help, click here.

If you wanted to find out about games played with marbles, you could enter "marbles AND games." Then you might get this list of web pages:

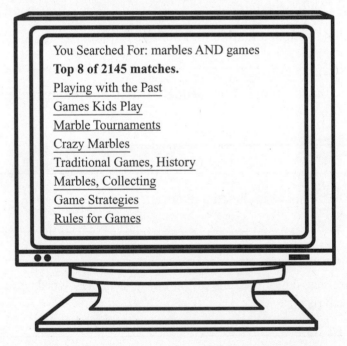

You Searched For: marbles AND games
Top 8 of 2145 matches.
Playing with the Past
Games Kids Play
Marble Tournaments
Crazy Marbles
Traditional Games, History
Marbles, Collecting
Game Strategies
Rules for Games

Web pages often include diagrams or scale drawings. A **diagram** is a special drawing with labels that usually show how something is made or done. A **scale drawing** is a diagram that uses a mathematical scale, such as 1 inch on the drawing equals 1 foot in real life.

© Scott Foresman 5

Name _____

Directions: The web page below explains how to play a game of marbles called Three Holes. It includes a diagram of the playing area. Use the instructions and the diagram to answer the questions that follow.

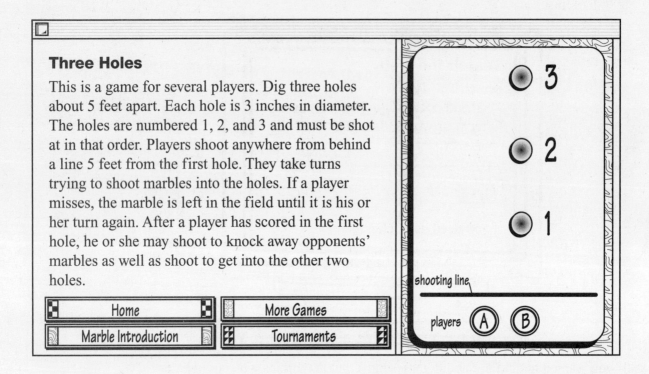

Three Holes

This is a game for several players. Dig three holes about 5 feet apart. Each hole is 3 inches in diameter. The holes are numbered 1, 2, and 3 and must be shot at in that order. Players shoot anywhere from behind a line 5 feet from the first hole. They take turns trying to shoot marbles into the holes. If a player misses, the marble is left in the field until it is his or her turn again. After a player has scored in the first hole, he or she may shoot to knock away opponents' marbles as well as shoot to get into the other two holes.

| Home | More Games |
| Marble Introduction | Tournaments |

shooting line

players (A) (B)

1. What does the line represent in the diagram? _____

2. Is player B in a good position to shoot a marble into hole 3? Explain. _____

_____

3. If the diagram were drawn using a scale of 1 inch equals 1 foot, how many inches apart should the holes be drawn? Explain.

_____

_____

4. Why do you think the web page above included a diagram?

_____

_____

5. If you wanted to find games that senior citizens might enjoy, what key words could you type to search the Internet for web pages?

_____

Notes for Home: Your child read a diagram and answered questions about it. *Home Activity:* Help your child draw a scale drawing of the playing field for the marble game described above using a scale of 1 inch equals 1 foot.

© Scott Foresman 5

Name _____

Text Structure

- **Text structure** is the way a piece of writing is organized. There are two main kinds of writing—fiction and nonfiction.

- Fiction tells stories of made-up people and events. Fiction is often organized in chronological order.

- Nonfiction tells stories of real people and events or gives real information. It can be organized in chronological order, by main ideas with supporting details, or as relationships such as cause and effect, problem and solution, and compare and contrast.

Directions: Reread "Bee Bodies." Then complete the table. Give two supporting details for each main idea in the article.

Main Ideas	Supporting Details
Body	1.
	2.
Eyes	3.
	4.
Mouth	5.
	6.
Wings	7.
	8.
Legs	9.
	10.

Notes for Home: Your child used a table to help show how information in an article has been organized. *Home Activity:* Read a newspaper or magazine article with your child. Have him or her identify the way the information is organized.

© Scott Foresman 5

Name _____

Vocabulary

Directions: Choose the word from the box that best completes each sentence.
Write the word on the line to the left.

_____ 1. Ants often live together in a _____.

_____ 2. See how they _____ from their anthill.

_____ 3. At a picnic, keep all your spare food
in _____.

_____ 4. If food is left out, the ants _____ to it
quickly.

_____ 5. What good _____ those ants are in!
Watch them lift that cracker!

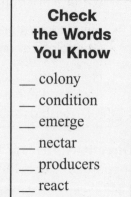

Check the Words You Know

__ colony
__ condition
__ emerge
__ nectar
__ producers
__ react
__ storage
__ venom

Directions: Choose the word from the box that best matches each clue.
Write the letters of the word on the blanks. The boxed letters spell something
that some ants in a colony might be.

6. sweet liquid   6. __ __ __ __ ▢ __

7. product makers   7. __ __ __ __ __ __ ▢ __ __

8. poison   8. __ __ ▢ __ __

9. state someone is in 9. __ __ __ __ __ ▢

10. state of being stored 10. ▢ __ __ __ __ __ __

What some ants in a colony might be: __ __ __ __ __

Write a Description

Imagine you are a scientist who has discovered a new creature. On a separate
sheet of paper, describe the creature. Give vivid details that tell what the
creature looks like, how it moves, what sounds it makes, and what it likes to eat.
Use as many vocabulary words as you can.

Notes for Home: Your child identified and used vocabulary words from "From Bees to
Honey." **Home Activity:** Find out more about an insect that interests your child. Create an
encyclopedia entry of text and a picture that describes the insect.

© Scott Foresman 5

Name _____

Text Structure

- **Text structure** is the way a piece of writing is organized.

- Fiction tells stories of made-up people and events. Fiction is usually organized in chronological order. Nonfiction tells of real people and events. It can be organized in chronological order, by main idea and supporting details, or as relationships such as cause and effect, problem and solution, or compare and contrast.

Directions: Reread this passage from "From Bees to Honey" about the history of beekeeping. Then answer the questions below.

The relationship between humans and honeybees goes back thousands of years. In prehistoric times, people took honey from the hives of wild bees in hollow trees. About four thousand years ago, the Egyptians kept bees in cigar-shaped hives made of clay. During the Middle Ages, beekeepers used dome-shaped hives called skeps, which were woven of straw.

John Wetzler, like most modern beekeepers, uses hives made of wood. A hive consists of several boxes, or *hive bodies,* which are open at the top and bottom. Hanging inside each hive body are ten movable wooden *frames.* The frames hold sheets of wax called *foundation,* on which bees build the six-sided cells of their combs.

From A BEEKEEPER'S YEAR by Sylvia Johnson. Copyright © 1994 by Sylvia Johnson (Text); Illustrations © by E.M. Peterson Books. By permission of Little, Brown and Company.

1. What four time periods does the passage mention?

   _____

   _____

2. Which period is the earliest example of beekeeping?

   _____

3. Which period is the most recent example of beekeeping?

   _____

4. Is this passage an example of fiction or nonfiction writing? Explain. Which kind or kinds of organization does the author use: chronological order, main idea and supporting details, cause and effect, problem and solution, or compare and contrast?

   _____

   _____

5. What kinds of organization do you find in "From Bees to Honey"? Give examples. Write your answer on a separate sheet of paper.

Notes for Home: Your child read a passage and identified the ways that information is organized. **Home Activity:** Read a newspaper article together with your child. Invite him or her to describe how the information is organized.

© Scott Foresman 5

Name _____

1.	Ⓐ	Ⓑ	Ⓒ	Ⓓ
2.	Ⓕ	Ⓖ	Ⓗ	Ⓙ
3.	Ⓐ	Ⓑ	Ⓒ	Ⓓ
4.	Ⓕ	Ⓖ	Ⓗ	Ⓙ
5.	Ⓐ	Ⓑ	Ⓒ	Ⓓ
6.	Ⓕ	Ⓖ	Ⓗ	Ⓙ
7.	Ⓐ	Ⓑ	Ⓒ	Ⓓ
8.	Ⓕ	Ⓖ	Ⓗ	Ⓙ
9.	Ⓐ	Ⓑ	Ⓒ	Ⓓ
10.	Ⓕ	Ⓖ	Ⓗ	Ⓙ
11.	Ⓐ	Ⓑ	Ⓒ	Ⓓ
12.	Ⓕ	Ⓖ	Ⓗ	Ⓙ
13.	Ⓐ	Ⓑ	Ⓒ	Ⓓ
14.	Ⓕ	Ⓖ	Ⓗ	Ⓙ
15.	Ⓐ	Ⓑ	Ⓒ	Ⓓ

© Scott Foresman 5

Selection Test

Directions: Choose the best answer to each item. Mark the letter for the answer you have chosen.

Part 1: Vocabulary

Find the answer choice that means about the same as the underlined word in each sentence.

1. The teacher told us about nectar.
   A. the main bee in a hive
   B. a sheet of wax made by bees
   C. a mixture of sugar and water
   D. the sweet liquid found in flowers

2. When José teases you, don't react.
   F. listen carefully
   G. complain to someone
   H. respond to something
   J. disappear

3. Those ants live in a colony.
   A. group of living things
   B. barn for storing hay
   C. cage for birds
   D. underground cave

4. Scientists studied the venom.
   F. poison from an insect or animal
   G. communication between animals
   H. home for bees
   J. sticky substance

5. What is the condition of the animal?
   A. diet
   B. state
   C. age
   D. name

6. Who are the producers of that jelly?
   F. people who make
   G. people who sell
   H. people who use
   J. people who like

7. The proper storage of food is important.
   A. cooking to kill germs
   B. preparing to mix flavors
   C. selecting for good quality
   D. saving for a later date

8. When will the children emerge?
   F. stop playing
   G. pay attention
   H. come out
   J. work together

Part 2: Comprehension

Use what you know about the selection to answer each item.

9. John Wetzler produces honey mainly because he likes to—
   A. make money.
   B. eat lots of sweet foods.
   C. work with bees.
   D. hire his neighbors to work for him.

10. The information in this selection is presented as—
    F. a series of comparisons and contrasts.
    G. a series of causes and effects.
    H. problems and solutions.
    J. events in chronological order.

GO ON

Name _____

From Bees to Honey

11. John uses a smoker when opening the hive because he—
   A. wants some of the bees to die.
   B. has to melt the bee glue.
   C. does not want to be stung.
   D. wants to keep the bees warm.

12. What is the main difference between worker bees under 20 days old and worker bees over 20 days old?
   F. Young worker bees cannot lay eggs, but older ones can.
   G. Young worker bees work inside the hive, and older worker bees collect nectar.
   H. Older worker bees mostly guard the hive from wasps, but younger ones don't.
   J. Young worker bees forage for nectar and pollen while older ones stay inside the hive.

13. What does John do just before placing a frame in the honey extractor?
   A. puts plastic bags over the hives
   B. removes impurities from the honey
   C. removes the supers from the hives
   D. uncaps the frames

14. Which detail suggests that John is good at thinking of creative solutions to problems?
   F. his use of the brick code
   G. his use of the bee tool
   H. his use of the honey extractor
   J. his use of hive bodies

15. The text structure helps you understand the content of this selection mainly by—
   A. illustrating the dangers of beekeeping.
   B. describing the natural order of a beekeeper's activities.
   C. suggesting unusual solutions to problems.
   D. comparing wild bees and domesticated bees.

STOP

© Scott Foresman 5

136 Selection Test

Name _____

Steps in a Process

REVIEW

Directions: Read the passage. Then read each question about the passage. Choose the best answer to each question. Mark the letter for the answer you have chosen.

Baking a Honeycake

To bake a honeycake, you will need these ingredients: flour, baking powder, baking soda, cinnamon, brown sugar, eggs, honey, and oil. You will need two large bowls and a tube baking pan.

Start making the honeycake by mixing together these ingredients in a large bowl:

$2\frac{1}{2}$ cups of flour, 2 teaspoons of baking powder, 1 teaspoon of baking soda, and 2 teaspoons of cinnamon.

Then in a second large bowl, mix $\frac{3}{4}$ cup of brown sugar with 3 eggs.

Next, add a cup of honey and $\frac{3}{4}$ cup of oil to the second bowl.

Pour the contents of the first bowl into the second. Mix until blended.

Pour the batter into a 10-inch tube pan.

Bake at 325°F for 1 hour. After an hour, remove the pan from the oven and let it cool. Then remove the cake from the pan.

1. The first step in the process of making a honeycake involves—
   A. sugar.
   B. eggs.
   C. oil.
   D. cinnamon.

2. Just before adding honey and oil, you—
   F. mix the batter.
   G. mix sugar and eggs.
   H. mix flour and cinnamon.
   J. pour the contents of one bowl into another.

3. Right after mixing the batter, you—
   A. add eggs and sugar.
   B. add oil and honey.
   C. pour it in a pan.
   D. bake at 325° F.

4. The contents of the two bowls are combined—
   F. before honey is used.
   G. after honey is used.
   H. before oil is used.
   J. while honey is being added.

5. The final step in the process is to—
   A. remove the cake from the pan.
   B. let cool for 20 minutes.
   C. add oil and honey.
   D. remove the cake from the oven.

Notes for Home: Your child read an explanation of a process and identified the order of the steps. *Home Activity:* Read a set of directions, such as a cookbook recipe, with your child. Then have your child tell you the order of the steps.

© Scott Foresman 5

Word Study: Possessives

Directions: Read the sentences below. Rewrite each underlined phrase using an **apostrophe (')** and **s** to show possession. For example, **the ball of the boy** can be written as **the boy's ball.** Write the new phrase on the line.

_____ 1. It is <u>the job of the worker bee</u> to look for flower nectar.

_____ 2. They visited <u>the hive that belongs to the beekeeper</u>.

_____ 3. <u>The wife of the beekeeper</u> shows visitors the honey house.

_____ 4. <u>The combs of the hive</u> were filled with honey.

_____ 5. Everyone enjoys <u>the flavor of honey</u>.

Directions: Read the phrases below. Rewrite each phrase using the possessive form. Write the new phrase on the line. Remember, for plural nouns that end in **-s,** add only an apostrophe, as in **the sisters' bikes.**

_____ 6. the job of bees

_____ 7. the honey of beekeepers

_____ 8. the market of farmers

_____ 9. the enjoyment of the families

_____ 10. the bees of a hive

_____ 11. the nectar of a flower

_____ 12. the responsibility of a farmer

_____ 13. the harvests of many seasons

_____ 14. the crops from many farms

_____ 15. the eggs of the queen bee

Notes for Home: Your child formed singular and plural possessives, such as *the boy's ball* and *the sisters' bikes.* **Home Activity:** Point out objects that belong to one person or more. Ask your child to use possessives to tell who owns them.

© Scott Foresman 5

Name _____

Outlining

An **outline** is a plan that shows how a story, article, report, or other text is organized. You can use an outline to better understand how a text is organized or as a way to organize your own thoughts before you write something of your own.

Directions: Read the following outline. Then answer the questions.

Occupations

I. Outdoor jobs
   A. Forest ranger
      1. Cut down dead trees
      2. Watch for forest fires
      3. Plant new trees
   B. Landscaper
      1. Plant gardens
      2. Mow lawns
II. Indoor jobs
   A. Lab technician
      1. Conduct experiments
      2. Analyze results
   B. School teacher
      1. Instruct students
      2. Evaluate students

1. What other main topic is shown in the outline besides outdoor jobs? _____

2. What two subtopics are listed under the first main topic? _____
_____

3. What subtopics are listed under the second main topic? _____
_____

4. What details are listed under the subtopic "Lab technician"? _____
_____

5. Which subtopic has the most details? _____

© Scott Foresman 5

Name _____

Directions: Read the following article. Then complete the outline below.

Where Would You Like to Work?

There are two main kinds of jobs you can have—outdoor jobs and indoor jobs. Working outdoors offers many benefits. For example, you get to enjoy fresh air. You also see pretty landscapes. In addition, you get to be more active. On the other hand, outdoor work can present disadvantages too. Sometimes you may have to work in the rain. Some days may be unbearably cold or hot.

Working indoors has its benefits. For example, you may be in a climate-controlled environment, so you don't get too hot or too cold. Also, it is usually easy to get from place to place, without any rough roads or hills to climb. On the other hand, indoor work also has disadvantages. You may start to feel "cooped up" on long days. You may have to work in a room with poor air circulation.

Occupations

I. _____

   A. Benefits

      1. Enjoy fresh air

      2. _____

      3. _____

   B. _____

      1. Work in rain

      2. _____

II. Indoor jobs

   A. _____

      1. _____

      2. _____

   B. Disadvantages

      1. _____

      2. _____

Notes for Home: Your child practiced organizing information in an outline. *Home Activity:* Talk with your child about the different jobs that people in your family have. Then invite your child to create an outline that organizes the information you discussed together.

© Scott Foresman 5

Summarizing

- **Summarizing** means telling just the main ideas of an article or the plot of a story.

- A good summary is brief. It does not include unnecessary details, repeated words or thoughts, or unimportant ideas.

Directions: Reread "What Do Animals Say?" Then complete the table. Write one sentence to summarize each portion of the article indicated. Then write a summary of the entire article.

Portion of Article	Summary
Paragraph 1	**1.**
Paragraphs 2–4	**2.**
Paragraph 5	**3.**
Paragraph 6	**4.**
Paragraph 7	**5.**

Notes for Home: Your child read an article and summarized each part of it. *Home Activity:* Read a story with your child. Stop at various points during the story and have your child summarize what happened in only a few sentences.

© Scott Foresman 5

Name _____

Vocabulary

Directions: Match each word on the left with its definition on the right.
Write the letter of the definition next to the word.

_____ **1.** civil   **a.** without warning

_____ **2.** instinct   **b.** having good judgment

_____ **3.** raid   **c.** inborn way of acting

_____ **4.** unexpected   **d.** polite

_____ **5.** sensible   **e.** sudden attack

Check the Words You Know
__ chaos
__ civil
__ confusion
__ instinct
__ raid
__ sensible
__ unexpected

Directions: Read the news report. Choose the word from
the box that best completes each sentence. Write the word
on the matching numbered line below.

BIG STORM HITS PRAIRIE TOWN

The storm was entirely **6.** _____. At first, there
was great **7.** _____. Everyone ran to a huge tree
on the prairie for shelter. Then a **8.** _____ young
girl said, "That's not safe. Lightning could strike
you!" Her **9.** _____ was right. In spite of the
10. _____, she led the people to safe shelter in
a nearby barn.

6. _____   **9.** _____

7. _____   **10.** _____

8. _____

Write a Story

On a separate sheet of paper, write a story that tells about a war
or battle that took place. Use as many vocabulary words as you can.

Notes for Home: Your child identified and used vocabulary words from "Babe to the
Rescue." **Home Activity:** Think of a word. Say a word to your child that means the opposite.
See if your child can guess your word. For example, the opposite of *foolish* is *sensible*.

© Scott Foresman 5

Summarizing

- **Summarizing** means telling just the main ideas of an article or the plot of a story. A good summary is brief. It does not include unnecessary details, repeated words or thoughts, or unimportant ideas.

Directions: Read the following four summaries of the opening of "Babe to the Rescue." Then answer the questions below.

A. Fly and Babe went to the pond where the ducks swam. After the ducks came out of the water, Babe tried to round them up and bring them to Fly. His efforts failed.

B. Fly and Babe went to the pond where the ducks swam. The pond was soupy green. Babe tried to round up the ducks after they came out of the water. His efforts failed.

C. Fly and Babe went to the pond where the ducks swam. Fly was a sheepdog. She was also a collie. Babe tried to round up the ducks when they came out of the water.

D. Fly and Babe went to the pond where the ducks swam. After the ducks came out of the water, Babe tried to round them up. When Babe spoke with Fly, he said, "Yes, Mum."

1. Which of the four summaries is best? Explain why.

_____

_____

2. What unnecessary detail is given in Summary B?

_____

_____

3. What unnecessary detail is given in Summary C?

_____

_____

4. What unnecessary detail is given in Summary D?

_____

_____

5. Summarize in a few sentences the part of the story about the sheep rustlers. Write your summary on a separate sheet of paper.

Notes for Home: Your child identified characteristics that make a good summary. *Home Activity:* Watch a TV show or movie with your child. Then ask your child to summarize the story. Discuss whether the summary included the most important parts of the story.

© Scott Foresman 5

Name _____

1.	(A)	(B)	(C)	(D)
2.	(F)	(G)	(H)	(J)
3.	(A)	(B)	(C)	(D)
4.	(F)	(G)	(H)	(J)
5.	(A)	(B)	(C)	(D)
6.	(F)	(G)	(H)	(J)
7.	(A)	(B)	(C)	(D)
8.	(F)	(G)	(H)	(J)
9.	(A)	(B)	(C)	(D)
10.	(F)	(G)	(H)	(J)
11.	(A)	(B)	(C)	(D)
12.	(F)	(G)	(H)	(J)
13.	(A)	(B)	(C)	(D)
14.	(F)	(G)	(H)	(J)
15.	(A)	(B)	(C)	(D)

© Scott Foresman 5

Selection Test

Directions: Choose the best answer to each item. Mark the letter for the answer you have chosen.

Part 1: Vocabulary

Find the answer choice that means about the same as the underlined word in each sentence.

1. Your telephone call was unexpected.
   A. too long
   B. made incorrectly
   C. not planned for
   D. not wanted

2. The cat followed its instinct.
   F. markings
   G. inborn way of acting
   H. owner
   J. sense of smell

3. The speaker stopped in confusion.
   A. state of being embarrassed
   B. state of feeling ill
   C. state of being frightened
   D. state of not knowing what to do

4. The salesperson was very civil.
   F. polite
   G. friendly
   H. eager
   J. cold

5. There was chaos on the field.
   A. joy
   B. lack of order
   C. sorrow
   D. movement

6. The raid was planned for Thursday.
   F. surprise party
   G. instructional gathering
   H. sudden attack
   J. formal test

7. Please try to be sensible.
   A. having good judgment
   B. being brave
   C. being generous
   D. having good taste

Part 2: Comprehension

Use what you know about the story to answer each item.

8. What does Babe first try to herd?
   F. puppies
   G. piglets
   H. ducks
   J. lambs

9. Unlike Fly, Babe tries to herd sheep by—
   A. shouting at them.
   B. standing in one place.
   C. speaking politely to them.
   D. nipping at their heels.

10. Why is Babe's style of herding different from a normal sheepdog's?
    F. Fly wants him to be different.
    G. Babe was not born with a sheepdog's instincts.
    H. Farmer Hoggett teaches Babe a new method of herding.
    J. Pigs are not intelligent animals.

11. Ma does not like sheepdogs because they—
    A. are rude to sheep.
    B. talk to sheep.
    C. try to herd sheep.
    D. are stupid.

© Scott Foresman 5

GO ON

Name _____

12. Which is the best summary of the first half of this story?
    F. Babe makes friends with Ma, an old ewe, by telling her she doesn't look old.
    G. Babe practices his herding skills with Fly's help and makes friends with Ma.
    H. Babe herds some ducks and talks with Fly.
    J. When Babe meets Ma, she tells him that she doesn't like sheepdogs, which she calls wolves.

13. Which is the best summary of the second half of this story?
    A. When Ma rejoins the flock and Mr. Hoggett goes away, Babe tries to steal the sheep.
    B. Mrs. Hoggett decides to keep Babe because he makes so much noise.
    C. Sheep rustlers come to the Hoggetts' farm one day while Mr. Hoggett and Fly are away.
    D. Babe saves the sheep from rustlers, and Mrs. Hoggett decides to keep him.

14. Which part of this story is fantasy?
    F. sheep stealers
    G. dogs that can herd sheep
    H. talking animals
    J. dogs that obey human commands

15. Based on her decision to keep Babe, you can tell that Mrs. Hoggett highly values—
    A. loyalty.
    B. money.
    C. an easy life.
    D. being meek and quiet.

STOP

© Scott Foresman 5

Compare and Contrast

Directions: Read the passage. Then read each question about the passage. Choose the best answer to each question. Mark the letter for the answer you have chosen.

Pigs and Sheep

Both pigs and sheep are common farm animals that are raised for the products they furnish to people. These animals provide food but also other things. Most pigs and sheep are raised in order for people to be able to have products made with their skin, hair, and meat.

Although pigs and sheep are never likely to be mistaken for one another, they actually share several qualities. That is, both of these animals are used by people for some of the same products.

First, both pigs and sheep provide people with meat. Sheep yield lamb chops and mutton, while pigs give ham, sausage, bacon, and pork chops. In addition, the fat and skin of both pigs and sheep are used to produce leather, soap, glue, and fertilizer.

Of course, you are aware of using the hair of sheep. It is the wool that is a common product for weaving into heavy warm clothing. You might not as quickly think of using the hair of pigs. In fact, you might not think of pigs as having much hair. Certainly, it is not as abundant as the wool of sheep. Although pigs do not grow wool, their hair is used as bristles for brushes. Pig hair is also used as stuffing for mattresses and for baseball gloves.

1. The article explains how pigs and sheep are—
   A. alike only.
   B. different only.
   C. alike and different.
   D. like other animals.

2. Both pigs and sheep are used to produce—
   F. mutton.
   G. ham.
   H. sausage.
   J. soap.

3. One difference between pigs and sheep is that—
   A. pigs live on farms.
   B. sheep grow wool.
   C. sheep supply meat.
   D. pigs supply meat.

4. One way that pigs and sheep are alike is that both—
   F. are used for leather.
   G. look the same.
   H. yield pork chops.
   J. yield bacon.

5. Bristles for brushes are a product supplied by—
   A. sheep only.
   B. pigs only.
   C. both pigs and sheep.
   D. neither pigs nor sheep.

Notes for Home: Your child read an article and identified comparisons and contrasts that the writer made. *Home Activity:* Choose two separate items in your home. Talk with your child about ways that the two items are alike and different.

© Scott Foresman 5

Name _____

Word Study: Unusual Possessives

Directions: Some plural nouns do not end in **-s.** To make them possessive, add
an **apostrophe (')** and the letter **s.** Rewrite each phrase using the possessive
form. Write the new phrase on the line.

_____ 1. the honks of the geese

_____ 2. the laughter of the children

_____ 3. the conversation of the men

_____ 4. the voices of the women

_____ 5. the squeaks of the mice

Directions: Some singular nouns end in **-s.** To make them possessive, add an
apostrophe (') and the **s.** Rewrite each phrase using the possessive form.
Write the new phrase on the line.

_____ 6. the orders of the boss

_____ 7. the desks of the class

_____ 8. the singing of the chorus

_____ 9. the color of the dress

_____ 10. the contents of the glass

Directions: Read each sentence. Circle the correct possessive form in ( ).

11. The animals heard the main (boss's/boss') words, and they started to make noise.

12. The farmer could hear the many (sheep's/sheep') cries.

13. Then he heard the (mens/men's) low voices.

14. He saw the two (thieves's/thieves') truck.

15. Quietly, he crept to the truck and let out all
    four of the (tires'/tire's) air.

Notes for Home: Your child learned how to form unusual possessives, such as *sheep's.* **Home**
Activity: Make a list of irregular plurals, such as *mice* and *men,* and singular nouns that end in
-s, such as *Chris.* Have your child write sentences using the possessive form of each word.

© Scott Foresman 5

Name _____

Babe to the Rescue

Magazines/Periodicals/Almanacs

Periodicals are materials published at regular time periods, such as weekly, monthly, and so on. **Magazines** are a type of periodical that contain news articles, opinion columns, advertisements, cartoons, reports, and so on. The *Readers' Guide to Periodic Literature* is a good resource for locating magazine articles about specific topics.

Directions: Suppose you found the following articles in the *Readers' Guide.* Use these sample entries to answer the questions that follow.

ANIMALS, FARM
    See also
  Farming

A horses's life: just say neigh. N. Johansen.
  Farming Mag Ap 4 '98 p 87–90
All vets are off: a shortage of animal doctors.
  L. Landon. Time Mag D 13 '98 p 45
An udder disgrace: the milk strike continues.
  J. Jackson. US News Report Ja '98 p 23–24
Chicks and ducks and geese better scurry: a
  cold winter's coming. Weather Gazette.
  N '98 p 12–13
Do pigs really eat like pigs? D. Taylor.
  Farmer's Guide F 16 '98 p 90–94
Don't be a chicken with your chickens.
  G. McMillan. Farming Mag Jl 16 '98
  p 44–45

Ducks and swans: what's the difference?
  B. Barello. Science Digest D 14 '98 p 34–35
Honk if you love geese! N. Michelson.
  Agriculture and You. My '98 p 56–58
Is any animal really as stubborn as a mule? M.
  Vicars. Science Digest F 12 '98 p 87–89
Never pull the wool over a sheep's eyes.
  T. Albright. Newsweek Mag Jl 14 '98
  p 29–32
New feed for a new age. G. O'Tooney.
  Science Digest Mr 14 '98 p 99–101
New ways to shear sheep at the baa-baa shop.
  P. Nelson. Farmer's Guide Ag '98 p 78–80
Should farmers clone sheep? J. Miller. Time
  Mag Mr 10 '98 p 55–58
Why did the chicken cross the road? and
  other farm animal jokes. F. Mock. Humor
  Mag F '98 p 17

1. In which magazine does the article "Honk If You Love Geese!" appear?

_____

2. What is the date of the *Farmer's Guide* that carries the article "Do Pigs Really Eat Like Pigs?"

_____

3. Who wrote the article "New Ways to Shear Sheep at the Baa-Baa Shop"?

_____

4. On what page or pages does the article "Never Pull the Wool Over a Sheep's Eyes" appear?

_____

5. What other listing is given by the *Readers' Guide* for more information about farm animals?

_____

© Scott Foresman 5

Research and Study Skills: Magazines/Periodicals/Almanacs **149**

Name _____

An **almanac** is a book published each year that contains calendars, weather information, dates of holidays, and charts and tables of current information in many different subject areas.

Directions: Use the almanac index to answer the questions that follow.

Agriculture, U.S.
Congressional committees 159
Corn blight 428
History 54
Income 498

Animals
Endangered wildlife 330
Farm animal revenues 229
Sheep cloning 109
Use in research 24

6. For a report on farm animals, would you find more helpful information under "Agriculture, U.S." or under "Animals"?

_____

7. On what page of the almanac would you find information on farm animal revenues?

_____

8. Information about what topic appears on page 109 of the almanac? _____

_____

9. If you wanted to learn about problems farmers have had with corn crops, which page would you turn to?

_____

10. When might an almanac be a more useful resource than a book? Explain.

_____

_____

Notes for Home: Your child learned how to find information in magazines and an almanac. *Home Activity:* With your child, look through the table of contents of a magazine or almanac. Choose a specific topic, and see if your child can find it in the magazine or almanac.

© Scott Foresman 5

Name _____

Compare and Contrast

- To **compare** is to tell how two or more things are alike. To **contrast** is to tell how two or more things are different.

- Authors sometimes use clue words such as *similar to, like,* or *as* to compare things. They may use clue words such as *different from, but,* or *unlike* to contrast things.

Directions: Reread "A Visitor from Japan." Then complete the diagram. Write what the story says and what you already know about people and places in Japan on the left. Write about the people and places in America on the right. Write things that both countries have in common in the middle. Some ideas have been given to help you get started.

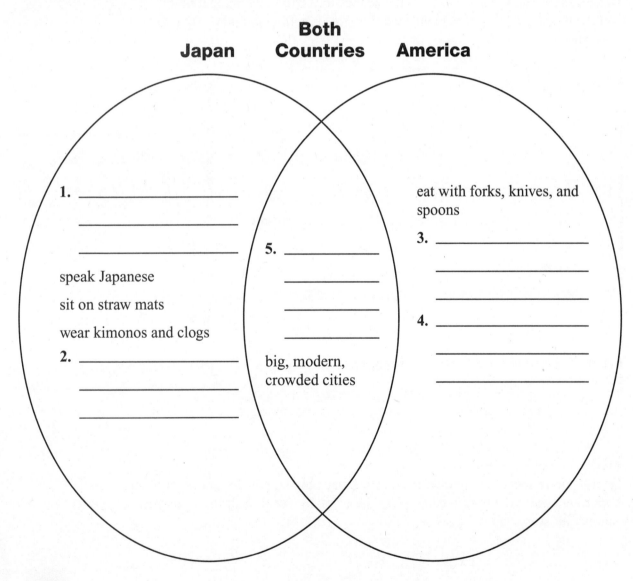

Japan   **Both Countries**   **America**

1. _____
_____
_____

speak Japanese

sit on straw mats

wear kimonos and clogs

2. _____
_____
_____

5. _____
_____
_____
_____

big, modern, crowded cities

eat with forks, knives, and spoons

3. _____
_____
_____

4. _____
_____
_____

Notes for Home: Your child read a story and learned how to compare and contrast. ***Home Activity:*** With your child, look at family photographs of two people, places, or things. Invite your child to describe how the people, places, or things in the photos are alike and different.

© Scott Foresman 5

Vocabulary

Directions: Choose the word from the box that best matches each definition. Write the word on the line.

Check the Words You Know

__ dismayed
__ impression
__ insult
__ records
__ sprouts
__ winced

_____ 1. say something rude

_____ 2. shoots of plants

_____ 3. drew back or flinched slightly

_____ 4. troubled greatly

_____ 5. department in hospital that keeps
                        written accounts

Directions: Read the diary entry. Choose the word from the box that best completes each sentence. Write the word on the matching numbered line to the right.

Dear Diary,

   Boy, am I upset! I couldn't be more

6. _____. We had our class potluck supper

tonight. I'm positive Amy Jones 7. _____ when

I brought out my casserole of eels and bean

8. _____. I never dreamed she would 9. _____

me like that! Could I be wrong? I don't

think so. Tomorrow I'll ask Leah if she

got the same 10. _____. More later.

6. _____

7. _____

8. _____

9. _____

10. _____

Write a Funny Story

On a separate sheet of paper, write a funny story about a holiday dinner or other important event your family celebrates. Use as many vocabulary words as you can in your story.

Notes for Home: Your child identified and used vocabulary words from "The Yangs' First Thanksgiving." **Home Activity:** Ask your child to make expressions that match the words *dismayed* and *winced*. Take turns doing the same for the other words about strong feelings.

© Scott Foresman 5

Name _____

The Yangs' First Thanksgiving

Compare and Contrast

- To **compare** is to tell how two or more things are alike. To **contrast** is to tell how two or more things are different.

- Authors sometimes use clue words such as *similar to, like,* or *as* to compare things. They may use clue words such as *different from, but,* or *unlike* to contrast things.

Directions: Reread what happens in "The Yangs' First Thanksgiving" after Mrs. Conner tries to get Mrs. Hanson to take a piece of pie. Then answer the questions below.

Mother was staring at Mrs. Hanson and Mrs. Conner during this exchange. We Chinese think that being fat is good. It's a sign of good fortune. Thin people are considered unfortunate and miserable.

But I knew here, being thin is supposed to be attractive. A lot of the girls in school are worried about their weight, and some of them even go on diets.

I saw Mother open her mouth. Don't say it, Mother, I wanted to shout. Don't say it!

But she did. Radiating good will, Mother said, "Why you're not skinny at all, Mrs. Hanson. You're actually quite fat!"

From YANG THE THIRD AND HER IMPOSSIBLE FAMILY by Lensey Namioka. Copyright © 1995 by Lensey Namioka (Text); Illustrations © by Kees de Kiefte. By permission of Little, Brown and Company.

1. What is the author contrasting in this scene?

_____

2. What clue word does the writer use to show contrast?

_____

3. How is Mother different from Mrs. Hanson and Mrs. Conner?

_____

_____

4. Tell why Mrs. Hanson will probably feel insulted by Mother's remark.

_____

_____

5. In what other ways are the Yangs different from the Conners and their guests? On a separate sheet of paper, describe another example of contrast from the story.

Notes for Home: Your child read a story and identified comparisons and contrasts. *Home Activity:* Work with your child to compare and contrast two people, places, or things.

Compare and Contrast **153**

Name _____

1.	Ⓐ	Ⓑ	Ⓒ	Ⓓ
2.	Ⓕ	Ⓖ	Ⓗ	Ⓙ
3.	Ⓐ	Ⓑ	Ⓒ	Ⓓ
4.	Ⓕ	Ⓖ	Ⓗ	Ⓙ
5.	Ⓐ	Ⓑ	Ⓒ	Ⓓ
6.	Ⓕ	Ⓖ	Ⓗ	Ⓙ
7.	Ⓐ	Ⓑ	Ⓒ	Ⓓ
8.	Ⓕ	Ⓖ	Ⓗ	Ⓙ
9.	Ⓐ	Ⓑ	Ⓒ	Ⓓ
10.	Ⓕ	Ⓖ	Ⓗ	Ⓙ
11.	Ⓐ	Ⓑ	Ⓒ	Ⓓ
12.	Ⓕ	Ⓖ	Ⓗ	Ⓙ
13.	Ⓐ	Ⓑ	Ⓒ	Ⓓ
14.	Ⓕ	Ⓖ	Ⓗ	Ⓙ
15.	Ⓐ	Ⓑ	Ⓒ	Ⓓ

© Scott Foresman 5

Selection Test

Directions: Choose the best answer to each item. Mark the letter for the answer you have chosen.

Part 1: Vocabulary

Find the answer choice that means about the same as the underlined word in each sentence.

1. She made a good underline impression.
   - A.   sound
   - B.   effect on people
   - C.   statement of facts
   - D.   look on one's face

2. Stefanie winced when she heard the yell.
   - F.   cried out
   - G.   burst into laughter
   - H.   shrugged
   - J.   drew back suddenly

3. Mr. Jackson got a bag of sprouts.
   - A.   shoots of plants
   - B.   small twigs
   - C.   flower buds
   - D.   small bushes

4. She is in charge of the records department.
   - F.   where products are made
   - G.   having information about patients or workers
   - H.   where medicines are stored
   - J.   for very ill patients

5. Why are you so dismayed?
   - A.   very sneaky
   - B.   shy
   - C.   greatly troubled
   - D.   quiet

6. Did Mark mean to insult his guest?
   - F.   pay no attention to
   - G.   invite again
   - H.   talk louder than
   - J.   say something rude to

Part 2: Comprehension

Use what you know about the story to answer each item.

7. The Yang family lives in—
   - A.   Shanghai, China.
   - B.   Washington, D.C.
   - C.   Seattle.
   - D.   Hong Kong.

8. What do most of the kids at the Thanksgiving meal have in common?
   - F.   playing music
   - G.   playing baseball
   - H.   doing carpentry
   - J.   taking care of pets

9. Mrs. Yang is horrified by the idea of—
   - A.   cooking anything.
   - B.   her children making new friends.
   - C.   roasting a turkey.
   - D.   shaking hands.

10. The narrator of this story is looking forward to dinner at the Conners' because she wants to—
    - F.   talk with Holly Hanson.
    - G.   try cranberries for the first time.
    - H.   get to know Matthew.
    - J.   learn how to prepare a turkey.

GO ON

© Scott Foresman 5

Name _____

The Yangs' First Thanksgiving

11. Why are the Yangs horrified when Mr. Conner starts to scoop stuffing out of the turkey?
   A. They do not want to eat food that has been served by a man.
   B. They do not like the taste of onions.
   C. They think the turkey has not been prepared properly.
   D. They think a lot of meat has been wasted.

12. Unlike in America, most people in China think that—
   F. young people should be served first.
   G. the hosts should serve themselves before serving others.
   H. every family should have a pet.
   J. it is an honor to be old.

13. Why does Mrs. Hanson become upset during dinner?
   A. She feels insulted by Mother.
   B. Mary spills cranberries on her dress.
   C. She does not like turkey.
   D. Mary says she plays viola better than Holly.

14. Unlike in America, people in China think that it is—
   F. very rude to discuss money.
   G. rude to ask questions about a person's family.
   H not proper for women to work outside the home.
   J. good to be fat.

15. What lesson does this story teach about meeting with people from other countries?
   A. Except for differences in language, people everywhere are the same.
   B. There may be misunderstandings between people who were raised to behave differently.
   C. It is impossible to learn what people from other countries believe.
   D. There is always one right way to behave, no matter where you were born and raised.

STOP

© Scott Foresman 5

156 Selection Test

Summarizing

Directions: Read the passage. Then read each question about the passage. Choose the best answer to each question. Mark the letter for the answer you have chosen.

America's Patriotic Holidays

Two of our nation's most important patriotic holidays are Memorial Day and Independence Day. Memorial Day is observed on the last Monday in May, regardless of the date. It honors all those who died in our nation's wars. Independence Day always falls on the fourth of July, regardless of the day of the week. It celebrates the signing of the Declaration of Independence.

Most Americans feel that Memorial Day is a serious occasion. Many towns hold parades in which war veterans march. Ceremonies are held to remember the war dead. Often an important citizen will give a speech, and a firing of guns and the playing of taps bring the ceremony to a close.

Independence Day, by contrast, is a time for celebration. Towns and families hold afternoon picnics in which there frequently are games, contests, music, and plenty of food. The high point comes at nightfall. In towns across America on Independence Day, fireworks explode in brilliant shades of red, silver, and blue.

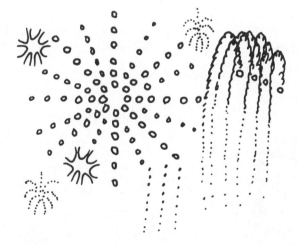

1. What is the main idea of the second paragraph?
   A. Memorial Day is a serious occasion.
   B. We should honor our war dead.
   C. Speeches should be kept short.
   D. Taps are an important custom.

2. What is the main idea of the third paragraph?
   F. Picnics are fun.
   G. Independence Day is a fun holiday.
   H. Fireworks are an important custom on Independence Day.
   J. Celebrations are an important American custom.

3. A summary of the details about Memorial Day should mention—
   A. taps.　　　　C. ceremonies.
   B. speeches.　　D. gun fire.

4. What would be the *least* important detail to include in a summary about Memorial Day?
   F. Memorial Day honors the many fallen soldiers.
   G. Memorial Day is a serious holiday.
   H. An important citizen may give a speech.
   J. Memorial Day is marked by parades and ceremonies.

5. Which would be the *most* important detail to include in a summary about Independence Day?
   A. food　　　　C. contests
   B. games　　　　D. fireworks

Notes for Home: Your child read a nonfiction article and practiced summarizing. *Home Activity:* Read a story with your child. Then have him or her summarize it. Encourage your child to keep the summary brief and to include only the most important ideas or events.

© Scott Foresman 5

Word Study: Inflected Endings -ed, -ing

Directions: Two endings that are commonly added to verbs are **-ed** and **-ing.** If the verbs end in **e,** drop the **e** before adding **-ed** or **-ing.** Read the words in the table. Find the words that dropped the **e** before adding the ending. Write the base word on the lines.

1. _____

2. _____

3. _____

4. _____

5. _____

Base Word	Add -ed	Add -ing
relieve	relieved	relieving
cook	cooked	cooking
illustrate	illustrated	illustrating
invite	invited	inviting
hope	hoped	hoping
embarrass	embarrassed	embarrassing
arrive	arrived	arriving
help	helped	helping

Directions: Add **-ed** and **-ing** to each base word. Write the new word on the line.

Base Word	Add -ed		Add -ing	
excite	6. _____		16. _____	
introduce	7. _____		17. _____	
work	8. _____		18. _____	
interest	9. _____		19. _____	
slice	10. _____		20. _____	
complain	11. _____		21. _____	
dine	12. _____		22. _____	
wince	13. _____		23. _____	
start	14. _____		24. _____	
boil	15. _____		25. _____	

Notes for Home: Your child read and wrote words with the endings *-ed* and *-ing*. **Home Activity:** Read a magazine article with your child. List any words with *-ed* or *-ing* endings. Discuss whether the spelling of each verb was changed before *-ed* or *-ing* was added.

© Scott Foresman 5

Name _____

Research Process/Evaluate Reference Sources

There are many different resources you can use to find information, such as atlases, almanacs, CD-ROMs, and the Internet. When beginning a research project, follow these steps to make the best use of your time.

Research Process

1. Set a purpose.
2. Form and revise questions.
3. Evaluate and choose sources.
4. Collect, organize, and present information.

© Scott Foresman 5

Name _____

Directions: Suppose you wanted to do a research report about holidays. Think about the research process and the resources you might use. Then answer the questions below.

1. First, narrow down the topic for your report on holidays. What holiday or aspect of holidays are you most interested in? Write your topic on the line below.

_____

2. What questions about your topic do you want to answer through your research? List at least two questions.

_____

_____

_____

_____

3. List two resources you might use to begin your research into the questions above and explain why these are good resources to use. Consider whether such resources are reliable, accurate, sufficient, and up-to-date.

_____

_____

_____

_____

4. What might your finished report look and sound like? For example, could you use a diagram, a map, or a recording of a speech or music? Describe how you could organize and present your report.

_____

_____

_____

_____

5. How might the research process help you make the best use of your time? Explain.

_____

_____

_____

_____

Notes for Home: Your child wrote about the steps in the research process. *Home Activity:* Watch a news report on television with your child. Talk about the research the news team probably had to do before giving the report.

© Scott Foresman 5

Main Idea and Supporting Details

- The **main idea** is the most important idea about the topic of a paragraph, article, or story. **Supporting details** tell more about the main idea.

- When the main idea is not directly stated, you will have to decide what is most important and put it in your own words.

Directions: Reread "Saving Nome." Then complete the table. Decide on the most important idea about the topic. Then list important supporting details that tell more about that idea.

Topic The diphtheria epidemic in Nome
Main Idea 1.
Detail Nome wasn't reachable by ship in winter.
Detail 2.
Detail 3.
Detail 4.
Detail 5.

 Notes for Home: Your child read a story, identified its main idea, and described important supporting details. ***Home Activity:*** With your child, read a small section of a simple magazine article. Ask your child to identify the main idea of the section and list some supporting details.

© Scott Foresman 5

Name _____

Vocabulary

Directions: Draw a line to connect each word on the left with its definition on the right.

1. skids

2. obstacles

3. cargo

4. injuries

5. overtakes

damages

catches up and moves ahead

slides

things that get in the way or slow you down

load of goods

```
Check
the Words
You Know
```
__ announcer
__ cargo
__ delays
__ injuries
__ obstacles
__ overtakes
__ skids
__ wilderness

Directions: Choose the word from the box that best completes each sentence. Write the word on the line to the left.

_____ 6. We awoke before dawn to load the _____ into the camper van.

_____ 7. Our plan was to drive to the mountains and spend two weeks in the _____.

_____ 8. As we drove, we listened to the radio _____ give a traffic report.

_____ 9. She said to expect long _____ on the mountain road.

_____ 10. I hope we don't face any other _____ on our vacation.

Write a Sports Announcement

Imagine you are a radio announcer covering a big sports event. How will you convey to your listeners what you see? Write your account of what happens, blow by blow. Use as many vocabulary words as you can.

Notes for Home: Your child identified and used new vocabulary words from "The Jr. Iditarod Race." *Home Activity:* With your child, write a postcard describing a real or imaginary trip to the wilderness. Encourage your child to use as many of the vocabulary words as possible.

© Scott Foresman 5

Main Idea and Supporting Details

- The **main idea** is the most important idea about the topic of a paragraph, article, or story. When the main idea is not stated, you have to figure it out and state it in your own words.

- **Supporting details** tell more about the main idea.

Directions: Reread what happens in "The Jr. Iditarod Race" as Dusty and his team enter the woods. Then answer the questions below.

They cross the lake safely, following the red plastic cones marking the route. But as they enter the woods, Dusty is on edge. He's never done this part of the trail, and it's crowded with obstacles. Snowmobiles roar along the same trail, and within ten miles he has to cross four roads. Sometimes the roads are so slick the dogs fall, or they get confused by the cars and spectators. Dusty knows he just needs to survive this part until he hits the main Iditarod trail.

From IDITAROD DREAM. Copyright © 1996 by Ted Wood. Reprinted with permission from Walker and Company. All Rights Reserved.

1. In a few words, write the topic of this paragraph.

_____

2. State the main idea of the paragraph in your own words.

_____

_____

3. List three supporting details for the main idea.

_____

_____

_____

4. Is the description of the red plastic cones marking the route a supporting detail? Why or why not?

_____

_____

5. What are the topic and main idea of "The Jr. Iditarod Race"? On a separate sheet of paper, identify the topic, state the main idea, and list supporting details.

Notes for Home: Your child read a paragraph from a nonfiction text and identified the main idea and supporting details. **Home Activity:** With your child, read a newspaper article. Help him or her to identify its main idea and supporting details.

© Scott Foresman 5

Name _____

1.	(A)	(B)	(C)	(D)
2.	(F)	(G)	(H)	(J)
3.	(A)	(B)	(C)	(D)
4.	(F)	(G)	(H)	(J)
5.	(A)	(B)	(C)	(D)
6.	(F)	(G)	(H)	(J)
7.	(A)	(B)	(C)	(D)
8.	(F)	(G)	(H)	(J)
9.	(A)	(B)	(C)	(D)
10.	(F)	(G)	(H)	(J)
11.	(A)	(B)	(C)	(D)
12.	(F)	(G)	(H)	(J)
13.	(A)	(B)	(C)	(D)
14.	(F)	(G)	(H)	(J)
15.	(A)	(B)	(C)	(D)

© Scott Foresman 5

Selection Test

Directions: Choose the best answer to each item. Mark the letter for the answer you have chosen.

Part 1: Vocabulary

Find the answer choice that means about the same as the underlined word in each sentence.

1. There were many <u>obstacles</u> in the street.
   A. people looking at something
   B. things that stand in the way
   C. large holes that need to be filled
   D. booths where people sell things

2. Jenna hiked into the <u>wilderness</u>.
   F. wild place with no people living in it
   G. piece of land surrounded by water
   H. area full of ancient buildings
   J. border separating two countries

3. What did the <u>announcer</u> just say?
   A. someone who acts on a stage
   B. person who introduces a program or event and tells what happens
   C. someone who writes news articles
   D. person who represents the government of a foreign country

4. Workers carried the <u>cargo</u>.
   F. passengers
   G. broken machines
   H. sails on a ship
   J. load of goods

5. What should you do if your car <u>skids</u>?
   A. stops suddenly
   B. catches on fire
   C. gets a flat tire
   D. slides

6. The hiker had some <u>injuries</u>.
   F. wounds; hurt body parts
   G. hot meals
   H. successes; wins
   J. favorite sights

7. My horse <u>overtakes</u> the leader.
   A. bumps into
   B. moves ahead of
   C. loses to
   D. makes a noise at

8. There were many <u>delays</u> during the trip.
   F. surprising events
   G. pleasant meetings
   H. stops along the way
   J. dangers to avoid

Part 2: Comprehension

Use what you know about the selection to answer each item.

9. Both the Iditarod and Jr. Iditarod races are held to honor—
   A. the coming of pioneers to Alaska.
   B. the earliest Eskimo mushers.
   C. a dog team that carried medicine to Nome.
   D. Alaska's natural beauty.

© Scott Foresman 5

GO ON

10. What is this selection mostly about?
    F. how Dusty Whittemore and his family became involved in mushing
    G. the fifteen young people who competed in the 1995 Jr. Iditarod
    H. how the Jr. Iditarod is different from the adults' race
    J. the experiences of the boy who won the 1995 Jr. Iditarod

11. Which detail supports the idea that sled dogs love to run and pull sleds?
    A. "It's zero degrees, which is perfect for the dogs."
    B. "Dusty has to walk each dog from the truck."
    C. "The dogs are so excited by the other teams it takes every hand to hold them in place."
    D. "QT and Blacky have splits in the webs between their toes."

12. What can you tell about Dusty from how he acts in the early part of the race?
    F. He doesn't realize that mushing can be a dangerous sport.
    G. He stays clear-headed when faced with a problem.
    H. He panics when something unexpected occurs.
    J. He keeps imagining victory and forgets to pay attention to what is happening.

13. You can tell from this selection that sled dogs—
    A. are very calm and patient.
    B. are more powerful than a moose.
    C. need no training to mush correctly.
    D. remember places they have been before.

14. Which sentence states an opinion?
    F. "The handlers step away and Dusty flies from the start."
    G. "Back on the trail, he uses his track brake to slow the dogs."
    H. "The team is running perfectly now, strong and fast."
    J. "It takes him five minutes to straighten them out and get under way."

15. What part of the story shows that Dusty follows the spirit of the race?
    A. People think Dusty has mistreated his dogs.
    B. Dusty got lost in the race the year before.
    C. Snowmobilers almost run into Dusty's dogs.
    D. Dusty helps the other racers build a fire.

STOP

© Scott Foresman 5

Generalizing

REVIEW

Directions: Read the passage. Then read each question about the passage. Choose the best answer to each question. Mark the letter for the answer you have chosen.

Siberian Huskies

Siberian Huskies were originally bred as sled dogs. These dogs were bred by the Chukchi people of northeastern Asia. In general, the breed's compact size, quickness, and endurance make it perfect for pulling loads over long distances.

In 1909, the first team of Siberian Huskies was brought to Alaska to compete in the All Alaska Sweepstakes Race. Soon, many Alaskan dog breeders were breeding Siberian Huskies. The dogs became popular in Alaska for racing, and they also became popular in other parts of the United States as family pets.

If you are thinking about getting a Siberian Husky for a pet, there are three important things to know about them. First, all Siberian Huskies love to run. A fenced-in yard is important so that your dog has plenty of room to run. Second, Siberian Huskies shed. If dog hair bothers you or anyone in your family, this is probably not the dog for you. Finally, Siberian Huskies are friendly and love company. If you will have to leave your dog alone for long periods of time, consider a different breed of dog.

1. What clue words in the first paragraph signal a generalization?
   A. originally
   B. in general
   C. perfect
   D. Siberian Huskies

2. Which generalization is valid based on information given in the passage?
   F. Siberian Huskies are loners.
   G. Siberian Huskies make great sled dogs.
   H. Siberian Huskies are slow, but steady runners.
   J. Siberian Huskies are easy dogs to care for.

3. Why isn't the first sentence of the second paragraph a generalization?
   A. It tells a historical fact.
   B. It doesn't give enough information about the team.
   C. It doesn't tell what most Huskies have in common.
   D. It doesn't say whether the team won the race.

4. What clue word in the third paragraph signals a generalization?
   F. all
   G. second
   H. first
   J. finally

5. Which of the following generalizations is faulty based on information given in the passage?
   A. Siberian Huskies are compact in size.
   B. Siberian Huskies love to run.
   C. Siberian Huskies originated in Siberia.
   D. Siberian Huskies are quick runners, but tire easily.

Notes for Home: Your child read an article and identified generalizations in it. **Home Activity:** Use the following clue words to take turns making generalizations with your child: *many, all, most, never, always, often.* For example: *All my children have dark hair.*

© Scott Foresman 5

Word Study: Inflected Endings -er, -est

Directions: The endings **-er** and **-est** are added to words to show comparisons. Read the base words below. Add **-er** and **-est** to each word. Write the new word on the line.

Base Word	Add -er	Add -est
warm	1. _____	2. _____
high	3. _____	4. _____
short	5. _____	6. _____
new	7. _____	8. _____

Directions: Read each sentence. Circle the word that ends with either **-er** or **-est**. Write the base word on the line.

_____ 9. The goal of any race is to be quicker than the competition.

_____ 10. In many sports, the team with the highest score wins.

_____ 11. In dogsled racing, the person with the coolest head often wins.

_____ 12. Dogsled races only occur in the north, where the weather is colder.

_____ 13. Lower temperatures usually mean good track conditions.

_____ 14. Warmer temperatures and melting snow can slow down a team.

_____ 15. A slower pace will lose a race.

_____ 16. It is important to stay away from the softer patches of snow.

_____ 17. Some races may be harder to win than others!

_____ 18. The last night of the race often seems like the longest.

_____ 19. It's always nice to get the loudest cheer at the finish line.

_____ 20. It feels great to know you have the fastest time among all the people racing.

 Notes for Home: Your child identified words with the endings *-er* and *-est*. ***Home Activity:*** Make a list of words that have these endings. Have your child use them to make comparisons about two objects (use *-er* words) and more than two objects (use *-est* words).

© Scott Foresman 5

Graphs

Graphs present information visually. **Circle graphs** have a pie shape and show the division of something into parts or percentages. **Bar graphs** use vertical or horizontal bars to show amounts that you can compare easily. **Line graphs** use lines to represent information that shows how something changes over a period of time.

Directions: Use the three graphs to answer the questions on the next page.

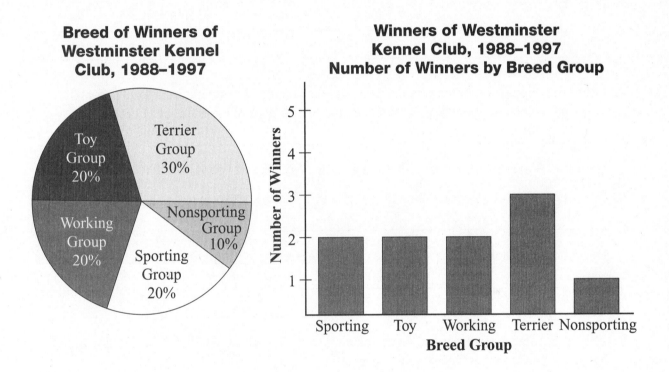

Breed of Winners of Westminster Kennel Club, 1988–1997

Winners of Westminster Kennel Club, 1988–1997 Number of Winners by Breed Group

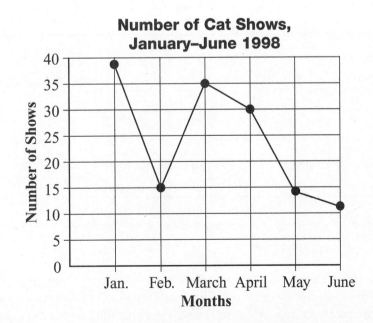

Number of Cat Shows, January–June 1998

© Scott Foresman 5

Name _____

1. From 1988 to 1997, what percentage of Westminster Kennel Club winners were dogs in the Terrier Group?

_____

2. From 1988 to 1997, how many Westminster Kennel Club winners were from the Nonsporting Group?

_____

3. Which dog breed groups had the same percentage of wins during the 10-year period? How do you know?

_____

_____

4. Between which two months was there the greatest change in the number of cat shows? Between which two months was there the smallest change in the number of cat shows?

_____

5. How many more cat shows were held in March 1998 than in February 1998? _____

6. Does the bar graph tell you which breed won in 1997? Explain. _____

_____

7. Does the line graph tell you where the cat shows were held? Explain. _____

_____

_____

8. If the percentages were not shown on the circle graph, could you still tell which dog breed had the greatest percentage of wins? Explain.

_____

_____

9. Suppose you had kept track of how much your dog weighed each month from birth until now. Which type of graph would best show how much your dog had grown? Explain.

_____

_____

10. Do you find one type of graph easier to read and understand than another? Explain.

_____

_____

Notes for Home: Your child analyzed three types of graphs. *Home Activity:* Help your child keep a weather record for one week. Then work together to make a line graph showing high and low temperatures or a bar or circle graph showing the number of cloudy or sunny days.

© Scott Foresman 5

Predicting

- To **predict** is to give a statement about what you think might happen next in a story or come next in an article. The statement you give is a **prediction.**

- You make predictions based on what you already know and what has already happened in the story or article.

- After you predict something, continue reading to check your prediction. As you learn new information, you might need to change your prediction.

Directions: Follow the directions for making predictions as you reread "Why Bears Have Short Tails." As you read each section of the story, tell what logical prediction can be made based on what you have read up to that point in the story. Give a reason for each prediction you make. One prediction has been done for you.

Paragraphs 1–5: Predict what will happen after Fox tells Bear how he caught the fish.

Prediction:
Bear will try what Fox told him. _____

  1. Reason: _____

_____

Paragraphs 6–9: Predict what will happen after Bear's tail freezes off.

  2. Prediction: _____

_____

  3. Reason: _____

_____

Paragraphs 10–13: Predict what will happen to Fox.

  4. Prediction: _____

_____

  5. Reason: _____

_____

Notes for Home: Your child read a legend and made predictions about what would happen next. *Home Activity:* Have your child read the first chapter of a book and predict what will happen next. Encourage your child to read the next chapter to see if his or her prediction was accurate.

© Scott Foresman 5

Vocabulary

Directions: Write the word from the box that belongs in each group.

1. careless, thoughtless, _____

2. bag, purse, _____

3. cabin, resort, _____

4. injured, damaged, _____

5. property, object owned, _____

Check the Words You Know

__ bruised
__ lodge
__ possession
__ pouch
__ reckless

Directions: Choose the word from the box that best matches each clue.
Write the letters of the word on the blanks. The boxed letters spell something
that you might wear or carry.

6. thing owned   6. ☐ __ __ __ __ __ __ __ __ __ __

7. dwelling   7. __ ☐ __ __ __

8. hurt   8. __ __ ☐ __ __ __ __

9. careless   9. __ __ ☐ __ __ __ __

10. bag or sack   10. __ __ __ ☐ __

Something you might wear or carry: __ __ __ __ __

Directions: Choose a word from the box that best completes each sentence.
Write the word on the line to the left.

_____ 11. When we visited the Rocky Mountains
we stayed in a _____.

_____ 12. Hanging from the wall was a leather _____.

_____ 13. My _____ little brother threw it across the room.

_____ 14. It hit me hard and _____ my arm.

_____ 15. I told him it hurt and that he shouldn't just grab someone
else's _____.

Write a Diary Entry

Imagine that you are spending the night alone in the woods. On a separate sheet
of paper, write a diary entry that describes your adventure. Tell what you see
and hear and how you feel. Use as many vocabulary words as you can.

Notes for Home: Your child identified and used new vocabulary words from "The Night
Alone." *Home Activity:* Help your child write a description of what it would be like to live in
the woods. Encourage your child to use as many vocabulary words as possible.

© Scott Foresman 5

Name _____

Predicting

> • To **predict** is to give a statement about what you think might happen next in a story or article, based on what has already happened and what you know.
>
> • The statement you give is a **prediction.**

Directions: Reread what happens in "The Night Alone" when Ohkwa'ri returns from his first night alone in his own lodge. Then answer the questions below.

As he walked down the rocky trail toward his canoe, which he had drawn up into the alders at the edge of the river, he wondered what food might be ready so early in the morning. His thoughts were divided between his hunger and his memory of Grabber's story. He began to walk faster as he thought of food. He no longer considered the possibility of danger. By the time Ohkwa'ri reached the place where the trail curved around a great stone to cross a rocky ledge, he was no longer watching where he put his feet.

From CHILDREN OF THE LONGHOUSE by Joseph Bruchac. Copyright © 1996 by Joseph Bruchac.
Used by permission of Dial Books for Young Readers, a division of Penguin Putnam Inc.

1. What clues help you predict what will happen next?

_____

_____

2. What prediction would you make after reading this paragraph?

_____

_____

3. How can you check your prediction?

_____

4. In the next paragraph, Ohkwa'ri almost steps on a rattlesnake. How does this event compare to your prediction? Explain.

_____

_____

5. On a separate sheet of paper, describe some of the predictions you made while reading "The Night Alone." Were there any events that surprised you? Did you have to change any of your predictions?

Notes for Home: Your child read a paragraph and predicted what would happen next. ***Home Activity:*** Watch a television show with your child. As you watch, take turns making predictions about what will happen next.

1.	Ⓐ	Ⓑ	Ⓒ	Ⓓ
2.	Ⓕ	Ⓖ	Ⓗ	Ⓙ
3.	Ⓐ	Ⓑ	Ⓒ	Ⓓ
4.	Ⓕ	Ⓖ	Ⓗ	Ⓙ
5.	Ⓐ	Ⓑ	Ⓒ	Ⓓ
6.	Ⓕ	Ⓖ	Ⓗ	Ⓙ
7.	Ⓐ	Ⓑ	Ⓒ	Ⓓ
8.	Ⓕ	Ⓖ	Ⓗ	Ⓙ
9.	Ⓐ	Ⓑ	Ⓒ	Ⓓ
10.	Ⓕ	Ⓖ	Ⓗ	Ⓙ
11.	Ⓐ	Ⓑ	Ⓒ	Ⓓ
12.	Ⓕ	Ⓖ	Ⓗ	Ⓙ
13.	Ⓐ	Ⓑ	Ⓒ	Ⓓ
14.	Ⓕ	Ⓖ	Ⓗ	Ⓙ
15.	Ⓐ	Ⓑ	Ⓒ	Ⓓ

© Scott Foresman 5

Selection Test

Directions: Choose the best answer to each item. Mark the space for the answer you have chosen.

Part 1: Vocabulary

Find the answer choice that means about the same as the underlined word in the sentence.

1. Nick's arms were <u>bruised</u>.
   - A. dirty
   - B. hurt
   - C. strong
   - D. tired

2. You shouldn't be <u>reckless</u>.
   - F. filled with fear
   - G. selfish
   - H. careless; ignoring danger
   - J. lazy

3. The mover picked up each <u>possession</u> and placed it in a box.
   - A. something owned by someone
   - B. chair
   - C. something that has been damaged
   - D. book

4. That is a model of an Indian <u>lodge</u>.
   - F. home
   - G. weapon
   - H. farming tool
   - J. toy

5. Put the coins in that <u>pouch</u>.
   - A. box
   - B. bag
   - C. drawer
   - D. hole

Part 2: Comprehension

Use what you know about the story to answer each question.

6. What does Ohkwa'ri reach for twice during the night?
   - F. a snack
   - G. his mother's hand
   - H. a special stone
   - J. a deerskin robe

7. Ohkwa'ri wakes up many times during the night because—
   - A. he is cold.
   - B. he is hungry.
   - C. bears are near his lodge.
   - D. his lodge is too quiet.

8. Ohkwa'ri seems to feel that the moon and the sun are like—
   - F. members of his family that keep him company.
   - G. giant stars that care nothing for him.
   - H. animals about to attack him.
   - J. mighty gods who will protect him.

9. During his first night and morning alone, Ohkwa'ri thinks mostly about—
   - A. the dangers he faces.
   - B. the future.
   - C. his family.
   - D. his own achievements.

© Scott Foresman 5

GO ON

10. According to this selection, the people of Ohkwa'ri's tribe used which of the following to teach lessons to young people?
   F. hunting maps
   G. diagrams
   H. scientific experiments
   J. spoken stories

11. The author most likely included the story of "Grabber" to—
   A. make the reader laugh.
   B. scare the reader.
   C. make the reader sad.
   D. teach the reader about bears.

12. When the story says that Ohkwa'ri was "no longer watching where he put his feet," a reader is most likely to predict that he will—
   F. die in the wilderness.
   G. kill a bear for food.
   H. soon run into danger.
   J. return to his little lodge instead of to his family.

13. The stories of Grabber and the two young men of the Turtle Clan suggest that—
   A. most young men in Ohkwa'ri's tribe are as wise as adults.
   B. wild animals are not very intelligent.
   C. it is the men, not the women, who rule Ohkwa'ri's tribe.
   D. young men sometimes do foolish things.

14. How does Ohkwa'ri's experience with the rattlesnake show that he is gaining in good judgment?
   F. He jumps when he hears the snake rattle.
   G. He decides to be more careful in the future.
   H. He realizes that he has bruised his shoulder.
   J. He realizes that he has missed breakfast back at the lodge.

15. You can tell from this story that the "Little People" probably are—
   A. Ohkwa'ri's brothers and sisters.
   B. spirits of the forest.
   C. members of the Turtle Clan.
   D. wild birds and animals.

STOP

© Scott Foresman 5

Setting/Compare and Contrast

REVIEW

Directions: Read the story. Then read each question about the story. Choose the best answer to each question. Mark the letter for the answer you have chosen.

A Taste of Independence

"Mom, can we go shopping?" Becky asked. She and her twin sister, Angela, were vacationing with their parents. At 12 years old, they had never gone shopping alone. Becky and Angela thought vacation time was a good time to start.

"All right," their mother said, "but be back for dinner." She was a little uncertain about letting the girls go by themselves, but she knew they were careful.

Three hours later, the girls hadn't returned. Dinner was long past. Becky and Angela's mother began to worry that she had made a mistake. She got in the car to look for them. Their father walked to the boardwalk on foot. He searched every video arcade, T-shirt shop, and ice cream parlor. Neon signs danced before his eyes. The din of voices and video games filled his head. He grew very worried. Where were his daughters?

Then he spotted the girls, far out on the sand. He breathed a sigh of relief. He walked out to them. There, unlike on the boardwalk, it was peaceful. The beach was deserted. Only the pounding surf and screaming gulls could be heard.

The girls waved to their dad and then ran up to him. They were surprised that he had come looking for them.

"We're sorry, Dad," Angela explained. "We had no idea it was so late. We finished shopping and came to the beach."

"After this we'll have to have more specific rules for going out alone," their father replied.

1. This story is set in a—
   A. mountain village.
   B. seaside town.
   C. big city.
   D. suburban mall.

2. This story takes place—
   F. in the present day.
   G. in the 1930s.
   H. a century ago.
   J. in the distant past.

3. What clue word signals a contrast in the fourth paragraph?
   A. then
   B. only
   C. there
   D. unlike

4. What is the writer contrasting in the fourth paragraph?
   F. Angela and Becky
   G. the boardwalk and the beach
   H. the mother and father
   J. the afternoon and the evening

5. As the setting changes from the boardwalk to the beach, the father's mood changes from—
   A. worried to angry.
   B. happy to sad.
   C. worried to relieved.
   D. angry to calm.

Notes for Home: Your child read a story and analyzed its setting and looked for comparisons and contrasts. **Home Activity:** Invite your child to compare and contrast two rooms in your home. Ask him or her to tell how these settings are alike and different.

© Scott Foresman 5

Word Study: Inflected Endings

When adding **-ed, -er,** or **-est** to words that end in a **consonant** and **y,** change the **y** to **i,** and then add **-ed.** For example, **fry** becomes **fried.**

When adding **-ed, -ing, -er,** or **-est** to words that end in a single consonant preceded by a single vowel, double the consonant and add the ending. For example, **hop** becomes **hopping. Thin** becomes **thinner.**

Directions: Add an ending to each word below. Write the new word on the line.

1. drop   +   -ing   =   _____
2. grab   +   -ing   =   _____
3. flat   +   -er   =   _____
4. big   +   -est   =   _____
5. cry   +   -ed   =   _____
6. pat   +   -ed   =   _____

Directions: Read the journal entry. Circle each word that ends in **-ed, -ing, -er,** or **-est.** Then write the base word for each circled word on the line.

Day 1

It is my first night alone in the forest. I'm worried. I tried to sleep, but I heard the strangest noises. I zipped and snapped all the tent flaps shut and buried my head in my pillow. But I'm still awake. I couldn't imagine a scarier place! I ran through the forest most of the day, only stopping twice to take a drink from my canteen. I'll be much happier when daylight comes.

7. _____
8. _____
9. _____
10. _____
11. _____
12. _____
13. _____
14. _____
15. _____

Notes for Home: Your child practiced changing *y* to *i* and doubling the final consonant when adding *-ed* and *-ing.* **Home Activity:** Read a short story with your child and find words with these endings. He or she can write the words with and without the endings.

© Scott Foresman 5

Name _____

Technology: Encyclopedia

Encyclopedias can be purchased on CD-ROMs or found on the Internet. The computer lets you search the entire encyclopedia for your topic using letters or a few key words. The welcome screen for an online encyclopedia might look like this:

If you wanted an article about Native Americans, you could either type key words: Native AND Americans, or you could click on the letter *N*. Clicking on a letter will give you a list of articles about topics that begin with that letter.

nasturtium
Natchez
national parks
Native Americans
navigation
navy
Nebraska
Neptune

Try another letter:
A B C D E F G H I J K L M N O P Q R S T U V W X Y Z

Search the Encyclopedia for:
[   ]

© Scott Foresman 5

Name _____

When you find an article about your topic, it will probably have links to other articles. The links will most likely be set in capital letters and underlined. Clicking on an underlined phrase will show you the other related articles.

Native American Art

The traditional arts of the indigenous native peoples of North America (see <u>NORTH AMERICA, INDIGENOUS PEOPLES OF</u>) were an important part of the everyday lives of Native Americans. Different arts were practiced in different regions. The cultures of the Eastern woodlands (see <u>IROQUOIS</u>) made pottery, baskets, beadwork, and <u>MASKS</u>. The Plains tribes (see <u>SIOUX</u>) used beads and quills to decorate hides. On the Northwest coast, native peoples used wood carving to make houses, large <u>CANOES</u>, and <u>TOTEM</u> poles. The <u>NAVAHO</u> of the Southwest had sophisticated techniques for making silver jewelry.

Directions: Use the sample computer screens to answer these questions.

1. What are two different ways to find an article about Native Americans using an online encyclopedia?

_____

2. In the second computer screen, what will you get if you click on *Nebraska?*

_____

3. In the first and second computer screens, what will you get if you click on the letter *B?*

_____

4. In the third computer screen, which link would you choose to see a related article about Native Americans who lived in the Eastern woodlands?

_____

5. Which links would you choose to find articles about the arts and crafts of the Northwest coast peoples?

_____

Notes for Home: Your child learned how to use an online encyclopedia. *Home Activity:* Ask your child to list possible key words to use to search for articles about native peoples in Alaska.

© Scott Foresman 5

Context Clues

- **Context clues** are words that can help you figure out a word that is unfamiliar to you.
- Look for specific clues by asking yourself questions like: "Does the sentence give a definition of the word or explain anything about it?"

Directions: Reread "Physical Fitness." Then complete the table. Use context clues to figure out the meaning of each word or phrase in the table.

Word or Phrase	Meaning
skills fitness	1.
agility	2.
balance	3.
coordination	4.
reaction time	5.

Notes for Home: Your child read an article and used context clues to figure out the meanings of unfamiliar words. *Home Activity:* Read a newspaper article with your child. Help your child use context clues to figure out the meanings of any unfamiliar words.

© Scott Foresman 5

Name _____

Vocabulary

Directions: Choose the word from the box that best matches each definition.
Write the word on the line.

_____ 1. joint that connects foot with leg

_____ 2. self-assured

_____ 3. conquered an obstacle

_____ 4. having the duty to take care of
someone or something

_____ 5. run a short way at top speed

Check the Words You Know

__ ankle
__ athlete
__ confident
__ overcame
__ relay
__ responsible
__ sprint

Directions: Choose the word from the box that best matches each clue.
Write the word on the line.

_____ 6. It's a compound word and you'll feel good if you've done it.

_____ 7. It's what you call a person who is good at sports.

_____ 8. It's the kind of person you would want to have baby-sit your
little brother.

_____ 9. It's how you feel when you know you can do something well.

_____ 10. It's something you can do for a short while, but not for too
long.

Directions: Read the news story. Choose the word from the box that best
completes each sentence. Write the word on the matching numbered line
to the right.

RUNNER SWEEPS STATE MEET
The city has never seen an **11.** _____ like Aysha Morgan. At Thursday's track competition, this young unknown rose to stardom. Despite a sore **12.** _____, she was able to **13.** _____ the 100-meter event in record time. She also **14.** _____ an early setback to win the quarter mile. Later, she led her team to victory by running the fastest leg in the 400-meter **15.** _____. Sports fans, this is a young woman to watch. Congratulations, Aysha!

11. _____

12. _____

13. _____

14. _____

15. _____

Write a Description

Whom do you respect? On a separate sheet of paper, describe a person whom
you respect and tell why you respect him or her. Use as many vocabulary words
as you can in your description.

Notes for Home: Your child identified and used vocabulary words from "The Heart of a
Runner." *Home Activity:* With your child, write a story about an athlete your child admires.
Encourage your child to use as many of the vocabulary words as possible.

© Scott Foresman 5

Context Clues

- **Context clues** are words that can help you figure out a word that is unfamiliar to you.

- Look for specific types of clues as you read. Context clues include synonyms, antonyms, definitions and explanations, examples, and descriptions.

Directions: Reread what happens in "The Heart of a Runner" when E.R. writes about the relay race. Then answer the questions below.

> I have to tell you what an anchor is. An anchor is the final leg of a relay, the fastest runner. The anchor has to overcome any slowness of the other three runners and power on to the end. The lead runner, or lead-off, is the first leg of a relay team. That runner has to be superfast, and confident, too.
>
> The runners in a relay depend on one another to be fast and not make mistakes. Like dropping one of the batons. I'm not mentioning any names, but you know who I mean!
>
> Excerpt from RUNNING GIRL: THE DIARY OF EBONEE ROSE, copyright © 1997 by Sharon Bell Mathis, reprinted by permission of Harcourt Brace & Company.

1. What is an *anchor?*

   _____

2. What kind of context clue helped you define *anchor?*

   _____

3. Give the meaning of *leg* in the first paragraph and tell what clues you used to figure it out.

   _____

   _____

4. Define *lead-off* and tell what type of context clue you used to define it.

   _____

   _____

5. Go back to the story and find the terms *baton-passing* and *field event.* Use context clues to figure out their meanings. On a separate sheet of paper, write the meanings and tell what clues you used. Then use a dictionary to see if your definitions were correct.

Notes for Home: Your child read a story and used context clues to define unfamiliar words. *Home Activity:* Read a challenging book with your child. Work together to use context clues to define words that are unfamiliar to your child.

© Scott Foresman 5

1.	Ⓐ	Ⓑ	Ⓒ	Ⓓ
2.	Ⓕ	Ⓖ	Ⓗ	Ⓙ
3.	Ⓐ	Ⓑ	Ⓒ	Ⓓ
4.	Ⓕ	Ⓖ	Ⓗ	Ⓙ
5.	Ⓐ	Ⓑ	Ⓒ	Ⓓ
6.	Ⓕ	Ⓖ	Ⓗ	Ⓙ
7.	Ⓐ	Ⓑ	Ⓒ	Ⓓ
8.	Ⓕ	Ⓖ	Ⓗ	Ⓙ
9.	Ⓐ	Ⓑ	Ⓒ	Ⓓ
10.	Ⓕ	Ⓖ	Ⓗ	Ⓙ
11.	Ⓐ	Ⓑ	Ⓒ	Ⓓ
12.	Ⓕ	Ⓖ	Ⓗ	Ⓙ
13.	Ⓐ	Ⓑ	Ⓒ	Ⓓ
14.	Ⓕ	Ⓖ	Ⓗ	Ⓙ
15.	Ⓐ	Ⓑ	Ⓒ	Ⓓ

© Scott Foresman 5

Name _____

Selection Test

Directions: Choose the best answer to each item. Mark the letter for the answer you have chosen.

Part 1: Vocabulary

Find the answer choice that means about the same as the underlined word in each sentence.

1. I hurt my ankle.
   A. bone in the knee
   B. part of the leg between the knee and hip
   C. bottom of the foot
   D. joint that connects the foot and leg

2. The other team looked confident.
   F. unfriendly
   G. full of energy
   H. large
   J. sure of themselves

3. Meghan is responsible for the picnic.
   A. signed up to attend
   B. having the duty to do something
   C. trying to stop
   D. curious about the reason for something

4. We watched Jeremy sprint down the sidewalk.
   F. ride
   G. walk slowly
   H. run at top speed
   J. hop

5. Alisha overcame her fears.
   A. talked about for a long time
   B. asked help for
   C. got the better of; defeated
   D. was ashamed of

6. The first event in the meet is a relay.
   F. long jump
   G. race in which each member of a team runs or swims for one part
   H. race in which a runner must leap over a series of gates
   J. event that involves throwing an object

7. My sister is a fine athlete.
   A. person who is skilled in physical games
   B. person who attends school
   C. person who makes crafts
   D. person who organizes others to get things done

Part 2: Comprehension

Use what you know about the story to answer each item.

8. Ebonee Rose was upset when she twisted her ankle because she—
   F. knew her mother would be angry.
   G. would be kicked off the team for the year.
   H. did not want to miss the All-City meet.
   J. was afraid to go to the hospital.

9. Which track star raced jackrabbits in the Mojave Desert as a child and won four medals in the 1988 Olympics?
   A. Evelyn Ashford
   B. Robin Campbell
   C. Florence Griffith Joyner
   D. Wyomia Tyus

© Scott Foresman 5

GO ON

10. The story says, "Our fans in the <u>bleachers</u> are going crazy." <u>Bleachers</u> are—
    F. long race tracks.
    G. benches for people to sit on.
    H. school buses.
    J. large crowds of people.

11. In this story, Ebonee Rose seems to think of "Dee" as—
    A. an opponent.
    B. a pacer.
    C. her mother.
    D. a friend.

12. The story says, "The name MAIN TRACK CLUB will be <u>inscribed</u> on the brass plate beneath the golden track shoe." <u>Inscribed</u> means—
    F. remembered.
    G. written on stone or metal.
    H. borrowed.
    J. carried by the winners.

13. How do E.R.'s parents feel before the All-City Meet?
    A. nervous but proud
    B. worried but calm
    C. bored and impatient
    D. happy and relaxed

14. The author most likely included information about African American track stars in this story to—
    F. show how heroes and heroines inspire young people.
    G. make readers think that Ebonee Rose is a real person.
    H. prove that Ebonee Rose is the greatest runner ever.
    J. show that good athletes can also be good writers.

15. The author probably focuses more on E.R.'s experience in the relay instead of the long jump to show the importance of—
    A. kindness.
    B. teamwork.
    C. independence.
    D. trying new sports.

STOP

© Scott Foresman 5

Author's Viewpoint   REVIEW

Directions: Read the passage. Then read each question about the passage. Choose the best answer to each question. Mark the letter for the answer you have chosen.

Run for Your Life

Couch potatoes of the world, listen carefully. There's a very good chance that you are ruining your health sitting right there on the couch. Throw down those television remote controls and lace up your sneakers! It's time to get moving!

As a whole, American children and young people are not getting nearly enough exercise. For American adults, the situation is even worse. Many Americans do not exercise on a regular basis. (Getting up to go to the refrigerator for a soda doesn't count!)

An inactive lifestyle is dangerous at any age. It puts a person at higher risk for serious health problems. Heart disease, diabetes, and other serious diseases become more likely for people who are not active.

How can you get on the road to good health? Start by getting some regular exercise. You might choose running, jogging, walking, bicycling, gardening, or aerobics. They are all good ways to get "heart smart"! You might actually find out that you enjoy getting healthier by exercising.

1. The first paragraph suggests the author will try to—
   A. describe.
   B. explain.
   C. tell a story.
   D. persuade.

2. Which of the following words reveals how the author feels about the subject of this article?
   F. couch potatoes
   G. remote controls
   H. children
   J. young people

3. The author's opening implies that—
   A. people should never watch television.
   B. people who watch television are more relaxed.
   C. people who watch too much television don't exercise enough.
   D. couch potatoes have diabetes.

4. In this article the author—
   F. criticizes all Americans.
   G. links exercise and health.
   H. describes aerobic exercises that are dangerous.
   J. recommends consulting a doctor as soon as possible.

5. The author is strongly—
   A. in favor of regular exercise.
   B. in favor of lace-up sneakers.
   C. in favor of an inactive lifestyle.
   D. against exercise.

Notes for Home: Your child read a passage and identified the author's viewpoint. *Home Activity:* Read an editorial or a letter to the editor with your child. Together, identify the author's viewpoint and look at how well the author's opinions are supported.

© Scott Foresman 5

Name _____

Phonics: Schwa Sound (Within Word)

Directions: The **schwa sound** is an indistinct vowel sound heard in unstressed syllables. For example, the **a** in **ago,** the **o** in **complete,** and the **e** in **agent** are all schwa sounds. Read each sentence. Say each underlined word aloud. Write each underlined word on the line and circle the syllable that has the **schwa sound.**

_____ 1. In most cultures, people <u>compete</u> in races.

_____ 2. For <u>today's</u> race, there are more runners than usual.

_____ 3. Before the race, runners stretch and <u>exercise</u> their legs.

_____ 4. They know that it isn't wise to run on a full <u>stomach</u>.

_____ 5. Many runners feel <u>nervous</u> before a big race.

_____ 6. One athlete wiped her face with her lucky <u>handkerchief</u>.

_____ 7. She was hoping for a big <u>victory</u>.

_____ 8. But, in order to win, she must <u>overcome</u> her fears.

_____ 9. She knows she has a <u>difficult</u> race ahead of her.

_____ 10. Many people <u>identify</u> with the runner's fears.

Directions: Each word below has two **schwa sounds.** Circle the **schwa sounds** in each word.

11. different	16. emigrant	21. orchestra
12. tolerance	17. gelatin	22. passable
13. confident	18. imitation	23. president
14. together	19. literally	24. consider
15. responsibility	20. nitrogen	25. singular

Notes for Home: Your child identified the schwa sound. ***Home Activity:*** Read an article with your child. Ask your child to write down words that might have the schwa sound. Check the words in a dictionary. The symbol for the schwa sound looks like an upside-down *e.*

© Scott Foresman 5

Organize and Present Information/Draw Conclusions

As you read, take notes about important information. You can use your notes to help you **organize information** for a report and to help you **present information** to others. You can also use your notes to help you **draw conclusions** about the information by telling what it means.

Directions: Suppose you were planning a research report. Use the notes shown to answer the questions on the next page.

Track and field events involve running, walking, jumping, and throwing.

Some athletes are good at other events but not at the track and field events. Other athletes excel in track and field as well as other sports.

Older outdoor tracks are dirt or cinders. Newer ones use a waterproof synthetic surface. Indoor tracks are a wooden or synthetic surface with banked turns.

Track and field events of the summer Olympic Games include: Men's—runs of 100, 200, 400, 800, 1500, 5000, and 10,000 meters; hurdles of 100 and 400 meters; relays of 400 and 1600 meters; 3000-meter steeplechase; walks of 20 and 50 meters; marathon; high, long, and triple jump; discus, hammer, and javelin throw; pole vault; 16-pound shot put; and decathlon. Women's—runs of 100, 200, 400, 800, 1500, 3000, 5000, and 10,000 meters; hurdles of 100 and 400 meters; relays of 400 and 1600 meters; 10-kilometer walk; marathon; high, long, and triple jump; discus and javelin throw; 8-pound, 13-ounce shot put; and heptathlon.

The first Olympic games in Greece took place in 776 B.C. The only event was a foot race—the first competitive track and field event.

The Olympic records for men's track and field go back to 1896. The women's records are from 1928.

© Scott Foresman 5

Name _____

> The first U.S. woman to win an Olympic track and field event was Elizabeth Robinson in 1928 (the first year of the records). In 1896, the first year of the men's records, there were six Olympic winners in track and field from the United States—Thomas Burke, Thomas Curtis, Ellery Clark, James Connolly, Robert Garrett, and William Hoyt.
>
> In the decathlon, heptathlon, and pentathlon, the athletes compete in several different events over a period of time.
>
> Jackie Joyner-Kersee holds the heptathlon record with 7,215 points, set in 1988.

1. The title of your report will give the main idea. What title will you give your report?

   _____

2. The information in the notes came from several different sources, but the notetaker made the mistake of not listing the sources. What reference sources could you use to verify the information in the notes and add to it?

   _____

   _____

3. If you wanted to present the information about the different Olympic track and field events for men and women, how might you organize this information so it is easier for readers to understand and compare?

   _____

   _____

   _____

4. Think of things that might make your report interesting to hear and see, such as videotapes, audiotapes, graphic organizers, drawings, or posters. What might you use in your report?

   _____

   _____

5. Why will taking good notes as you read help you organize and present information and then draw conclusions about it? Will you use every note you wrote in your report? Explain.

   _____

   _____

   _____

Notes for Home: Your child described how information might be organized and presented for a report. *Home Activity:* Together with your child, make a poster using information from the notes shown.

© Scott Foresman 5

Author's Purpose

- An **author's purpose** is the reason or reasons an author has for writing.

- Authors don't usually state a purpose so it helps to remember that the four common purposes for writing are to persuade, inform, entertain, and express.

Directions: Reread "Your Life Remembered." Then complete the web. Write the author's purpose or purposes in the middle. In the outer ovals, write words or phrases from the article that helped you identify the purpose or purposes.

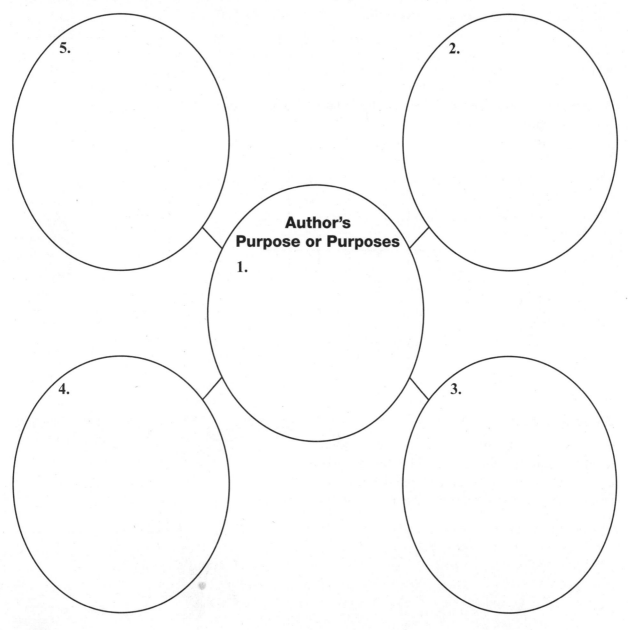

5.

2.

Author's Purpose or Purposes

1.

4.

3.

Notes for Home: Your child read an article and identified the author's purpose. *Home Activity:* Look through a magazine with your child. Invite your child to identify the author's purpose for various kinds of writing, such as editorials, poems, profiles, how-to articles, ads, or cartoons.

© Scott Foresman 5

Vocabulary

Directions: Choose the word from the box that best completes each statement.
Write the word on the line to the left.

_____   1. *Inflated* is to *blew up* as *flattened* is to
_____.

_____   2. *Journals* are to *diaries* as *keepsakes* are to
_____.

_____   3. *Think* is to *act* as *forget* is to _____.

_____   4. *Hand* is to *glove* as *knife* is to _____.

_____   5. *Throw* is to *catch* as *cast* is to _____.

**Check
the Words
You Know**

__ recall
__ reel
__ sheath
__ souvenirs
__ squished
__ traditions

Directions: Choose the word from the box that best matches each clue.
Write the word in the puzzle.

Down

6. to draw in by winding
7. keepsakes
8. case or covering for a knife

Across

9. remember
10. beliefs and customs handed down from parents to children

Write a Letter

On a separate sheet of paper, write a thank-you
letter to a family member for all the things he or she
has done for you. Describe your good memories.
Use as many vocabulary words as you can in your letter.

Notes for Home: Your child identified and used vocabulary words in *The Memory Box*. **Home**
Activity: Invite your child to draw a picture for at least three vocabulary words. Work together
to write sentences under the pictures that use the vocabulary words.

© Scott Foresman 5

Name _____

Author's Purpose

- An **author's purpose** is the reason or reasons an author has for writing. Sometimes an author has more than one reason for writing.

- Four common purposes for writing are to persuade (convince), to inform (explain something), to entertain (amuse), or to express (describe something to help you see or feel a scene).

Directions: Reread what happens in *The Memory Box* after Zach's first dinner with Gramps and Gram. Then answer the questions below.

After dinner, we dragged our fish-full bellies to the porch to watch the sun slip into the lake. Crickets fiddled and owls hoo-ooted, but the rest of the world was quiet. All except Gram and Gramps and me in our rickety rockers on the wooden porch.

"Hmm-mmmm-m." Gramps was settling in, getting ready for another true tale. He's a great storyteller. Gram thinks so, I know, because she always puts down her cross-stitch when he begins.

THE MEMORY BOX by Mary Bahr. Text copyright © 1992 by Mary Bahr. Excerpt reprinted by permission of Albert Whitman & Company.

1. What is happening in this scene?

_____

_____

2. How do you think Zach feels when he and Gram and Gramps are on the porch?

_____

3. What are some of the unusual words and phrases the author uses in writing this part of the story?

_____

4. What do you think is the author's purpose for writing this scene? Explain what makes you think so.

_____

_____

5. On a separate sheet of paper, tell what you think is the author's reason (or reasons) for writing *The Memory Box*. Support your answer with examples from the story.

Notes for Home: Your child read a story and identified the author's purpose for writing. ***Home Activity:*** Discuss each of the four common purposes for writing described above. Name a favorite book, story, or article that is an example of each purpose.

© Scott Foresman 5

Name _____

1.	Ⓐ	Ⓑ	Ⓒ	Ⓓ
2.	Ⓕ	Ⓖ	Ⓗ	Ⓙ
3.	Ⓐ	Ⓑ	Ⓒ	Ⓓ
4.	Ⓕ	Ⓖ	Ⓗ	Ⓙ
5.	Ⓐ	Ⓑ	Ⓒ	Ⓓ
6.	Ⓕ	Ⓖ	Ⓗ	Ⓙ
7.	Ⓐ	Ⓑ	Ⓒ	Ⓓ
8.	Ⓕ	Ⓖ	Ⓗ	Ⓙ
9.	Ⓐ	Ⓑ	Ⓒ	Ⓓ
10.	Ⓕ	Ⓖ	Ⓗ	Ⓙ
11.	Ⓐ	Ⓑ	Ⓒ	Ⓓ
12.	Ⓕ	Ⓖ	Ⓗ	Ⓙ
13.	Ⓐ	Ⓑ	Ⓒ	Ⓓ
14.	Ⓕ	Ⓖ	Ⓗ	Ⓙ
15.	Ⓐ	Ⓑ	Ⓒ	Ⓓ

© Scott Foresman 5

Selection Test

Directions: Choose the best answer to each item. Mark the letter for the answer you have chosen.

Part 1: Vocabulary

Find the answer choice that means about the same as the underlined word in each sentence.

1. Mariah put her <u>souvenirs</u> in a box.
   A. rings meant to be worn
   B. food for a light meal
   C. things that bring back memories
   D. important papers

2. I <u>recall</u> a trip to Niagara Falls.
   F. remember
   G. plan
   H. photograph
   J. describe

3. What <u>traditions</u> does your family have?
   A. pets
   B. silly names
   C. valuable objects kept for a long time
   D. beliefs and customs handed down through time

4. The baby happily <u>squished</u> the chocolate pudding.
   F. pressed something soft and wet
   G. licked something cold
   H. pointed at something far away
   J. grabbed something hard

5. It was difficult to <u>reel</u> in the kite.
   A. draw in by winding
   B. pack up
   C. sew together
   D. put in a certain order

6. Put it in the <u>sheath</u>.
   F. drawer
   G. case or covering
   H. envelope
   J. trash bag or can

Part 2: Comprehension

Use what you know about the story to answer each item.

7. What do Zach and Gramps do the first day of Zach's visit?
   A. take a hike
   B. go fishing
   C. build a box
   D. cook a meal together

8. From whose point of view is this story told?
   F. Zach's
   G. Gramps's
   H. Gram's
   J. Francie's

9. How does Zach react when Gramps says, "No matter what happens to the old person, the memories are saved forever"?
   A. He is happy to know he will always have memories of Gramps.
   B. He is bored that he will have to listen to more old stories.
   C. He realizes that Gramps has Alzheimer's.
   D. He is confused and worried that something is wrong.

© Scott Foresman 5

GO ON

10. Which of these events happens first?
    F.   Gramps gets lost.
    G.   Zach sees Gramps talking to someone who is not there.
    H.   Zach wonders why Gramps has not shaved.
    J.   Gramps gives Zach the special knife.

11. Why does Gramps think that Zach's mom is "going to hurt"?
    A.   Zach will not spend any more summers with Gram and Gramps.
    B.   She will not like how Zach has changed.
    C.   Zach has decided to live with Gram and Gramps instead of with his mom.
    D.   She will feel sad to see Gramps when his memory is gone.

12. The author's main purpose in this story is to—
    F.   entertain the reader with funny tales about a forgetful man.
    G.   persuade kids to spend summers with their grandparents.
    H.   express what it feels like for a family to deal with Alzheimer's.
    J.   inform people about the causes of memory loss.

13. When Zach finally gets the knife he wanted, he realizes that—
    A.   other things are more important than having a knife.
    B.   he would rather have a newer and more valuable knife.
    C.   he will have to return the knife to Gram.
    D.   he will never go fishing again.

14. A "memory-box day" is best described as something that—
    F.   happens when a person is alone.
    G.   two people want to remember sharing with each other.
    H.   happens when a man or woman gets very old.
    J.   causes worry for everyone in a family.

15. What does the ending of this story suggest about Zach's view of life?
    A.   He accepts things as they are.
    B.   He does not take responsibility for himself.
    C.   He always sees the worst in everything.
    D.   He is too hopeful most of the time.

STOP

© Scott Foresman 5

Name _____

Plot and Theme

Directions: Read the story. Then read each question about the story. Choose the best answer to each question. Mark the letter for the answer you have chosen.

The Scrapbook

When Aunt Rose got sick and went to the hospital, Misha and his little sister Emily were both very upset. She was their favorite aunt. She often brought them books and entertained them with stories about when she was young.

Misha decided to make a scrapbook for Aunt Rose. Emily felt jealous of his idea. It seemed to her that Misha always thought of everything first and could do it better. She wanted to do something too, but her ideas didn't seem as interesting as Misha's. Misha offered to let her help, but she refused.

For the next few days, Misha worked on Aunt Rose's scrapbook. He wrote a poem, and he drew pictures. He chose favorite family snapshots. He put everything into the scrapbook. He decorated the pages with some of his favorite stickers.

Emily, meanwhile, spent a lot of time sulking. Whenever Misha tried to talk to her, she turned on her heel and walked away.

On the day they had planned to visit Aunt Rose, Misha stormed into the kitchen.

"Where's my scrapbook?" he said accusingly to Emily. She burst into tears.

"I took it," she sobbed. "I want it to be from me too."

Misha put his arm around Emily and hugged her. Emily said she was sorry. Misha told Emily to hurry and get ready to go so they could give Aunt Rose their scrapbook together.

1. What is the conflict, or problem, in this story?
   A. Aunt Rose is in the hospital.
   B. Misha and Emily are upset.
   C. Emily is jealous of Misha.
   D. Misha has to make a scrapbook.

2. The rising action of the story, where the action builds, is in—
   F. the first two paragraphs.
   G. the third and fourth paragraphs.
   H. the fifth and sixth paragraphs.
   J. the seventh and eighth paragraphs.

3. The climax, or the high point, of the story comes when—
   A. Misha confronts Emily and she cries.
   B. Emily turns on her heel and walks away.
   C. Misha finishes the scrapbook.
   D. Misha hugs Emily.

4. How is the conflict, or problem, resolved?
   F. Emily has a good cry.
   G. Misha finishes the scrapbook.
   H. Misha apologizes to Emily.
   J. Emily apologizes to Misha, who agrees to share the scrapbook.

5. Which of following best states a theme for this story.
   A. Jealous feelings should always be kept hidden.
   B. Jealousy is harmful.
   C. Jealousy is not harmful if it's kept hidden.
   D. Jealousy should be ignored.

Notes for Home: Your child read a story and identified elements of the plot and the theme. *Home Activity:* Watch a movie with your child. Then work with him or her to write a movie review, outlining the plot and identifying the theme.

© Scott Foresman 5

Name _____

Phonics: Schwa Sound (Final Syllable)

Directions: The **schwa sound** is often found in a final, unstressed syllable. For example, the final syllables of **table, summer,** and **natural** have the schwa sound. Read the words in the box. Say each word to yourself. Sort the words by their final **schwa sounds.** Write each word in the correct column.

freckle	soccer	tackle
professional	festival	flower
water	normal	circle

Sounds like *table* | **Sounds like *summer*** | **Sounds like *natural***

1. _____ 4. _____ 7. _____

2. _____ 5. _____ 8. _____

3. _____ 6. _____ 9. _____

Directions: Read each sentence. Listen for the word that has the **schwa sound** in the final syllable. Circle the word and write it on the line.

_____ **10.** I remember taking trips to go fishing.

_____ **11.** Uncle Ted always caught the biggest fish.

_____ **12.** We would take a photo of it for the photo album.

_____ **13.** Then the fresh fish was cooked for dinner.

_____ **14.** We ate, and then we would sit on the porch and whistle songs.

_____ **15.** I could not think of anything I liked better.

Notes for Home: Your child identified the schwa sound heard at the end of words, such as *table, summer,* and *natural.* **Home Activity:** In the car, read signs and billboards with your child. Take note of words with the schwa sound in the final syllables.

© Scott Foresman 5

Name _____

Alphabetical Order

Resources such as encyclopedias, dictionaries, glossaries, indexes, and telephone directories list information in **alphabetical order** to make it easier for readers to find information quickly. Remember to use the first letter of the first word in each entry when you order alphabetically. If the first letters are the same, use the second letters. If the second letters are the same, use the third letters, and so on.

Directions: Suppose you wanted to find a particular photograph among the boxes of photographs below. The boxes are labeled, but they are not in any order. Someone has started to put them in alphabetical order on a shelf. On the next page, answer the questions about organizing the rest of the boxes in alphabetical order.

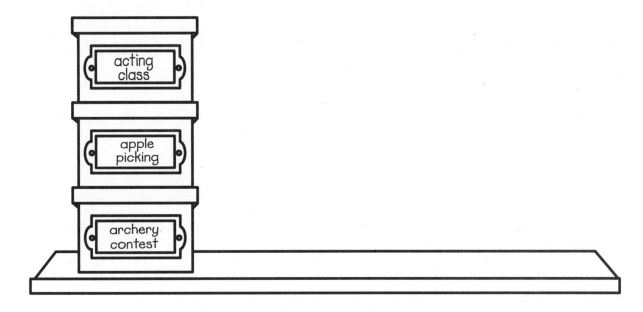

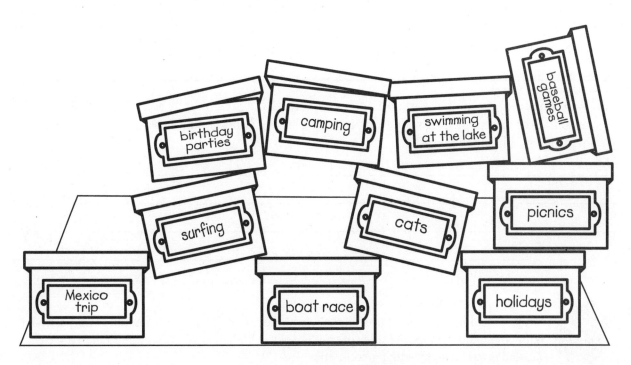

Name _____

Directions: Write the names of the photo boxes not on the shelf in alphabetical order.

1. _____
2. _____
3. _____
4. _____
5. _____
6. _____
7. _____
8. _____
9. _____
10. _____

11. For which boxes did you have to use the second letter of the words on the labels to alphabetize the boxes?

_____

_____

12. For which boxes did you have to use the third letter of the words on the labels to alphabetize the boxes?

_____

13. Between which two boxes would you put a photo box labeled *school trips?*

_____

14. Between which two boxes would you put a box labeled *canoeing?* _____

_____

15. Why might it be useful to sort and organize materials at school or at home by alphabetical order? Give an example of something in your class or at home that it would be helpful to organize by alphabetical order.

_____

_____

_____

_____

Notes for Home: Your child used alphabetical order to organize information. *Home Activity:* With your child, arrange the titles of some books in alphabetical order. Ignore the articles *a, the,* and *an* when alphabetizing book titles.

© Scott Foresman 5

Setting

- The **setting** is the time and place in which a story happens.

- In some stories, the author tells you exactly when and where the story takes place. In other stories, the author tells about the setting through details and you have to figure out the time and place.

Directions: Reread "The Year of Mother Jones." Then complete the table.
Provide details from the story to support each statement about the setting.

Setting	How I Know (Supporting Details from the Story)
The story takes place in Philadelphia.	1.
The story begins in November, 1903.	2.
The children work in a mill.	3.
The mill is dirty and dangerous.	4.
The strike takes place in the summer of 1903.	5.

Notes for Home: Your child read a story and identified details about its setting. *Home Activity:* Read a story with your child. Have him or her point out details that help identify when and where the story takes place. Talk about how important the setting is to the story.

© Scott Foresman 5

Name _____

Vocabulary

Directions: Choose the word from the box that best completes each sentence. Write the word on the line.

Check the Words You Know

__ banners
__ headlines
__ parlor
__ pavement
__ splattered
__ stockings
__ trolley

_____ **1.** Kate stared at the _____ on the newspapers: FAIR WAGES NOW!

_____ **2.** Kate rode the _____ through town to the factory.

_____ **3.** She saw striking workers marching along, carrying _____ and signs.

_____ **4.** Even when they began to be _____ by rain, they didn't quit.

_____ **5.** So much rain had fallen that the _____ was covered with deep puddles.

_____ **6.** A few striking workers complained that the rainwater had soaked their shoes and _____.

Directions: Choose the word from the box that best matches each clue. Write the word on the line.

_____ **7.** I am something you can ride in to travel throughout the city.

_____ **8.** I am a sitting room in which you entertain guests.

_____ **9.** I am a road or sidewalk covered with a hard surface.

_____ **10.** I am worn over your feet and under your shoes.

Write a Song

On a separate sheet of paper, write a political song that suffragists might sing at marches, parades, or demonstrations. Use as many vocabulary words as you can.

Notes for Home: Your child identified and used vocabulary words from the story "I Want to Vote!" *Home Activity*: If possible, show your child pictures of suffragists from the 1910s and 1920s. Invite your child to make up his or her own story about the fight for the right to vote.

© Scott Foresman 5

Name _____

Setting

- The **setting** is the time and place in which a story happens. It may be directly identified or only described through details.

- In some stories, the setting is very important. It affects what happens and why it happens.

Directions: Reread the section of "I Want to Vote!" in which the parade begins. Then answer the questions below. Think about where and when the story takes place.

All at once, all the bands were playing and the columns of women began to move. Left, left. Lila was marching. Above her, the yellow banners streamed.

Out of Washington Square they marched and onto Fifth Avenue. Before and behind came the sound of the drums, and the flags snapped in the breeze. Left, left. On they went up the street, marching in time to the music.

From the curbs came the sound of whistles and cheers. Yellow streamers flew from the shop doors. White-gloved policemen held back the crowds as the bands and the marchers passed.

From A LONG WAY TO GO by Zibby Oneal. Copyright © 1990 by Zibby Oneal. Used by permission of Viking Penguin, a division of Penguin Putnam Inc.

1. Where is the parade taking place?

_____

_____

2. Is the setting directly identified or implied through details? Explain.

_____

_____

3. Which details make the setting come alive for the reader?

_____

_____

4. How does the setting affect the marchers?

_____

5. How important is the time period in which the story is set? Explain your answer on a separate sheet of paper.

Notes for Home: Your child read a story and analyzed how the time and place affected the characters and events. *Home Activity:* Read a story with your child. Then talk about the way the setting (time and place) affects the characters and events.

© Scott Foresman 5

Name _____

1.	Ⓐ	Ⓑ	Ⓒ	Ⓓ
2.	Ⓕ	Ⓖ	Ⓗ	Ⓙ
3.	Ⓐ	Ⓑ	Ⓒ	Ⓓ
4.	Ⓕ	Ⓖ	Ⓗ	Ⓙ
5.	Ⓐ	Ⓑ	Ⓒ	Ⓓ
6.	Ⓕ	Ⓖ	Ⓗ	Ⓙ
7.	Ⓐ	Ⓑ	Ⓒ	Ⓓ
8.	Ⓕ	Ⓖ	Ⓗ	Ⓙ
9.	Ⓐ	Ⓑ	Ⓒ	Ⓓ
10.	Ⓕ	Ⓖ	Ⓗ	Ⓙ
11.	Ⓐ	Ⓑ	Ⓒ	Ⓓ
12.	Ⓕ	Ⓖ	Ⓗ	Ⓙ
13.	Ⓐ	Ⓑ	Ⓒ	Ⓓ
14.	Ⓕ	Ⓖ	Ⓗ	Ⓙ
15.	Ⓐ	Ⓑ	Ⓒ	Ⓓ

© Scott Foresman 5

Selection Test

Directions: Choose the best answer to each item. Mark the letter for the answer you have chosen.

Part 1: Vocabulary

Find the answer choice that means about the same as the underlined word in each sentence.

1. Lou rode the trolley.
   A. station wagon
   B. bicycle
   C. horse-drawn carriage
   D. streetcar

2. The milk splattered everywhere.
   F. splashed
   G. grew wildly
   H. smelled
   J. froze

3. The marchers carried banners.
   A. protective coverings
   B. signs made of cloth
   C. musical instruments
   D. small children

4. Her stockings were dirty.
   F. coverings for the hand
   G. drawers in a cabinet
   H. glasses used to improve eyesight
   J. coverings for the foot or leg

5. George is in the parlor.
   A. park
   B. garage
   C. living room
   D. basement

6. We stood on the pavement.
   F. street or sidewalk
   G. upper floor of a theater
   H. long, wooden porch
   J. flat stretch of sand by the sea

7. These headlines are not very exciting.
   A. small wrinkles on a person's face
   B. coverings or decorations for the head
   C. long lines at the store
   D. lines printed at the top of newspaper articles

Part 2: Comprehension

Use what you know about the story to answer each item.

8. At the beginning of the story, Lila and Mike were—
   F. marching in a parade.
   G. selling newspapers.
   H. fighting a fire.
   J. printing newspapers.

9. Lila read about women in Washington who refused to eat because they—
   A. were angry at the cook.
   B. did not like the food they got in jail.
   C. could not afford to buy food.
   D. would rather starve than not have the right to vote.

10. How did things change for the women in the story because there was a war on?
    F. They were allowed to vote.
    G. They had the same rights as men.
    H. They were working in offices and factories.
    J. They were not allowed to make speeches.

© Scott Foresman 5

GO ON

11. Where does this story take place?
   A. New York
   B. Washington, D.C.
   C. Georgia
   D. California

12. When does this story take place?
   F. at the time of the Civil War
   G. in the early 1900s
   H. after World War II
   J. in the 1960s

13. How did Lila's father react to her speech?
   A. He became angry.
   B. He pretended to be bored.
   C. He was annoyed.
   D. He was impressed.

14. This story supports the idea that—
   F. women deserve the same rights as men.
   G. boys are smarter than girls.
   H. women should not be allowed to vote.
   J. women don't need to know how to drive.

15. Lila's father was wrong in thinking that she—
   A. was not as smart as George.
   B. would grow into a beautiful lady.
   C. would prefer dances and parties to learning to drive.
   D. would make speeches when she was older.

STOP

© Scott Foresman 5

Making Judgments

Directions: Read the story. Then read each question about the story. Choose the best answer to each question. Mark the letter for the answer you have chosen.

Forward March!

Jack and Paul were going all the way to Washington to march in the parade with their friends Sally and Roberto. They woud travel down by train the day before. Jack had been thinking about it all week. He and Paul were good friends, and they would have a great time at the parade.

The night before, Jack and Paul got together to pack their bags. Paul noticed that Jack didn't pack an umbrella.

"Aren't you taking your umbrella, Jack? I read that it may rain tomorrow."

"I can't be bothered with an umbrella," objected Jack. "My pack is heavy enough already. Besides, why would it rain? The weather has been great all week."

Paul said nothing. He went back to his packing.

Jack watched as Paul stuffed a sweater into his pack. "Why are you taking that? Your pack will be so heavy you won't want to go anywhere! Besides, it's warm out."

"Sally travels on those trains all the time, and she says they're always cold," Paul explained. "They always have the air conditioning on full blast."

"Oh, what does she know?" scoffed Jack. "Sally always thinks it's cold. Bring that sweater if you want to, but I'm not taking one."

Paul grinned at his friend and zipped his full pack. "All set?" he asked. "We should get some sleep if we want to be awake in time for our train tomorrow!"

1. Jack thinks he won't need an umbrella because—
   A. it's too big to fit into his backpack.
   B. he has no room for it.
   C. he doesn't believe it will rain.
   D. Paul has an umbrella.

2. Jack should take an umbrella because—
   F. Paul tells him to.
   G. Paul read a forecast that predicted rain.
   H. they can sell it later.
   J. it will balance the weight of his pack.

3. Paul takes a sweater because—
   A. Sally told him it would snow.
   B. he likes to wear sweaters.
   C. he thinks it will amuse Jack.
   D. Sally told him the train would be cold.

4. Which character do you think is best prepared for whatever may happen?
   F. Jack
   G. Paul
   H. Sally
   J. Roberto

5. Which character do you think is least prepared for whatever may happen?
   A. Jack
   B. Paul
   C. Sally
   D. Roberto

Notes for Home: Your child read a story and made judgments about the characters and their actions. *Home Activity:* Talk with your child about some of the decisions he or she made recently. Together, discuss your opinion of each decision.

© Scott Foresman 5

Phonics: Complex Spelling Patterns

Directions: In some words, the sound **/sh/** is spelled **ci, sci,** or **ti.** Read the list of words. Say each word to yourself. Underline the letters that represent the sound **/sh/.**

1. official
2. special
3. commotion
4. spacious
5. occupation

6. imagination
7. dictionary
8. conscious
9. delicious
10. caution

11. conscience
12. luscious
13. socially
14. artificial
15. motion

Directions: Read the diary entry. Circle the words with the sound /sh/. Write the words on the lines.

May 29

Dear Diary,

    Today was a special day for our family. It was election day, and Mom just got elected to the city council! We worked very hard on her campaign. We passed out flyers and asked people to sign petitions saying they would vote for Mom. We ran commercials on the local radio and television stations. We reminded everyone we talked to that it was their constitutional right to vote. Mom told me that not so long ago women did not have the right to vote. Can you imagine that such a large percent of our population had no say in how the nation was run? It made me realize how precious our rights are, especially the right to vote. Now I can't wait till I turn 18 and can cast my own vote!

16. _____
17. _____
18. _____
19. _____
20. _____
21. _____
22. _____
23. _____
24. _____
25. _____

Notes for Home: Your child identified words with the sound /sh/ spelled *ci, sci,* and *ti.* **Home Activity:** Make a list of words with your child that end in *-tion* and have the sound /sh/. Make up rhymes with these words.

© Scott Foresman 5

Technology: Electronic Media

Electronic media includes audiotapes, videotapes, films, and computers. You can use computers to locate information on CD-ROMs and to search the Internet. To find a topic on the Internet, use a search engine and type in your key words.

Directions: Suppose you type "voting AND registration" in a search engine. You might get the following list that links you to related web pages. Use the list to answer the questions on the next page.

You Searched For:

| voting AND registration | **Top 6 of 3789 matches.**

CENSUS - Voting and Registration Data Information about who votes and is registered to vote according to characteristics such as age, gender, race, amount of money earned, and so on.

Programs — Voting Rights Voting for Everyone is a group that works to eliminate any discriminatory obstacles that might prevent Asian Pacific Americans from participating in the voting process. This includes working to enforce the protections of the Voting Rights Act, encouraging voter registration through enforcement of the National Voter Registration Act, and providing data about Asian Pacific American participation.

Voting Information for Minnesota To vote, you must be: A U.S. citizen, at least 18 years old, a Minnesota resident for at least 20 days on election day, and properly registered. Election Dates and Absentee Ballot Application provided here.

Voting in Oregon Casting a ballot is as easy as mailing a letter in Oregon. Vote by mail started in 1981 when the Legislature authorized it for special district elections. Since then, it has become extremely popular and common for many elections.

League of Women Voters: Austin, Texas Qualifications for Voting: You must be a citizen of the United States. You must be at least 18 years old on the day of the election. You must be registered to vote. You may register to vote at any time.

Voting Information in Delaware, Maryland Voting Information: To be eligible to vote, one must be eighteen (18) years of age by the day after the election.

© Scott Foresman 5

Name _____

1. Which web page has information about eliminating discrimination?

_____

2. How long must you live in Minnesota to be able to vote in that state?

_____

3. In which state listed can you vote by mail? _____

4. Which web page would you go to for data about how different groups of people voted in past elections?

_____

5. What is the difference between the voting age requirement in Texas and the voting age requirement in Maryland?

_____

_____

6. What key words could you use to find out about voting in Ohio on the Internet?

_____

7. What key words could you use to find out about the history of voting rights for women?

_____

8. Suppose your library has an audiotape of interviews of older women describing their struggles to win the right to vote. How might you use a resource like this in a report on the history of women's voting rights?

_____

_____

_____

9. Suppose your library had a videotape that showed how to use a voting booth. For what kind of report might this resource be useful?

_____

_____

10. What are the advantages to searching the Internet for information? _____

_____

_____

_____

 Notes for Home: Your child analyzed the results of a web page search on the Internet. *Home Activity:* Work with your child to find the requirements for voting in your area. Help your child use a telephone directory or online resources to find the voting requirements.

© Scott Foresman 5

Paraphrasing

- **Paraphrasing** is explaining something in your own words.

- After you read a sentence or paragraph, think about what the author is trying to say. Then put the sentence or paragraph into your own words without changing the meaning or adding your own opinion.

Directions: Reread "A Dream of Equal Rights." Then complete the table. Paraphrase each original statement in your own words. (The beginning words of each sentence will help you find the sentence to paraphrase.)

Original Statement	My Paraphrase
Paragraph 1, Sentence 1 "Movements are born. . . ."	1.
Paragraph 1, Sentence 3 "Often, it takes. . . ."	2.
Paragraph 2, Sentence 2 "People around the nation. . . ."	3.
Paragraph 3, Sentence 3 "Many people had. . . ."	4.
Paragraph 3, Sentence 6 "His dream was. . . ."	5.

© Scott Foresman 5

Notes for Home: Your child read an article and restated its ideas in his or her own words. *Home Activity:* Read a newspaper article with your child. Have your child restate sentences or paragraphs in his or her own words.

Vocabulary

Directions: Draw a line to connect each word on the left with its definition on the right.

**Check
the Words
You Know**
__ liberty
__ plantation
__ quickened
__ runaway
__ slavery
__ unconscious
__ vow

1. liberty   a solemn promise

2. slavery   a large farm or estate

3. vow   freedom

4. plantation   fugitive

5. runaway   holding people against their will

Directions: Choose a word from the box that is the most opposite in meaning for each word or words below. Write the word on the line.

_____ **6.** captivity

_____ **7.** broken promise

_____ **8.** slowed

_____ **9.** conscious

_____ **10.** freedom

Directions: Choose the word from the box that best completes each sentence. Write the word on the line on the left.

_____ **11.** _____ was a way of life for Annie and her family for as long as Annie could remember.

_____ **12.** The master's _____ had more than fifty slaves working in the fields and the house.

_____ **13.** Annie made a _____ to herself that she would not die a slave.

_____ **14.** The punishment for a _____ slave who was caught was severe.

_____ **15.** However, for Annie, the chance for true _____ was worth any risk.

Write a Speech

On a separate sheet of paper, write a speech that a person in the 1850s might have delivered in the fight against slavery. Use as many vocabulary words as you can.

Notes for Home: Your child identified and used vocabulary words from "The Long Path to Freedom." *Home Activity:* Talk with your child about what kind of life a slave had. Use the vocabulary words in the conversation.

© Scott Foresman 5

Paraphrasing

- **Paraphrasing** is explaining something in your own words.

- A paraphrase should include only the author's ideas and opinions. When paraphrasing, don't change the meaning or add your own opinions.

Directions: Reread what happened in "The Long Path to Freedom" when Harriet ran away with her brothers. Then answer the questions below.

> That night Harriet waited until her husband, John, fell asleep. Then she slid silently out of their cabin. She met her brothers, and they started off through the woods. Harriet took the lead. She knew the woods. They did not. Every owl that hooted, every frog that croaked startled them. They did not move very fast. And to Harriet they seemed to stomp and crash like a herd of cattle.
>
> Harriet kept encouraging them on. But at last her brothers stopped. They were frightened. They were going back.
>
> Harriet began to protest. They must go on!

From THE STORY OF HARRIET TUBMAN by Kate McMullan. Copyright © 1991 by Parachute Press, Inc. Used by permission of Dell Books, a division of Bantam Doubleday Dell Publishing Group, Inc.

1. How might you paraphrase the first two sentences as a single sentence?

_____

_____

2. How might you paraphrase the last sentence in the first paragraph?

_____

_____

3. How might you paraphrase the second paragraph as a single sentence?

_____

_____

4. How might you paraphrase the final two sentences as a single sentence?

_____

_____

5. When you paraphrase, why is it important to use your own words and not the author's exact words? Explain your thinking on a separate sheet of paper.

Notes for Home: Your child read a story and then retold parts of it in his or her own words. *Home Activity:* Read a newspaper article with your child. Challenge your child to restate individual sentences in his or her own words.

© Scott Foresman 5

Name _____

1.	Ⓐ	Ⓑ	Ⓒ	Ⓓ
2.	Ⓕ	Ⓖ	Ⓗ	Ⓙ
3.	Ⓐ	Ⓑ	Ⓒ	Ⓓ
4.	Ⓕ	Ⓖ	Ⓗ	Ⓙ
5.	Ⓐ	Ⓑ	Ⓒ	Ⓓ
6.	Ⓕ	Ⓖ	Ⓗ	Ⓙ
7.	Ⓐ	Ⓑ	Ⓒ	Ⓓ
8.	Ⓕ	Ⓖ	Ⓗ	Ⓙ
9.	Ⓐ	Ⓑ	Ⓒ	Ⓓ
10.	Ⓕ	Ⓖ	Ⓗ	Ⓙ
11.	Ⓐ	Ⓑ	Ⓒ	Ⓓ
12.	Ⓕ	Ⓖ	Ⓗ	Ⓙ
13.	Ⓐ	Ⓑ	Ⓒ	Ⓓ
14.	Ⓕ	Ⓖ	Ⓗ	Ⓙ
15.	Ⓐ	Ⓑ	Ⓒ	Ⓓ

© Scott Foresman 5

Name _____

Selection Test

Directions: Choose the best answer to each item. Mark the letter for the answer you have chosen.

Part 1: Vocabulary

Find the answer choice that means about the same as the underlined word in each sentence.

1. Patrick fights for liberty.
   A. freedom
   B. life
   C. food
   D. shelter

2. Mercy lived on a plantation.
   F. boat
   G. large farm
   H. busy road
   J. government-owned housing

3. Ben told us about his vow.
   A. experience
   B. promise
   C. secret
   D. project

4. When we found the child, he was unconscious.
   F. chilled
   G. very hungry
   H. happy
   J. not able to think or feel

5. Slavery existed in ancient Greece.
   A. a system in which one person can own another
   B. type of building with columns
   C. the study of the universe
   D. a system of measurement

6. The hikers quickened the pace.
   F. took a rest
   G. felt better
   H. cleaned up
   J. speeded up

7. The runaway asked for help.
   A. person with no money
   B. person who is sick
   C. person who is from another country
   D. person who has left somewhere secretly

Part 2: Comprehension

Use what you know about the selection to answer each item.

8. According to this selection, Harriet's master was—
   F. Dr. Thompson.
   G. John Tubman.
   H. Mr. Trent.
   J. Ezekiel Hunn.

9. When Harriet Tubman realized that her mother had been tricked into remaining a slave, she knew that she—
   A. had to hire a lawyer to become free herself.
   B. would never be free.
   C. would have to go outside the legal system to become free.
   D. had to go to a judge to free her mother.

10. Harriet trusted the Quaker woman who approached her one morning because—
    F. the stranger was a female.
    G. Quakers did not believe in slavery.
    H. the woman asked Harriet's name
    J. the woman lived near Dr. Thompson's plantation.

GO ON

© Scott Foresman 5

11. How were Harriet's brothers different from her?

    A.   They did not mind being slaves.

    B.   They wanted to be sold South.

    C.   They were not as brave as she was.

    D.   They were not as physically strong as she was.

12. Just before Harriet reached the Hunns' house, she—

    F.   got a pair of new shoes from Thomas Garrett.

    G.   heard slave hunters talking about a runaway girl.

    H.   sold her quilt.

    J.   put on elegant clothes to wear to the Pennsylvania border.

13. "She wanted to repay her kindness. She had no money, but she had one thing she valued." Which is the best paraphrase of these sentences?

    A.   She wanted to show she was thankful. Although she had no money, she did own one valuable item.

    B.   She wanted to get something back for being so kind. She didn't care about money, but she loved nice things.

    C.   She decided that the only way to repay the woman was with kindness, since she had no money.

    D.   She didn't want to have to pay the woman, since she had no money and only one valuable possession.

14. Harriet knows that she has found the right man in the cemetery when he—

    F.   tips his hat toward her.

    G.   says he has a ticket for the railroad.

    H.   gives her a pair of shoes.

    J.   tells her that he is a Quaker.

15. Ezekiel Hunn and Thomas Garrett would likely agree that—

    A.   slaves are property and should be returned to their owners.

    B.   a runaway slave is worth about the same as a bale of cotton.

    C.   Harriet Tubman did a foolish thing when she tried to escape.

    D.   no one has the right to own another human being.

STOP

© Scott Foresman 5

Main Idea and Supporting Details/Summarizing

REVIEW

Directions: Read the passage. Then read each question about the passage. Choose the best answer to each question. Mark the letter for the answer you have chosen.

Slavery

The practice of human slavery is something we would like to think had a short history that has long since ceased to be. It is hard to imagine how any group of people could think they could own another group of people.

It is a sad truth, however, that slavery has a long history. There is evidence that slavery was first practiced in prehistoric times. It became widespread in Greece and in the Roman Empire. During the 1500s and 1600s, slavery was established in the New World as Europeans established colonies in the Americas. They brought slaves from Africa to work on sugar plantations in the West Indies and South America. Later, slavery spread to North America.

Eventually, changing attitudes about human rights brought an end to slavery in most parts of the world. But slavery is still practiced today in parts of Africa, Asia, and South America. While the number of people living in slavery is unknown, most slaves are believed to be captives of war or persons sold into slavery to pay debts.

People who are enslaved are almost always restricted in many ways. Often they cannot legally marry or have a family. They cannot testify in court, vote, or own property. They are forced to work hard for little or no pay.

1. The main idea in the second paragraph is that—
   A. Greece had slaves.
   B. Slavery ended in places.
   C. Asia still has slavery.
   D. The practice of slavery is very old.

2. A detail that supports the main idea of the second paragraph is that—
   F. slaves are restricted.
   G. there was slavery in prehistoric times.
   H. slavery is very old.
   J. slaves can't vote.

3. The main idea in the fourth paragraph is that—
   A. slaves are restricted.
   B. slaves can't testify in court.
   C. Africa has slavery.
   D. attitudes have changed.

4. A detail that supports the main idea of the fourth paragraph is that—
   F. the New World had slavery.
   G. slavery is historic.
   H. attitudes have changed.
   J. slaves can't testify in court.

5. Which statement best summarizes the article?
   A. Slavery is everywhere.
   B. Slavery is an old and inhumane practice.
   C. Slavery has now ended.
   D. Slavery means hard work.

© Scott Foresman 5

Notes for Home: Your child identified the main ideas and supporting details of an article and summarized it. **Home Activity:** Read a newspaper article with your child. Together, identify its main ideas and supporting details. Then have your child summarize the article.

Word Study: Suffixes

Directions: Letters added to the ends of words are called **suffixes.** Suffixes can change the meaning of the base word. Add a suffix to each word below to make a new word. Write each new word on the line.

Base Word		Suffix		New Word
1. free	+	-dom	=	_____
2. legal	+	-ly	=	_____
3. own	+	-er	=	_____
4. grate	+	-ful	=	_____
5. joy	+	-ous	=	_____
6. risk	+	-y	=	_____

Directions: Read the diary entry below. Find nine words that have the suffix **-ly, -er, -ful, -ous,** or **-y.** Circle the words. Then write the base word and the suffix on the line connected by a + sign. For example, for **slowly,** you would write **slow + ly.**

June 9, 1863

On a dark and rainy night, I packed my things into a bundle. Silently, I slipped from the cabin and quickly disappeared into the woods. The journey was dangerous and lonely. Each day I feared that a slave tracker was following me. But when I crossed the state line, my heart set up a thunderous beat. A joyful feeling came over me. I was on my own! I was free! And it felt wonderful!

7. _____
8. _____
9. _____
10. _____
11. _____
12. _____
13. _____
14. _____
15. _____

Notes for Home: Your child added suffixes to base words to make new words, such as *slow + ly = slowly.* **Home Activity:** Read an advertisement with your child. Help your child notice words with suffixes. Ask your child to write down the words and circle the suffixes.

© Scott Foresman 5

Name _____

Time Line

A **time line** is a line divided into years or other periods of time. The line is labeled
with events that show when events happened or will happen in time order.

Directions: The time line below shows when slavery was abolished, or outlawed,
in various parts of the world. Use it to answer the questions on the next page.

The Decline of Slavery 1800–1900

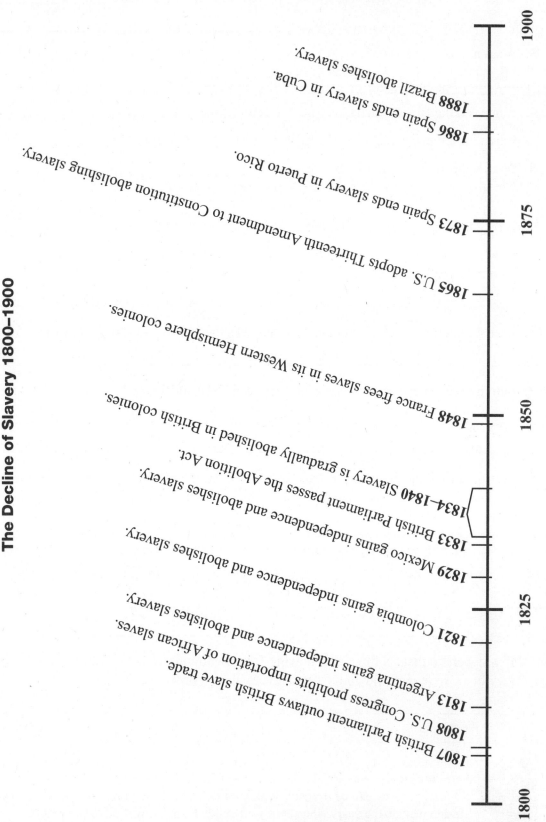

1900

1888 Brazil abolishes slavery.

1886 Spain ends slavery in Cuba.

1875

1873 Spain ends slavery in Puerto Rico.

1865 U.S. adopts Thirteenth Amendment to Constitution abolishing slavery.

1850

1848 France frees slaves in its Western Hemisphere colonies.

1834–1840 Slavery is gradually abolished in British colonies.

1833 British Parliament passes the Abolition Act.

1829 Mexico gains independence and abolishes slavery.

1825

1821 Colombia gains independence and abolishes slavery.

1813 Argentina gains independence and abolishes slavery.

1808 U.S. Congress prohibits importation of African slaves.

1807 British Parliament outlaws British slave trade.

1800

© Scott Foresman 5

Name _____

1. How many years does the time line show? _____

2. How many years does each of the four sections of the time line represent? _____

3. When did it become illegal to import slaves into the United States? _____

4. When was slavery abolished in Brazil? _____

5. What happened in 1865? _____

_____

6. When did the British Parliament pass the Abolition Act? _____

7. When did France end slavery in its Western Hemisphere colonies? _____

8. What happened between 1834 and 1840? _____

_____

9. Who ended its slave trade first, Great Britain or the United States? _____

10. How many years passed between the abolition of slave importation and the abolition of slavery in the United States?

_____

11. Which nation—Britain, Spain, or France—was the last to end slavery in its colonies?

_____

12. Summarize the events that took place between 1810 and 1830.

_____

_____

13. President Lincoln signed the Emancipation Proclamation in January 1863. This document freed all slaves in the Confederate states. Between which two events would you place this event on the time line?

_____

14. Do you think a time line is a useful way to present this information about slavery? Explain.

_____

_____

15. If you were to make a time line showing five upcoming events in your future, what would they be? Give a date and and list each event in time order.

_____

_____

Notes for Home: Your child read and interpreted a time line showing when slavery ended in various countries. *Home Activity:* With your child, list several important events in your child's life and include the years. Then help your child create a time line of the events.

© Scott Foresman 5

Visualizing

- **Visualizing** is creating a picture in your mind as you read.

- An author may help you visualize by using imagery. This happens when an author uses words that give you a strong mental picture or image. *Enormous billowing clouds* is an example of imagery.

- Another way an author may help you become part of what you are reading is through sensory details. Authors use words that describe how something looks, sounds, smells, tastes, or feels to do this.

Directions: Reread "Little Billy's Swan Rides." Then complete the table. List examples of words and phrases from the story that appeal to one of the five senses.

Example	Sense
house was quiet	hearing
curtains were drawn back	1.
2.	3.
4.	5.
6.	7.
8.	9.
10.	11.
12.	13.
14.	15.

Notes for Home: Your child read a story and identified words and phrases that helped create a mental picture of story events. *Home Activity:* Choose a familiar place. Give clues about how this place looks, smells, and sounds. Have your child guess the place.

© Scott Foresman 5

Vocabulary

Directions: Read the following paragraph. Choose the word from the box that best completes each sentence. Write the word on the matching numbered line to the right.

Tom Cat's whiskers acted as **1.** _____ to help him find his way in the dark. Suddenly, a shadow came swooping down and swept him up in the air! As Tom Cat rose into the air, the very strong winds felt like a **2.** _____ against his face. **3.** _____ to whatever had snatched him, Tom yelled for help. Then he heard a deep chuckle and tilted his head back to see Harry Hawk! "Doesn't it give you a **4.** _____ to fly on exciting **5.** _____ such as these?" asked Harry innocently.

1. _____

2. _____

3. _____

4. _____

5. _____

Check the Words You Know
__ clinging
__ excursions
__ feelers
__ gale
__ thrill

Directions: Choose the word from the box that has the same or nearly the same meaning as each word or phrase below. Write the word on the line.

6. clutching _____

7. high wind _____

8. trips _____

9. excitement _____

10. an animal's sensors _____

Write a Travel Log

Where do your journeys take you? On a separate sheet of paper, write an entry in a travel log describing a real or imaginary journey. Describe the people you meet, the animals you see, and the adventures you have. Use as many vocabulary words as you can in your travel log.

Notes for Home: Your child identified and used vocabulary words from *Chester Cricket's Pigeon Ride.* **Home Activity:** Invite your child to draw a cartoon describing an adventure on a first flight. Help him or her use as many vocabulary words as possible in the speech balloons.

© Scott Foresman 5

Visualizing

- **Visualizing** is creating a picture in your mind as you read.

- Authors may help you visualize by using imagery. These are words that give you a strong mental picture, or image.

- Another way an author may help you visualize is through sensory details. These are words that describe how something looks, sounds, smells, tastes, or feels.

Directions: Reread what happens in *Chester Cricket's Pigeon Ride* when Lulu takes Chester to Central Park. Then answer the questions below. Think about how the author uses imagery and sensory details to help you visualize.

"Here's Central Park," Lulu screeched against the wind.

And now Chester had another thrill. For there weren't only sycamore trees in the park. The cricket could smell birches, beeches, and maples—elms, oaks—almost as many kinds of trees as Connecticut itself had to offer. And there was the moon!—the crescent moon—reflected in a little lake. Sounds, too, rose up to him: the shooshing of leaves, the nighttime countryside whispering of insects and little animals, and—best of all—a brook that was arguing with itself, as it splashed over rocks. The miracle of Central Park, a sheltered wilderness in the midst of the city, pierced Chester's heart with joy.

From CHESTER CRICKET'S PIGEON RIDE by George Selden, pictures by Garth Williams. Text copyright © 1981 by George Selden Thompson. Illustrations copyright © 1981 by Garth Williams. Reprinted by permission of Farrar, Straus, & Giroux, Inc.

1. Which details in the passage help you visualize what the park smells like?

_____

2. Which details in the passage help you visualize what the park sounds like?

_____

3. Which details help you visualize what the park looks like?

_____

4. What sound reminds Chester of an argument?

_____

5. How does the author help you visualize the view from the top of the Empire State Building? On a separate sheet of paper, list the sensory details and imagery he uses.

Notes for Home: Your child read a story and pictured the scene in his or her mind. ***Home Activity:*** Have your child listen as you describe how an object looks, sounds, smells, feels, or tastes. See if your child can guess what it is. Then switch roles and repeat.

© Scott Foresman 5

Name _____

1.	Ⓐ	Ⓑ	Ⓒ	Ⓓ
2.	Ⓕ	Ⓖ	Ⓗ	Ⓙ
3.	Ⓐ	Ⓑ	Ⓒ	Ⓓ
4.	Ⓕ	Ⓖ	Ⓗ	Ⓙ
5.	Ⓐ	Ⓑ	Ⓒ	Ⓓ
6.	Ⓕ	Ⓖ	Ⓗ	Ⓙ
7.	Ⓐ	Ⓑ	Ⓒ	Ⓓ
8.	Ⓕ	Ⓖ	Ⓗ	Ⓙ
9.	Ⓐ	Ⓑ	Ⓒ	Ⓓ
10.	Ⓕ	Ⓖ	Ⓗ	Ⓙ
11.	Ⓐ	Ⓑ	Ⓒ	Ⓓ
12.	Ⓕ	Ⓖ	Ⓗ	Ⓙ
13.	Ⓐ	Ⓑ	Ⓒ	Ⓓ
14.	Ⓕ	Ⓖ	Ⓗ	Ⓙ
15.	Ⓐ	Ⓑ	Ⓒ	Ⓓ

© Scott Foresman 5

Selection Test

Directions: Choose the best answer to each item. Mark the letter for the answer
you have chosen.

Part 1: Vocabulary

Find the answer choice that means about the
same as the underlined word in each sentence.

1. This is such a <u>thrill</u>!
   - A. scary movie
   - B. exciting feeling
   - C. grand performance
   - D. sudden storm

2. He was <u>clinging</u> to his mother.
   - F. speaking in a soft voice
   - G. singing words over and over again
   - H. sitting next to
   - J. holding on tightly

3. They flew into the <u>gale</u>.
   - A. side of a mountain
   - B. tall building in a city
   - C. very strong wind
   - D. large storm cloud

4. Margo has taken many <u>excursions</u>.
   - F. photographs
   - G. tests
   - H. helpings
   - J. trips

5. A cricket has several <u>feelers</u>.
   - A. close friends
   - B. parts of an insect's body used for
         sensing
   - C. family members
   - D. strong emotions

Part 2: Comprehension

Use what you know about the story to answer
each item.

6. Chester's friend Lulu is a—
   - F. pigeon.
   - G. cricket.
   - H. mouse.
   - J. cat.

7. How did Chester get from Connecticut to
   the city?
   - A. He crossed the Atlantic on a sailing
         vessel.
   - B. He was carried there inside a picnic
         basket.
   - C. He took an airplane ride.
   - D. He flew there on a pigeon's back.

8. Lulu gives Chester a—
   - F. ride on the subway.
   - G. free trip to Connecticut.
   - H. place to stay in Bryant Park.
   - J. tour of New York.

9. Which phrase best helps you see in your
   mind what Central Park looks like?
   - A. "Big beautiful Central Park!"
   - B. "coasted down through the air"
   - C. "a sheltered wilderness in the midst
         of the city"
   - D. "the best place in the city"

10. How does Chester feel about flying?
    - F. completely terrified
    - G. extremely bored
    - H. a little afraid, but excited
    - J. somewhat embarrassed

11. While flying down into Central Park, Lulu
    probably looks most like a—
    - A. paper airplane.
    - B. hunting bird.
    - C. hot-air balloon.
    - D. speeding bullet.

© Scott Foresman 5

GO ON

Name _____

from **Chester Cricket's**
Pigeon Ride

12. How can you tell that Chester is very happy in Central Park?
　F.　He jumps up and down.
　G.　He dances around with Lulu.
　H.　He holds on to Lulu's claw.
　J.　He chirps to his heart's content.

13. Which sentence from the story gives an opinion?
　A.　"Lulu gripped the pinnacle of the TV antenna with both her claws."
　B.　"They reached the Battery, . . . part of lower New York."
　C.　"The finest shops in all the world are on Fifth Avenue."
　D.　"Her right hand was holding something up."

14. After being blown off the Empire State Building, Chester most likely wants to return to the drainpipe because he—
　F.　is angry at Lulu for putting his life in danger.
　G.　needs to feel safe again.
　H.　wants to tell everyone about his adventure.
　J.　wants to pack up and leave New York.

15. Which part of this story is fantasy?
　A.　A cricket talks to a pigeon.
　B.　A pigeon flies over New York.
　C.　A cricket chirps in Central Park.
　D.　A pigeon looks at the Statue of Liberty.

© Scott Foresman 5

226 **Selection Test**

Paraphrasing

Directions: Read the story. Then read each question about the story. Choose the best answer to each question. Mark the letter for the answer you have chosen.

Strange Planet

Maria, the nation's newest astronaut, journeyed to the planet Backwards. No one had ever explored the territory before. Maria was overwhelmed by what she found there.

On this planet, everything appeared upside down and backwards from the way it appeared on Earth. The planet had a ground of clouds and a sky of grass. The trees grew with their leaves down and their roots up. When it rained, the rain actually traveled upward.

The people of Backwards had their faces on the backs of their heads. They greeted Maria with a "good-bye." And when they were ready to leave, they said "hello."

"This planet certainly deserves its name," Maria said to herself. She couldn't wait to get back to Earth, where everything and everyone was right side up and forward!

1. Which of the following best paraphrases the first two sentences in the first paragraph?
   A. Astronaut Maria wasn't sure she wanted to go to Backwards.
   B. Astronaut Maria was sent to the planet Backwards.
   C. Astronaut Maria was the first to explore the planet Backwards.
   D. Maria, the nation's newest astronaut, journeyed to the planet Backwards.

2. Which of the following best paraphrases the second and third sentences in the second paragraph?
   F. Clouds and grass were reversed, and trees grew upside down.
   G. The sky was grass, and the ground was clouds.

   H. Leaves grew down, and roots grew up on trees.
   J. The trees had no roots, and the leaves grew underground.

3. Which of the following best paraphrases the third paragraph?
   A. People had backward heads, feet, and arms.
   B. People had backward heads and said "good-bye" first and "hello" last.
   C. The people of Backwards had their faces on the backs of their heads.
   D. People had backward heads and said "hello" last.

4. Which of the following best paraphrases the last paragraph?
   F. Maria was frightened by the planet Backwards.
   G. Maria couldn't wait to get back to Earth and return to a normal life.
   H. Maria was ready to leave Backwards and return to Earth.
   J. Maria found Backwards deserving of its name and was eager to return to a right side up and forward Earth.

5. Which of the following best paraphrases the whole story?
   A. Maria traveled to Backwards and never returned to Earth.
   B. Maria loved being an astronaut.
   C. The people of Backwards do everything in reverse.
   D. Astronaut Maria explored Backwards, a planet where everything is backwards or upside down.

Notes for Home: Your child identified statements that best paraphrase a story. *Home Activity:* Say a pair of sentences to your child, such as *It would be fun to take a vacation. We could go camping.* Challenge your child to restate the same idea in a single sentence.

© Scott Foresman 5

Word Study: Suffixes

Directions: Sometimes the spelling of a base word changes when a suffix is added. In most words, when the base word ends in **-e,** drop the **-e** and add the suffix. In most words, when the base word ends in **-y,** change the **-y** to **-i** and add the suffix. Read each sentence. Combine the base word and suffix in ( ) to make one word. Write the new word on the line.

_____ 1. Traveling with my cousin is always a (please + ure).

_____ 2. Something fantastic (usual + ly) happens on our trips.

_____ 3. Our adventures make for a very interesting (converse + ation).

_____ 4. (Fortunate + ly), we have plenty of time for traveling.

_____ 5. On our last trip, we saw some (remark + able) ruins in the jungle.

_____ 6. A hidden (pass + age) led us to an amazing treasure room.

_____ 7. We were thrilled to find the (plenty + ful) riches.

_____ 8. Finding treasure is a (respect + able) way to get rich!

_____ 9. For us, the (excite + ment) of traveling never wears off.

Directions: Read the words below. Write each base word and the suffix in the correct column.

	Base word		Suffix
10. lazily	_____	+	_____
11. direction	_____	+	_____
12. sorrowful	_____	+	_____
13. sleepy	_____	+	_____
14. possibly	_____	+	_____
15. disappointment	_____	+	_____
16. dizziness	_____	+	_____
17. beautiful	_____	+	_____
18. imaginable	_____	+	_____
19. famous	_____	+	_____
20. musician	_____	+	_____

Notes for Home: Your child made new words by adding suffixes to base words, such as *please* + *ure* = *pleasure.* **Home Activity:** Read a newspaper article with your child. Ask your child to find words with suffixes. Have your child break each word into the base word and suffix.

© Scott Foresman 5

Following Directions

Following directions involves reading or listening and then doing or making
something.

Directions: Follow these directions to complete the Unusual Journey puzzle.
Read all the directions before you begin. Follow each step closely. Some letters
have been filled in for you.

1. What is the name for a book of maps? Write the word in both columns marked **1.** (The first
   letter in each column is written in for you.)

2. What is the name of a book of facts that is published each year? Write the word in both
   columns marked **2.**

3. What is the name of a book you use to learn about a subject in school? Write the word in
   both columns marked **3.**

4. What is the name of a book that has words and their definitions? Write the word in both
   columns marked **4.**

5. What is the name for a set of books that has information about many different subjects?
   Write the word in both columns marked **5.**

6. Use a colored pencil or crayon to shade the space marked **6.**

7. Use different colored pencils or crayons to shade the spaces marked **7a** and **7b.**

8. Write your name in the box marked **8.**

9. Find all the letters that are set inside a diamond. Write the word the letters make after **Hot** in
   the box marked **9.**

10. Find all the letters that are circled. Write the word the letters make in the box marked **10.**

11. Use a pencil or crayon to color in all the empty boxes.

Directions: Use the completed puzzle to answer the questions below.

12. What type of unusual flying machine does the complete puzzle show?

_____

13. Where would you travel to have an unusual journey?

_____

14. Why is it important to read all the directions before you begin?

_____

_____

15. Why is it important to follow directions in the order they are given?

_____

_____

© Scott Foresman 5

Name _____

from **Chester Cricket's
Pigeon Ride**

Unusual Journey

				5 e	6	5					
			4 d				4				
		3 t	◇					3			
	2 ◇ a								2		
1 a										1 a	
				⬭		⬭					
		⬭ b					⬭				
								⬭	⬭		
			⬭								
							◇				
					7a						
					7b						
		8						's			
			9 Hot								
			10								

Notes for Home: Your child followed detailed directions to fill in a puzzle. *Home Activity:* With your child, make several lists of numbered directions to follow for writing words on a page. For example: *1. Write your name. 2. Cross out every other letter. 3. Write the letters that are left.*

230 Research and Study Skills: Following Directions

© Scott Foresman 5

Context Clues

- **Context clues** are words that help explain an unfamiliar word.

- Context clues can appear just before or after an unfamiliar word. But sometimes they are in a different part of the story or article, far from the unfamiliar word.

- Look for specific context clues such as definitions, explanations, examples, and descriptions.

Directions: Reread "Butterfly Memorial." Then complete the table. Write the meaning of each word in the table. Tell what context clue helped you figure out the meaning and where you found it.

Word	Meaning	Context Clues
ghetto	1.	The definition appears just before the word in the first paragraph.
Holocaust	2.	3.
remembrance	4.	5.

Notes for Home: Your child read an article and figured out the meanings of unfamiliar words by using context clues. *Home Activity:* Read a magazine article with your child. When you come to a word your child doesn't know, use context clues to figure out its meaning.

© Scott Foresman 5

Vocabulary

Directions: Choose a word from the box that best completes each
sentence. Write the word on the line to the left.

	Check the Words You Know
	__ agreement
	__ cable
	__ disobey
	__ issue
	__ permission
	__ representatives
	__ superiors
	__ translated

_____ 1. We elected _____ to speak for the rest
of us.

_____ 2. They approached an official who had
the power to _____ passports to our
group.

_____ 3. We needed this official's _____ to
leave the island.

_____ 4. He was worried we might _____ his
orders.

_____ 5. After much discussion, we finally reached an _____.

Directions: Choose the word from the box that best matches each clue. Write
the letters of the word on the blanks. The boxed letters spell something that a
happy child does.

6. consent   6. ☐ __ __ __ __ __ __ __

7. insulated bundle of wires   7. __ __ __ ☐ __
   for carrying electric current

8. changed from one   8. __ __ ☐ __ __ __ __ __ __
   language to another

9. refuse to obey   9. __ __ __ __ __ __ ☐

10. people who are higher in rank   10. ☐ __ __ __ __ __ __ __ __ __

Something a happy child does: __ __ __ __ __

Write an Award Citation

Imagine that one of your classmates has won an award for helping others. On a
separate sheet of paper, write a paragraph to go with the award. Describe what
the person did and the result of his or her actions. Try to use as many vocabulary
words as you can.

Notes for Home: Your child identified and used vocabulary words from *Passage to Freedom:
The Sugihara Story.* **Home Activity:** With your child, take turns telling a story using the
vocabulary words. At each turn, the teller may choose any unused word.

© Scott Foresman 5

Name _____

Context Clues

- **Context clues** are words that help explain an unfamiliar word. Context clues can appear just before or after an unfamiliar word. Sometimes, they are in a different part of the story or article.

- Context clues include synonyms, antonyms, definitions and explanations, examples, and descriptions.

Directions: Reread what happened in *Passage to Freedom: The Sugihara Story* when a crowd gathered outside the Sugiharas' home. Then answer the questions below.

I couldn't help but stare out the window and watch the crowd, while downstairs, for two hours, my father listened to frightening stories. These people were refugees—people who ran away from their homes because, if they stayed, they would be killed. They were Jews from Poland, escaping from the Nazi soldiers who had taken over their country.

The five men had heard my father could give them visas—official written permission to travel through another country. The hundreds of Jewish refugees outside hoped to travel east through the Soviet Union and end up in Japan. Once in Japan, they could go to another country. Was it true? the men asked. Could my father issue these visas?

Text copyright © 1997 Ken Mochizuki. Excerpt from PASSAGE TO FREEDOM: THE SUGIHARA STORY. Reprinted by arrangement with Lee & Low Books, Inc.

1. What does the word *refugees* mean?

_____

_____

2. What type of context clue did you use to determine the meaning of *refugees?*

_____

3. What does the word *visas* mean?

_____

_____

4. What type of context clue did you use to determine the meaning of *visas?*

_____

5. How can you be sure if you have determined the correct meaning of a word after using context clues?

Notes for Home: Your child used clues within a story to figure out the meanings of unfamiliar words. **Home Activity:** Read a story with your child. Help your child try to figure out the meaning of an unfamiliar word by looking at words surrounding it.

© Scott Foresman 5

Name _____

1.	Ⓐ	Ⓑ	Ⓒ	Ⓓ
2.	Ⓕ	Ⓖ	Ⓗ	Ⓙ
3.	Ⓐ	Ⓑ	Ⓒ	Ⓓ
4.	Ⓕ	Ⓖ	Ⓗ	Ⓙ
5.	Ⓐ	Ⓑ	Ⓒ	Ⓓ
6.	Ⓕ	Ⓖ	Ⓗ	Ⓙ
7.	Ⓐ	Ⓑ	Ⓒ	Ⓓ
8.	Ⓕ	Ⓖ	Ⓗ	Ⓙ
9.	Ⓐ	Ⓑ	Ⓒ	Ⓓ
10.	Ⓕ	Ⓖ	Ⓗ	Ⓙ
11.	Ⓐ	Ⓑ	Ⓒ	Ⓓ
12.	Ⓕ	Ⓖ	Ⓗ	Ⓙ
13.	Ⓐ	Ⓑ	Ⓒ	Ⓓ
14.	Ⓕ	Ⓖ	Ⓗ	Ⓙ
15.	Ⓐ	Ⓑ	Ⓒ	Ⓓ

© Scott Foresman 5

Selection Test

Directions: Choose the best answer to each item. Mark the letter for the answer you have chosen.

Part 1: Vocabulary

Find the answer choice that means about the same as the underlined word in each sentence.

1. Mr. Park <u>translated</u> for me.
   - A. wrote out by hand
   - B. read carefully
   - C. changed into a different language
   - D. learned by heart

2. The leaders were in <u>agreement</u>.
   - F. official stopping of work by a group of employees
   - G. loud protest
   - H. sudden rise in banking costs
   - J. understanding between two or more parties

3. Did the government <u>issue</u> those uniforms?
   - A. take back
   - B. design
   - C. forbid
   - D. give out

4. Captain Jones reported to his <u>superiors</u>.
   - F. bosses
   - G. people who buy goods
   - H. friends
   - J. people who are related

5. The <u>cable</u> was damaged in the storm.
   - A. tall tower
   - B. wooden structure in a body of water
   - C. bundle of wires for sending messages electronically
   - D. power station

6. Did you <u>disobey</u> the orders?
   - F. refuse to go along with
   - G. hear
   - H. misunderstand
   - J. give

7. Several <u>representatives</u> of the company spoke at the meeting.
   - A. people who dislike something
   - B. people appointed or elected to speak or act for others
   - C. people who refuse to take charge
   - D. people who have just paid money

8. Dad gave his <u>permission</u>.
   - F. money
   - G. help
   - H. decision to allow something
   - J. words of advice

Part 2: Comprehension

Use what you know about the selection to answer each item.

9. The major events in this story take place in—
   - A. Israel.
   - B. Germany.
   - C. Poland.
   - D. Lithuania.

10. This story is told from the point of view of—
    - F. a Japanese diplomat.
    - G. a Jewish refugee.
    - H. the diplomat's son.
    - J. the diplomat's wife.

11. Why do all the refugees come to talk to the diplomat?
    - A. They want visas so they can leave the country.
    - B. They want someone to speak out against the Germans.
    - C. They want his help in returning to the homes they have left.
    - D. They want him to hide them from the German army.

© Scott Foresman 5

GO ON

Name _____

12. The selection says, "Grown-ups <u>embraced</u> each other, and some reached to the sky."
<u>Embraced</u> means—
F. hugged.
G. yelled at.
H. struck.
J. cheered for.

13. The selection says, ". . . and when we finally returned to Japan, my father was asked to <u>resign</u> from diplomatic service."
<u>Resign</u> means—
A. join.
B. return.
C. quit.
D change.

14. The most important thing to Mr. Sugihara was to—
F. protect his family.
G. obey his government.
H. save people's lives.
J. make money.

15. The author's main purpose in this selection is to—
A. honor a brave act.
B. explain the causes of the war.
C. describe what it was like to be a refugee.
D. entertain readers.

STOP

© Scott Foresman 5

Main Idea and Supporting Details/Generalizing

REVIEW

Directions: Read the passage. Then read each question about the passage. Choose the best answer to each question. Mark the letter for the answer you have chosen.

D-Day

The D-Day invasion was an important event during World War II that made a big difference in the outcome of the war. That event occurred on June 6, 1944. On that day the Allied forces crossed the English Channel and attacked the German forces on the northern coast of France. The forces made this surprise landing on open beaches in the French region of Normandy.

The D-Day invasion required great planning. England, Canada, and the United States brought together some 3 million soldiers and 16 million tons of supplies in Great Britain. The Allies had 5,000 large ships, 4,000 small craft, and over 11,000 airplanes.

Months before the D-Day invasion, Allied planes bombed the Normandy coast to prevent Germans from taking over in the area. Allied soldiers cut rail lines, blew up bridges, and took control of landing strips to prepare for the invasion.

During the night of June 5, troops, jeeps, and even small tanks were brought in on gliders and warships. Beginning at 6:30 A.M. on June 6, German groups of soldiers on the coast were attacked by shells from Allied warships. All was ready for the largest land invasion in recent history—D-Day.

1. The main idea of the article is that—
   A. 3 million men fought.
   B. the D-Day invasion took planning.
   C. bridges were blown up.
   D. the D-Day invasion was June 6, 1944.

2. A detail that supports the main idea is that—
   F. 11,000 planes were used.
   G. Germans built up their forces.
   H. Britain was attacked.
   J. it happened in Normandy.

3. A detail that does **not** support the main idea is that—
   A. rail lines were cut.
   B. 5,000 ships were used.
   C. bridges were blown up.
   D. Normandy is in France.

4. A valid generalization you could make about the last paragraph is that—
   F. few warships were needed.
   G. all the troops, jeeps, and tanks were loaded on the morning of June 6.
   H. gliders and warships were important to the D-Day invasion.
   J. the D-Day invasion occurred on June 6, 1944.

5. A generalization you could make about the D-Day invasion is that—
   A. Germany was the enemy.
   B. Canada was in the war.
   C. many people took part in the invasion.
   D. the invasion was in June.

Notes for Home: Your child identified a main idea, supporting details, and general statements about an article. *Home Activity:* Read an article with your child. Invite him or her to tell you the main idea and supporting details. Look for generalizations.

© Scott Foresman 5

Name _____

Word Study: Syllabication, Common Syllable Patterns

Directions: A **syllable** is an individual part of a word that you say or hear. When a word is a compound word, it is usually divided between the two words that make up the compound word: **base • ball.** When two consonants come between two vowels (VCCV), the word is divided between the two consonants **(num • ber).** Separate each word into its syllables, using a dot **(base • ball).**

1. office _____

2. poster _____

3. downstairs _____

4. issue _____

5. outside _____

6. written _____

7. cannot _____

8. window _____

Directions: Read the words in the box. Separate each word into its syllables, using a dot **(base • ball).** Write each divided word in the correct column.

something	winter	curtains	suitcase	almost	tractor
indoors	danger	basket	flashbulb	daylight	nowhere
doctor	mittens	uptown	common	popcorn	

Compound Words

9. _____

10. _____

11. _____

12. _____

13. _____

14. _____

15. _____

16. _____

VCCV

17. _____

18. _____

19. _____

20. _____

21. _____

22. _____

23. _____

24. _____

25. _____

Notes for Home: Your child separated words into their syllable parts, such as *baseball* (*base • ball*). **Home Activity:** Read recipes, food packages, and game notes. Look for two-syllable words. Say each word aloud and clap to show its syllables.

© Scott Foresman 5

Name _____

Schedule

A **schedule** is a special chart that lists events and tells when they take place, such as the arrival and departure times of planes, trains, and buses.

Directions: The schedules below show airline flights and times between Boston, Massachusetts, and St. Louis, Missouri. Use these schedules to answer the questions on the next page.

To St. Louis, Missouri			
Flight Number	**Leave Boston**	**Arrive St. Louis**	**Frequency**
123	5:50 A.M.	8:06 A.M.	Daily
321	8:15 A.M.	10:21 A.M.	Daily
557	11:20 A.M.	1:24 P.M.	Daily
55	2:00 P.M.	4:10 P.M.	Daily
287	5:20 P.M.	7:40 P.M.	Daily
727	7:35 P.M.	9:46 P.M.	Daily Ex. Sat.

To Boston, Massachusetts			
Flight Number	**Leave St. Louis**	**Arrive Boston**	**Frequency**
222	7:54 A.M.	11:35 A.M.	Daily
354	10:23 A.M.	2:04 P.M.	Daily
408	12:50 P.M.	4:26 P.M.	Daily
292	4:20 P.M.	7:45 P.M.	Daily
156	6:55 P.M.	10:40 P.M.	Daily
166	9:30 P.M.	1:04 A.M.	Daily Ex. Sat.

© Scott Foresman 5

1. Sara has been visiting her brother in St. Louis for the weekend. She needs to be back in Boston by noon on Monday. What is the latest flight she can take on Monday morning? What time will she arrive in Boston?

_____

_____

_____

2. Gary is attending a meeting in Boston. His meeting ends at 5:00 P.M. on Friday. It takes one hour to get to the airport. Will he be able to get home to St. Louis on Friday night, or will he have to wait until Saturday? Explain.

_____

_____

_____

3. Flights that arrive at their destinations between midnight and 5:00 A.M. are less expensive than other flights. What flight would qualify for the less expensive rate? Explain.

_____

_____

_____

4. Gayle likes to travel between 10:00 A.M. and 4:30 P.M. She wants to fly from St. Louis to Boston on Monday. She wants to return to St. Louis on Saturday. What flights could she take to make this trip during the hours she prefers?

_____

_____

_____

5. Henry lives and works in St. Louis. On Wednesday at 10:00 A.M., Henry received a call at work from a family member in Boston. He has to fly to Boston as soon as possible. It will take him an hour and a half to go home, pack, and get to the airport. What is the earliest he can arrive in Boston? Explain how you figured out the answer.

_____

_____

_____

_____

Notes for Home: Your child has read and interpreted an airline schedule. *Home Activity:* Find a schedule of television programs. Read the schedule with your child. Take turns saying what each line means. For example: The news is on today at 5:00 P.M. and at 10:00 P.M.

© Scott Foresman 5

Name _____

Paraphrasing

- **Paraphrasing** is explaining something in your own words.
- When you paraphrase, you restate ideas without changing their original meaning or adding your own opinion.

Directions: Reread "Samuel Adams." Then complete the table. Paraphrase each original statement in your own words. (The beginning words of each sentence will help you find the sentence to paraphrase.)

Original Statement	My Paraphrase
Introduction, Paragraph 1, Sentence 1 "Samuel Adams didn't want. . . ."	1.
Paragraph 3, Sentence 1 "On April 18 the redcoats. . . ."	2.
Paragraph 3, Sentence 3 "The more trouble there was. . . ."	3.
Paragraph 6, Sentence 1 "Samuel jumped out. . . ."	4.
Paragraph 6, Sentence 3 "John also jumped out. . . ."	5.

Notes for Home: Your child read an article and restated its ideas in his or her own words. *Home Activity:* Challenge your child to listen to part of a family conversation and then paraphrase what each speaker said.

© Scott Foresman 5

Name _____

Vocabulary

Directions: Match each word on the left with its definition on the right.
Write the letter of the definition next to the word.

_____ 1. lingers   **a.** destiny

_____ 2. magnified   **b.** delays in starting

_____ 3. tread   **c.** faint, unsteady light

_____ 4. fate   **d.** walk

_____ 5. somber   **e.** caused to look larger

_____ 6. glimmer   **f.** gloomy

Check the Words You Know
__ fate
__ fearless
__ glimmer
__ lingers
__ magnified
__ somber
__ steed
__ tread

Directions: Read the help-wanted advertisement. Choose the word from
the box that best completes each sentence. Write the word on the matching
numbered line to the right.

7. _____

8. _____

9. _____

10. _____

HERO WANTED

Bold, **7.** _____ hero needed to help
American colonists fight for
freedom. The cause is serious and
the situation is **8.** _____. Must be
steady and willing to work hard.
Fast horseback riding required, so
must provide own **9.** _____. The
10. _____ of the nation may be in
your hands.

Write a Poem

On a separate sheet of paper, write a poem that alerts people to an important
problem, such as the destruction of the rain forests. Describe the problem and
some possible solutions. Use as many vocabulary words as you can.

Notes for Home: Your child identified and used vocabulary words from *Paul Revere's Ride*.
Home Activity: Have your child write a telegram announcing a heroic act by a friend, family
member, or public figure.

© Scott Foresman 5

Paraphrasing

- **Paraphrasing** is explaining something in your own words.

- When you paraphrase, include only the author's ideas and opinions and do not change the author's meaning.

Directions: Reread what happened in *Paul Revere's Ride* when Paul watched for the tower signal. Then answer the questions below.

But mostly he watched with eager search
The belfry tower of the Old North Church,
As it rose above the graves on the hill,
Lonely and spectral and somber and still.
And lo! as he looks, on the belfry's height
A glimmer, and then a gleam of light!
He springs to the saddle, the bridle he turns,
But lingers and gazes, till full on his sight
A second lamp in the belfry burns!

From "Paul Revere's Ride" from TALES OF THE WAYSIDE INN by Henry Wadsworth Longfellow, 1863.

1. How might you paraphrase lines 1 and 2 as a single sentence?

_____

_____

2. How might you paraphrase lines 5 and 6 as a single sentence?

_____

_____

3. How might you paraphrase line 7 as a single sentence?

_____

_____

4. How might you paraphrase lines 8 and 9 as a single sentence?

_____

_____

5. When you paraphrase, why is it important not to change the author's ideas and opinions?

Notes for Home: Your child read a poem and then retold parts of it in his or her own words. *Home Activity:* Read a story with your child. Have him pick out sentences and restate the same ideas in his or her own words.

© Scott Foresman 5

Name _____

1.	Ⓐ	Ⓑ	Ⓒ	Ⓓ
2.	Ⓕ	Ⓖ	Ⓗ	Ⓙ
3.	Ⓐ	Ⓑ	Ⓒ	Ⓓ
4.	Ⓕ	Ⓖ	Ⓗ	Ⓙ
5.	Ⓐ	Ⓑ	Ⓒ	Ⓓ
6.	Ⓕ	Ⓖ	Ⓗ	Ⓙ
7.	Ⓐ	Ⓑ	Ⓒ	Ⓓ
8.	Ⓕ	Ⓖ	Ⓗ	Ⓙ
9.	Ⓐ	Ⓑ	Ⓒ	Ⓓ
10.	Ⓕ	Ⓖ	Ⓗ	Ⓙ
11.	Ⓐ	Ⓑ	Ⓒ	Ⓓ
12.	Ⓕ	Ⓖ	Ⓗ	Ⓙ
13.	Ⓐ	Ⓑ	Ⓒ	Ⓓ
14.	Ⓕ	Ⓖ	Ⓗ	Ⓙ
15.	Ⓐ	Ⓑ	Ⓒ	Ⓓ

© Scott Foresman 5

Selection Test

Directions: Choose the best answer to each item. Mark the letter for the answer
you have chosen.

Part 1: Vocabulary

Find the answer choice that means about the
same as the underlined word in each sentence.

1. Sarah is completely <u>fearless</u>.
   A. making others afraid
   B. without fear
   C. very clever
   D. acting in a frightened way

2. The window <u>magnified</u> the tree outside.
   F. caused to look darker
   G. hid
   H. showed
   J. caused to look larger

3. Philip saw a <u>glimmer</u> in the woods.
   A. faint light
   B. dark shape
   C. tall tree
   D. red bird

4. The building looked very <u>somber</u>.
   F. wealthy
   G. elegant
   H. proper
   J. gloomy

5. The soldier wondered what his <u>fate</u> would
   be.
   A. position in the army
   B. what happens in the future
   C. meal
   D. punishment

6. The last guest <u>lingers</u>.
   F. delays in starting
   G. leaves
   H. travels
   J. is repaired

7. I heard the man's <u>tread</u> on the stairs.
   A. footstep
   B. loud crash
   C. squeaking noise
   D. ringing bell

8. The prince called for his <u>steed</u>.
   F. protective clothing for battle
   G. helper
   H. old-fashioned weapon
   J. horse

Part 2: Comprehension

Use what you know about the poem to answer
each item.

9. Where did Paul Revere wait for the signal?
   A. in the belfry of the North Church
   B. on a farm in Lexington
   C. on the bridge in Concord
   D. across the water from the North
       Church

10. Revere's friend in the North Church belfry
    noticed that the British were—
    F. marching toward Connecticut.
    G. returning quietly to their camps.
    H. heading to Concord by boat.
    J. heading toward Paul Revere's hiding
        place.

© Scott Foresman 5

GO ON

11. "He heard the bleating of the flock, / And the twitter of birds among the trees." Which is the best paraphrase of these lines?
- A. He scared the flock of sheep as he rode by.
- B. The bleating of sheep made him keep riding.
- C. He heard the sounds made by sheep and birds.
- D. Birds and a flock of sheep waved to him.

12. "And one was safe and asleep in his bed / Who at the bridge would be first to fall." Which is the best paraphrase of these lines?
- F. The man who would die first that day was still sleeping.
- G. The bridge was still safe, but it fell that day.
- H. While everyone else was sleeping, a man fell off the bridge.
- J. A man dreamed that he would be the first to die.

13. What can you conclude from the information in this poem?
- A. The British wanted the patriots to know they were coming.
- B. Paul Revere's friend discovered the British troops by accident.
- C. The patriots in Concord and Lexington were waiting for the British.
- D. Paul Revere was secretly working for the British.

14. The speaker in this poem often mentions shadows, silence, and graveyards to—
- F. show that Revere was a gloomy fellow.
- G. remind the reader that war and death were coming soon.
- H. suggest that Paul Revere's ride was all a bad dream.
- J. give the poem a peaceful, happy mood.

15. The end of this poem suggests that Paul Revere's ride stands for—
- A. the horror of war.
- B. cleverness and secrecy.
- C. fear and alarm.
- D. the struggle for freedom.

STOP

© Scott Foresman 5

Visualizing

Directions: Read the story. Then read each question about the story. Choose the best answer to each question. Mark the letter for the answer you have chosen.

The Battle of Bunker Hill

Johnny was only eighteen years old, yet he was doing a man's job. He stood on Breed's Hill, next to Bunker Hill, overlooking the city of Boston. Other armed patriots stood all around him. They watched silently as the British prepared to attack.

Time stood still as Johnny waited with the others. Finally a long line of redcoats began marching up the steep hill. To Johnny, the long line of enemy soldiers looked like one huge, red monster. A drummer beat a steady rhythm as the British troops came toward him.

As the soldiers drew near, Johnny took aim with his rough, heavy rifle. It felt uncomfortable in his hands. On the captain's order, a tremendous blast of gunfire erupted. It sounded like an explosion.

Smoke from the muskets filled the air and Johnny's lungs. His mouth went dry suddenly, as if he had been chewing on cotton. Johnny reloaded his musket and prepared to fire again.

Twice, the British charged up the hill and both times the patriots drove them back. At the third charge, Johnny found he was out of gunpowder. He left the battle field, along with most of the other Americans. It didn't matter. They had won what would come to be called the Battle of Bunker Hill.

1. The image "a long line of enemy began marching" appeals to the sense of—
   A. hearing
   B. sight
   C. touch
   D. taste

2. The image "a drummer beat a steady rhythm" appeals to the sense of—
   F. hearing
   G. sight
   H. touch
   J. smell

3. The image "rough, heavy rifle" appeals to the sense of —
   A. hearing
   B. sight
   C. touch
   D. taste

4. The image "smoke from the muskets filled the air and Johnny's lungs" appeals to the sense of—
   F. hearing
   G. sight
   H. touch
   J. smell

5. The image "chewing on cotton" appeals to the sense of—
   A. hearing
   B. sight
   C. touch
   D. taste

Notes for Home: Your child read a story and used its sensory details to picture the story in his or her mind. **Home Activity:** Read a poem with descriptive details. Have your child describe what he or she sees, hears, tastes, feels, or smells, based on the details.

© Scott Foresman 5

Word Study: Word Building

Directions: Say each pair of related words to yourself. Listen for the syllable that is stressed in each word. Write **same** if the same word part is stressed in each pair. Write **different** if different word parts are stressed in each pair.

_____ **1.** real   reality

_____ **2.** oppose   opposite

_____ **3.** sorrow   sorrowful

_____ **4.** history   historical

_____ **5.** office   officer

Directions: When you add a suffix to a word, you have built a new word. Most of the time, the base word still sounds the same. But sometimes when you add a suffix, you change the way the base word sounds. Read the paragraph below. Say each underlined word to yourself. Write each word in the correct column.

> The patriot's <u>curiosity</u> was aroused by a strange ship moored on the <u>opposite</u> shore. He sent a <u>respectful</u> <u>inquiry</u> to the ship's captain to ask its purpose. No one responded. <u>Plainly</u>, he thought, the newcomers are up to no good. He feared that they were <u>dangerous</u>. He leaped onto his horse. This journey would not be a <u>pleasure</u>. By riding hard under the cover of <u>darkness</u>, he could get a <u>signal</u> to his compatriots. The <u>sooner</u> they learned the news, the better.

Base Word Sound Unchanged

6. _____

7. _____

8. _____

9. _____

10. _____

Base Word Sound Changed

11. _____

12. _____

13. _____

14. _____

15. _____

 Notes for Home: Your child recognized sound changes when building new words by adding suffixes to base words. **Home Activity:** Read a magazine article with your child. Look for words with suffixes, and ask your child to identify which base words sound different with the suffix added.

© Scott Foresman 5

Name _____

Study Strategies

Learning and using different **study strategies** can help you better understand what you read and help you focus on the most important information.

Directions: Three different study strategies are described on the index cards below. Each one is a little different. Read about them and then answer the questions that follow.

Skim and Scan

When you skim, you glance through a piece of writing quickly to get a general idea of what it is about. When you scan, you read quickly to locate specific information, key words or ideas, or to answer a specific question.

SQ2R

SQ2R stands for Survey, Question, Read, and Recite. First you survey a new work by looking at its title, author, chapter titles, headings, picture captions, and so on. Then think of questions you want to find out about that you think might be answered in the reading. Then, as you read, look for answers to the questions. Finally, recite by telling what you learned.

K-W-L

"K-W-L" stands for "What I Know," "What I Want to Know," and "What I Learned." The letters go at the top of a chart. Before reading, list what you already know in the K column. Write questions you still have in the W column. As you read, write answers to your questions in the L column. Also write in the L column additional interesting information you discovered.

K What I Know	W What I Want to Know	L What I Learned

1. Which strategy would you use if you wanted to find major battles with their dates in an encyclopedia article about the Revolution? Explain.

_____

_____

2. Which strategy would you use for reading an article from *American History Magazine* about the winter of 1777 at Valley Forge? Explain.

_____

_____

© Scott Foresman 5

3. Which strategy would you use for reading a new biography of Paul Revere? Explain.

_____

_____

4. Which strategy would you use to review a chapter of your textbook for a test on the American Revolution? Explain.

_____

_____

5. Which strategy would you use to decide whether to read a historical novel about Abigail Adams? Explain.

_____

_____

6. Which strategy would you use for reading a nonfiction book about the role Native Americans played in the American Revolution? Explain.

_____

_____

7. Which strategy would you use to decide whether a historical atlas would be a useful resource for your Revolutionary War research? Explain.

_____

_____

8. Which strategy would you use for reading an illustrated history of the American Revolution? Explain.

_____

_____

9. Which strategy would you use for reading a collection of letters and diaries by American colonists during the Revolution? Explain.

_____

_____

10. Suppose you were reading a nonfiction text about Paul Revere's ride. What are some questions you might ask yourself that you could then use one of the study strategies to help you find the answers?

_____

_____

 Notes for Home: Your child made decisions about which of three study strategies works best with different kinds of texts. *Home Activity:* Discuss with your child a subject you would like to know more about. Make and complete a K-W-L chart like the one shown.

© Scott Foresman 5

Theme

- **Theme** is an underlying meaning or message of a story. Themes can be statements, lessons, or generalizations that stand on their own, such as: *Life is what you make of it.*

- Sometimes the author states the theme directly. Sometimes readers have to figure out a theme on their own by asking, "What did I learn from reading this story?"

Directions: Reread "King Midas." Then complete the table. Answer the questions in order to determine the story's theme.

Questions	Answers
What did King Midas wish for?	1.
Why did King Midas make the wish that he did?	2.
Why was Bacchus disappointed by King Midas' wish?	3.
What ultimately happened to King Midas?	4.
What lesson does this story teach you?	5.

 Notes for Home: Your child read a story and identified its theme, or message. ***Home Activity:*** Read a story with your child. Later, talk about the lesson that it teaches. Discuss what the main characters learn from their experiences in the story.

© Scott Foresman 5

Vocabulary

Directions: Choose the word from the box that best matches each clue.
Write the word on the line.

Check the Words You Know
__ fragrance
__ inspects
__ pastries
__ pleasures
__ privilege
__ scowling
__ trial

_____ 1. A grumpy person is always doing it.

_____ 2. This decides if a person is guilty or
not guilty.

_____ 3. Don't eat too many of these sweet treats.

_____ 4. It's what an inspector does.

_____ 5. It appeals to the sense of smell.

Directions: Choose the word from the box that best completes each sentence.
Write the word on the line to the left.

_____ 6. A good baker _____ his ingredients before he
starts to bake.

_____ 7. He uses only the finest flour, sugar, and butter
to make _____.

_____ 8. A delicious _____ wafts from the bakery.

_____ 9. His neighbors feel it is a _____ to live next door.

_____ 10. There are so many _____ to being a baker's
good friend!

Write a Recipe

What is your favorite dish? On a separate sheet of paper, write a recipe for it. List
the ingredients and steps in the preparation. Don't forget to tell how good the
food tastes and smells! Use as many vocabulary words as you can in your recipe.

Notes for Home: Your child identified and used vocabulary words from "The Baker's
Neighbor." **Home Activity:** Act out with your child a conversation between a baker and a
customer. Use as many listed vocabulary words as you can.

© Scott Foresman 5

Theme

- **Theme** is an underlying meaning or message of a story. Themes can be statements, lessons, or generalizations that stand on their own, such as: *Life is what you make of it.*

- Sometimes the author states the theme directly. Sometimes readers have to figure out a theme on their own by asking, "What did I learn from reading this story?"

Directions: Reread what happens in "The Baker's Neighbor" when the judge makes his ruling. Then answer the questions below.

JUDGE: No, I did not tell him to pay it to you. I told him to put it on this table. Then I instructed you to count the money, which you did. In doing so, you enjoyed Pablo's money the way he enjoyed your cakes and pies. In other words, he has smelled your pastry and you have touched his gold. Therefore, I hereby declare that the case is now settled. *(He raps twice with his gavel.*

MANUEL *shamefacedly shoves purse across table to* PABLO *and turns to leave.* JUDGE *stops him.)* Just a moment, Manuel! I hope this has been a lesson to you. In the future, think less about making money and more about making friends. Good friends and neighbors are better than gold. And now, if you please—my fee!

Reprinted by permission. From PLAYS FROM FAVORITE FOLKTALES, edited by Sylvia E. Kamerman. Copyright © 1987 by Sylvia K. Burack.

1. Why does the judge tell Manuel to count Pablo's money?

_____

_____

2. What is the final judgment in the case?

_____

_____

3. What lesson does the Judge want Manuel to learn?

_____

_____

4. Which sentence might be a statement of the play's theme?

_____

_____

5. Read "The Baker's Neighbor" again. On a separate sheet of paper, restate the theme in your own words.

Notes for Home: Your child read a play and identified its theme. *Home Activity:* With your child, read a fable or folk tale and identify its theme, or big idea. Discuss what lessons the story might be trying to teach its readers.

© Scott Foresman 5

Name _____

1.	Ⓐ	Ⓑ	Ⓒ	Ⓓ
2.	Ⓕ	Ⓖ	Ⓗ	Ⓙ
3.	Ⓐ	Ⓑ	Ⓒ	Ⓓ
4.	Ⓕ	Ⓖ	Ⓗ	Ⓙ
5.	Ⓐ	Ⓑ	Ⓒ	Ⓓ
6.	Ⓕ	Ⓖ	Ⓗ	Ⓙ
7.	Ⓐ	Ⓑ	Ⓒ	Ⓓ
8.	Ⓕ	Ⓖ	Ⓗ	Ⓙ
9.	Ⓐ	Ⓑ	Ⓒ	Ⓓ
10.	Ⓕ	Ⓖ	Ⓗ	Ⓙ
11.	Ⓐ	Ⓑ	Ⓒ	Ⓓ
12.	Ⓕ	Ⓖ	Ⓗ	Ⓙ
13.	Ⓐ	Ⓑ	Ⓒ	Ⓓ
14.	Ⓕ	Ⓖ	Ⓗ	Ⓙ
15.	Ⓐ	Ⓑ	Ⓒ	Ⓓ

© Scott Foresman 5

254 Answer Key

Selection Test

Directions: Choose the best answer to each item. Mark the letter for the answer you have chosen.

Part 1: Vocabulary

Find the answer choice that means about the same as the underlined word in each sentence.

1. The traveler inspects the hotel.
   - A.   enters
   - B.   describes in words
   - C.   visits again
   - D.   looks at closely

2. Aunt Melanie brought pastries to the party.
   - F.   gifts
   - G.   bakery goods
   - H.   things for decorating
   - J.   guests

3. What is that wonderful fragrance?
   - A.   smell
   - B.   music
   - C.   color
   - D.   flavor

4. Jasper was scowling throughout the game.
   - F.   clapping loudly
   - G.   yelling
   - H.   looking angry
   - J.   whispering

5. Niki acts as if she has some special privilege.
   - A.   gift
   - B.   information
   - C.   right
   - D.   skill

6. The trial was covered in the newspaper.
   - F.   big party
   - G.   recount of votes in an election
   - H.   championship game
   - J.   deciding of a case of law

7. Mom wrote us a letter describing the pleasures of her trip.
   - A.   problems
   - B.   things that are enjoyed
   - C.   places where one stops
   - D.   reasons for doing something

Part 2: Comprehension

Use what you know about the play to answer each item.

8. After Manuel sets his pies out in the morning, he—
   - F.   lies down to rest.
   - G.   travels from door to door selling his pies.
   - H.   invites the neighborhood children to sample his pies.
   - J.   counts his money.

9. At the beginning of the play, why is Manuel angry with Pablo?
   - A.   Pablo does not think Manuel's pies are very good.
   - B.   Pablo makes more money than Manuel.
   - C.   Pablo enjoys Manuel's pies without paying for them.
   - D.   Pablo sends children to Manuel's to beg for free pies.

10. What is Pablo's attitude about work?
   - F.   He works when he has to.
   - G.   He thinks work is the most important thing in life.
   - H.   A man should have his children support him.
   - J.   He would like to work part time for Manuel.

© Scott Foresman 5

GO ON

11. When the children ask what sound Pablo would like to be, he says that —
    A. he would like to be a song.
    B. he would like to be gold coins jingling.
    C. the question is a foolish waste of time.
    D. only children could think up such a question.

12. Which best states a theme of this play?
    F. People need to work hard to get ahead in life.
    G. When people grow up, they should stop acting like children.
    H. Some of life's simple pleasures don't have a price.
    J. It is just as bad to be greedy for food as to be greedy for money.

13. Which sentences from the story best help support the theme?
    A. "It has not yet been proved that Pablo is a thief. First he must have a fair trial."
    B. "Every night I mix the flour and knead the dough and slave over a hot oven while that shiftless, good-for-nothing Pablo sleeps."
    C. "I am a man of simple pleasures. Just the smell of a bakery makes me happy!"
    D. "I must make sure I haven't been cheated. How kind of you to remind me!"

14. The Judge decided the case the way he did because he wanted to—
    F. show everyone that stealing is punished severely.
    G. have people make fun of Manuel.
    H. scare Pablo so that he would stop smelling the pies.
    J. make Manuel truly understand why Pablo was innocent.

15. The writer probably ends the play with the Judge and Pablo eating the same pie in order to—
    A. have it end in a funny way.
    B. show that the Judge is just as greedy as Manuel.
    C. add an air of excitement.
    D. prove that the pies really taste good.

© Scott Foresman 5

STOP

Name _____

Name _____

REVIEW

Compare and Contrast

Directions: Read the story. Then read each question about the story. Choose the best answer to each question. Mark the letter for the answer you have chosen.

Resolving Conflict

Maggie and Beth both tend to have many conflicts with their friends. They handle these conflicts differently, however. Maggie tries to resolve problems by sitting down and talking with her friends. Beth, on the other hand, tends to dwell on the misunderstandings.

When Maggie has a disagreement with her friends, she listens to them and they listen to her. They come to understand each other's point of view and work out a resolution to their problem. Maggie's friendships don't seem to suffer from the fact that there are conflicts.

Beth refuses to sit down and talk out the differences honestly with the person with whom she disagrees. As a result, the conflicts between Beth and her friends never get resolved. The fights go on and on.

When the girls have conflicts with their parents, they use the same approaches as they do with their friends. Last week, for instance, both girls had trouble with their parents over their math grades.

Maggie agreed to sit down with her parents and talk about her math grade. She explained that she just didn't understand the new material and was too embarrassed to ask her teacher for extra help. Then she let her parents talk.

Beth, however, simply got angry when her parents brought up the subject of her math grade. She threw her math book on the floor, stormed out of the kitchen, slammed the door of her room, and sulked.

1. From the first paragraph, we learn that Maggie and Beth both—
   A. settle conflicts by talking.
   B. dwell on conflicts.
   C. tend to argue with friends.
   D. have a lot of friends.

2. In the first paragraph, the author shows contrast with the clue words—
   F. however, on the other hand.
   G. both, conflicts.
   H. resolve, dwell.
   J. sitting down, talking.

3. In the fourth paragraph, the author shows comparison with the clue word—
   A. for instance.
   B. both.
   C. when.
   D. conflicts.

4. In the fourth and fifth paragraphs, the author contrasts—
   F. the girls' grades in math.
   G. how the girls deal with their parents.
   H. the reactions of the girls' parents.
   J. the difficulty of growing up.

5. Overall, the girls are—
   A. exactly alike.
   B. completely different.
   C. alike in the way they handle conflicts.
   D. different in the way they handle conflicts.

Notes for Home: Your child read a story and identified comparisons and contrasts in the text. *Home Activity:* Have your child compare and contrast the ways that different family members or friends settle conflicts.

© Scott Foresman 5

Phonics: Vowel Digraphs

Directions: Read the words in the box. Each word contains the vowel combination **ea,** but the words have different vowel sounds. Write each word in the correct column.

steal	please	pleasure
tread	treat	break
great	steak	instead

Long e Sound

1. _____

2. _____

3. _____

Short e Sound

4. _____

5. _____

6. _____

Long a Sound

7. _____

8. _____

9. _____

Directions: Read the words in the box. Even though some words have the same vowel combination, the vowels have different vowel sounds. Write each word in the correct column.

pies	tough	belief	dough	tries
enough	pieces	ties	though	thief

Long o Sound

10. _____

11. _____

Long e Sound

12. _____

13. _____

14. _____

Short u Sound

15. _____

16. _____

Long i Sound

17. _____

18. _____

19. _____

Directions: Write six words that have the **long a** sound spelled **ay** as in **way** on the lines below.

20. _____

21. _____

22. _____

23. _____

24. _____

25. _____

Notes for Home: Your child distinguished between different vowel sounds for words with *ea, ou, ie,* and *ay.* **Home Activity:** With your child, write words with these vowel combinations on slips of paper. Say each word aloud and group the words that have the same vowel sounds and spellings.

© Scott Foresman 5

Name _____

Advertisement/Order Form

An **advertisement** is an announcement that tries to persuade readers, viewers, or listeners to do something, buy something, or feel a particular way about something. An **order form** is a chart that allows a person to respond to an advertisement or catalog.

Directions: Read the advertisement and order form below. Then answer the questions on the next page.

Momma's Marvelous Muffins Can't seem to wake up? One taste of Momma's Marvelous Muffins will wake you up and make you smile!

Just ask the basketball star, Harriet Hoopster. She eats Momma's Muffins every single morning, and her team has not lost a game all year.

Momma's Marvelous Muffins come in six delicious flavors: outrageous orange, raisin razzmatazz, strawberry surprise, peanut butter perfection, lemon zip, and blueberry bonanza.

Every bite is loaded with great flavor.

Order your muffins by phone, fax, mail, or in person.

Call 1-888-555-2020 today, or use the handy order form below.

Visit our web site at www.marvmuffins.com. for more information.

---

1. Ship to:

   Name _____

   Address _____

   _____

   Phone Number _____

2. Method of payment

   ____ check

   ____ credit card

   Card number: _____

3. Muffins ordered (order in boxes of six each)

ITEM	Quantity	Price per box	Cost
Outrageous Orange		$12.00	
Raisin Razzmatazz		$12.00	
Strawberry Surprise		$12.00	
Peanut Butter Perfection		$10.00	
Lemon Zip		$10.00	
Blueberry Bonanza		$14.00	

Mail to *Momma's Marvelous Muffins,* 15390 Delicious Drive, Bakerville, MD 20888.

Or fax your completed order form to 1-888-555-2025.

Subtotal	
Add shipping and handling.	
$10–$24 $1.50	
$25–$49 $2.50	
over $50 $3.50	
Subtotal, shipping and handling	
TOTAL	

© Scott Foresman 5

Name _____

1. What information in this advertisement are statements of fact? _____

_____

_____

_____

2. What information in this advertisement are statements of opinion? _____

_____

_____

_____

3. What exaggerated claim does this advertisement make? _____

_____

_____

4. What conclusion does the advertiser want you to draw about Harriet Hoopster's team's winning record?

_____

_____

5. If you order muffins by mail, how can you pay for them? _____

_____

6. How many muffins come in a box? _____

7. What is the price of a box of Lemon Zip muffins? _____

8. What would the shipping and handling costs be on an order worth $34.00? How do you know?

_____

_____

9. How can you send the order form to the company? _____

_____

10. Suppose your class decided to order two boxes of Outrageous Orange, one box of Strawberry Surprise, and three boxes of Blueberry Bonanza muffins. Fill out the order form. Then write the total amount you must pay on the line below.

_____

_____

Notes for Home: Your child read and interpreted an advertisement and filled out an order form. *Home Activity:* Look through magazines with your child. Talk about the ways the advertisers try to sell their merchandise. Then study an order form together and help your child fill it out.

© Scott Foresman 5

Name _____

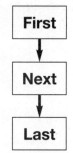

Steps in a Process

> - **Steps in a process** are the actions you take to reach a goal or to make something.
> - Sometimes steps in a process are shown by numbers or clue words *(first, next, then,* and *last)*. If there are no clues, use common sense to picture the steps.

First
↓
Next
↓
Last

Directions: Reread "Beetle Research." Then write the following steps in the order that they should be performed. The first step is done for you.

Steps

Compare beetles caught at different times of the day.
Cover the cup with the stones and the wood.
Gather a jar or plastic cup, four stones, and a small piece of wood.
Remove the trap when you have finished.
Bury the cup level with the surface.
Put food in the cup to see what attracts certain species.

Making a Pitfall Trap

Gather a jar or plastic cup, four stones, and a small piece of wood.

↓

1.

↓

2.

↓

3.

↓

4.

↓

5.

Notes for Home: Your child read about a process and then identified its steps in order. **_Home Activity:_** Choose a job that your child performs, such as doing the laundry or setting the dinner table. Work together to list all the steps of the process in order.

© Scott Foresman 5

Vocabulary

Directions: Draw a line to connect each word on the left with its definition on the right.

Check the Words You Know

__ clenched
__ comparing
__ cornmeal
__ essay
__ flyer
__ grease
__ primitive

1. essay   of early times

2. flyer   seeing similarities and differences

3. primitive   written composition

4. comparing   coarsely ground dried corn

5. cornmeal   brochure

Directions: Read the recipe. Choose the word from the box that best completes each sentence. Write the word on the matching numbered line to the right.

Fried Worms

This old family recipe dates all the way back to **6.** _____ times. I **7.** _____ my teeth when I first tried them, but I love them now. **8.** _____ the taste to chicken, I'd say worms are sweeter and less chewy.

Step 1: Dip one dozen fat, juicy earthworms in a beaten egg.

Step 2: Roll the worms in 1 cup of **9.** _____ or flour.

Step 3: Melt 2 tablespoons butter or **10.** _____ in a skillet.

Step 4: Fry the worms in the hot fat for 2–3 minutes, or until brown and crispy. Drain on a paper towel. Enjoy!

6. _____

7. _____

8. _____

9. _____

10. _____

Write Contest Rules

Imagine you are in charge of a creative cooking contest. On a separate sheet of paper, write the contest rules. Explain the type of contest, who can enter, and the prizes. Use as many vocabulary words as you can.

Notes for Home: Your child identified and used vocabulary words from "Andy's Secret Ingredient." **Home Activity:** Have your child write a story about the strangest food he or she has ever tasted. Guide your child to use as many vocabulary words as possible.

© Scott Foresman 5

Steps in a Process

- **Steps in a process** are the actions you take to reach a goal or to make something.
- Sometimes steps in a process are shown by numbers or clue words *(first, next, then,* and *last)*. If there are no clues, use common sense to picture the steps.

Directions: Reread what happens in "Andy's Secret Ingredient" when Andy makes his special brownies. Then answer the questions below.

> The batter was dark and moist. When the flour and eggs and sugar had been mixed, Andy put in a quarter of a cup of chopped walnuts and then, his teeth clenched, a quarter of a cup of chopped beetle.
>
> All the time the brownies were baking, Andy wondered if he could smell the beetles.
>
> When the brownies were done, he took them out, cooled them for twenty minutes, then cut them into squares and piled them onto a platter. He was just washing out the bowl and spoon in the sink when Wendell came into the kitchen, a screwdriver hanging out of one pocket.
>
> Reprinted with the permission of Atheneum Books for Young Readers, an imprint of Simon & Schuster Children's Publishing Division from BEETLES, LIGHTLY TOASTED by Phyllis Reynolds Naylor. Copyright © 1987 by Phyllis Reynolds Naylor.

1. What is the first step in the process described here?

_____

_____

2. What are the second and third steps in the process?

_____

_____

3. What steps does Andy take when the brownies are done?

_____

_____

4. What is the last thing Andy does?

_____

_____

5. On a separate sheet of paper, tell how Andy prepares the beetles he has found for baking. List the steps in order.

Notes for Home: Your child read a story and identified the order of steps in a process. *Home Activity:* Using a simple recipe, bake cookies or brownies with your child. Check to make sure he or she follows the recipe steps in the correct order.

© Scott Foresman 5

Name _____

1.	Ⓐ	Ⓑ	Ⓒ	Ⓓ
2.	Ⓕ	Ⓖ	Ⓗ	Ⓙ
3.	Ⓐ	Ⓑ	Ⓒ	Ⓓ
4.	Ⓕ	Ⓖ	Ⓗ	Ⓙ
5.	Ⓐ	Ⓑ	Ⓒ	Ⓓ
6.	Ⓕ	Ⓖ	Ⓗ	Ⓙ
7.	Ⓐ	Ⓑ	Ⓒ	Ⓓ
8.	Ⓕ	Ⓖ	Ⓗ	Ⓙ
9.	Ⓐ	Ⓑ	Ⓒ	Ⓓ
10.	Ⓕ	Ⓖ	Ⓗ	Ⓙ
11.	Ⓐ	Ⓑ	Ⓒ	Ⓓ
12.	Ⓕ	Ⓖ	Ⓗ	Ⓙ
13.	Ⓐ	Ⓑ	Ⓒ	Ⓓ
14.	Ⓕ	Ⓖ	Ⓗ	Ⓙ
15.	Ⓐ	Ⓑ	Ⓒ	Ⓓ

© Scott Foresman 5

Selection Test

Directions: Choose the best answer to each item. Mark the letter for the answer you have chosen.

Part 1: Vocabulary

Find the answer choice that means about the same as the underlined word in each sentence.

1. Marisol <u>clenched</u> her fists.
   A. cleaned
   B. looked at carefully
   C. closed tightly
   D. raised

2. Jan studies how <u>primitive</u> people lived.
   F. simple, as in early times
   G. from a different country
   H. very smart
   J. of the forest

3. Grandma bought some <u>cornmeal</u>.
   A. corn kernels
   B. pancakes made from corn
   C. coarsely ground dried corn
   D. corn syrup

4. She placed the fish in the hot <u>grease</u>.
   F. oil
   G. salt
   H. spice
   J. oven

5. Our teacher was <u>comparing</u> two countries.
   A. traveling to
   B. seeing how things are alike in
   C. discussing the history of
   D. listing all the things wrong with

6. A woman handed me a <u>flyer</u>.
   F. free sample of food
   G. young turkey
   H. ticket for an airplane flight
   J. paper handed out for advertising

7. Kala finished her <u>essay</u>.
   A. daily chore
   B. speech read aloud
   C. physical exercise
   D. written composition

Part 2: Comprehension

Use what you know about the story to answer each item.

8. In what kind of project is Andy involved?
   F. an essay contest
   G. a cooking contest
   H. an animal-raising project
   J. a project to raise money

9. What is Andy's attitude toward his cousin Jack?
   A. Andy feels sorry for Jack and wants to help him.
   B. Andy feels that he and Jack make a great team.
   C. Andy feels that he and Jack are always in a competition.
   D. Andy doesn't want to do anything that Jack does.

10. Andy begins planning for his essay by—
    F. running away from the turkey.
    G. writing a letter to the university.
    H. deciding that he does not like catfish.
    J. letting Wendell eat a brownie.

11. What is the first step Andy takes in preparing the beetles?
    A. He puts them in the freezer.
    B. He washes them.
    C. He puts them in a cookie tin with a tight lid.
    D. He feeds them cornmeal.

12. Just before Andy chops the beetles into pieces, he—
    F. rolls them in cornmeal.
    G. freezes them.
    H. peels off the wings and legs.
    J. toasts them.

GO ON

© Scott Foresman 5

13. Through his experiment with the beetles, Andy wants to show that—
    A. beetles can live in a freezer.
    B. people don't care what is in their food as long as it tastes good.
    C. he can bake as well as his mother can.
    D. people can eat bugs.

14. What will Andy probably do when he takes his brownies to school?
    F. decide that he cannot continue with his experiment
    G. let his classmates eat the brownies before he tells them about the beetles
    H. write an essay about eating soul food
    J. make a flyer to help sell his beetle brownies

15. Andy's approach to writing his essay is a good example of how to—
    A. get along better with people.
    B. solve problems in creative ways.
    C. impress a girl who is a good cook.
    D. get by without much money.

STOP

© Scott Foresman 5

Name _____

Fact and Opinion/ Author's Viewpoint

REVIEW

Directions: Read the passage. Then read each question about the passage. Choose the best answer to each question. Mark the letter for the answer you have chosen.

Insects as Food

You probably think that you would never eat an insect, even if you were starving. Insects are ugly and disgusting, right?

But chances are you do eat them, or at least you use products that come from insects. Beeswax, for example, is used in lip balms. Honeycomb is sold in most American supermarkets.

Around the world, insects have long been an important food source. Insects were once a major food for Australian aborigines. In some countries, grasshoppers and large palm weevil grubs are still eaten. In South Africa, some people snack on roasted termites as if they were popcorn. In the Sinai Desert, some people eat the dry, scaly parts of certain bugs. In Mexico, a popular cake is made with the eggs of a water insect. In the United States, chocolate-covered ants are a delicacy sold in many food stores.

As someone who has eaten dishes made from insects, let me tell you that they are delicious. They are very nutritious, too, because insects are an excellent source of protein. It is simply prejudice that keeps most people from enjoying these delicacies. As with any new food, you have to give it a chance. You might be surprised at just how tasty insects can be!

1. In the first paragraph, the author assumes that most people—
   A. like insects.
   B. hate insects.
   C. have eaten insects.
   D. think insects are useful.

2. In the second and third paragraphs, the author supports his or her viewpoint by—
   F. quoting an expert.
   G. providing a variety of opinions.
   H. repeating the main idea.
   J. giving facts.

3. Which of the following is a statement of opinion?
   A. Insects have long been an important food source.
   B. Australian aborigines ate bugs.
   C. Insects are delicious.
   D. Beeswax is used in lip balms.

4. Which statement best sums up the author's viewpoint?
   F. Insects are unfairly rejected as a food source.
   G. Insects are better than most foods.
   H. Insects have no place in a modern diet.
   J. Insects are the food of the future.

5. This article is best described as—
   A. balanced.
   B. unbalanced.
   C. emotional.
   D. inaccurate.

Notes for Home: Your child read an article and identified statements of fact and opinion, as well as the author's viewpoint. **Home Activity:** Read a newspaper editorial with your child. Have him or her identify the facts, opinions, and author's viewpoint.

© Scott Foresman 5

Phonics: Diphthongs and Vowel Digraphs

Directions: Read the words in the box. Each word has the letters **ow,** but the letters stand for different vowel sounds. Say each word to yourself. Listen for the words with the same vowel sound as **cow** and those with the same vowel sound as **low.** Write each word in the correct column.

brownies
bowl
swallow
down
showing
however

Vowel sound in *cow*

1. _____
2. _____
3. _____

Vowel sound in *low*

4. _____
5. _____
6. _____

Directions: Read each sentence below. One word in each sentence has a word with the vowel sound heard at the beginning of **author.** Write the word on the line. Circle the letters that stand for that vowel sound.

_____ 7. August is a good time to catch beetles.

_____ 8. The cook needed beetles because he is making a special dessert.

_____ 9. He placed the beetles on a saucer, then stored them in the freezer.

_____ 10. He rinsed them under the faucet in the sink.

Directions: Read the announcement below. Listen for words that have a vowel sound like **boy** or **oil.** Circle the words and write them on the lines.

▮▮▮▮▮▮▮▮▮▮▮▮▮▮
Everyone! Join in!
Make your choice!
Sign up for the school
science fair!
Don't boycott it this year!
You're sure to enjoy it!
You won't be disappointed!
See Mr. Keller for more details.

11. _____
12. _____
13. _____
14. _____
15. _____

Notes for Home: Your child worked with the vowel sounds represented by *oi* as in *join,* *oy* as in *boy,* *ow* as in *brownies* or *low,* and *au* as in *author.* **Home Activity:** As you read with your child, look and listen for these spellings and vowel sounds.

© Scott Foresman 5

Recipe

A **recipe** is a set of directions for preparing something to eat.

Directions: Use the recipe below to answer the questions on the next page.

Sharon's Spicy Scrambled Eggs

3 eggs	dash of pepper	$\frac{1}{4}$ cup minced onion
1 tablespoon milk	dash of hot pepper sauce	1 tablespoon butter or margarine
dash of salt	$\frac{1}{4}$ cup grated cheddar cheese	

Break an egg into a cup. Pick out any shell. Then pour the egg into a bowl.

Repeat for the other two eggs.

Add milk, salt, pepper, and hot sauce to eggs.

Beat eggs gently.

Melt butter or margarine in skillet over medium heat.

Add onion to the melted butter and cook for 2–3 minutes until you can see through the onion pieces. Be careful not to burn the butter or margarine.

Add egg mixture and cheese.

Stir occasionally with spatula until eggs are firm.

Sharon's suggestions for experimenting:

Use cottage cheese instead of cheddar cheese.

Separate 2 eggs into yolks and egg whites, and substitute the 2 egg whites for 2 whole eggs.

Add diced cooked potatoes.

Add chopped green chilies.

Add crumbled bacon or a nonmeat bacon substitute.

Put in more hot sauce!

© Scott Foresman 5

1. What is the first step in preparing this recipe? _____

   _____

2. Why does the recipe say to break each egg into a cup before pouring it into a bowl?

   _____

   _____

3. Which ingredients do you add before beating the eggs? _____

   _____

4. What do you do after beating the eggs gently? _____

   _____

5. What does the second illustration show? _____

   _____

6. What "experimental" ingredients do you think you would like in this recipe? Explain why.

   _____

   _____

7. Write your own suggestion for experimenting with this recipe. _____

   _____

   _____

8. What are the advantages to watching a cooking show on television? What are the
   disadvantages?

   _____

   _____

   _____

   _____

9. Why is it important to follow a recipe's directions in the order that they are given?

   _____

   _____

10. Are illustrations or photographs helpful in a recipe? Explain. _____

    _____

    _____

Notes for Home: Your child read and answered questions about a recipe and an illustration.
Home Activity: Find a simple recipe for something your child likes. Read the recipe together
and talk about the steps involved in following the recipe. Then make the dish together.

© Scott Foresman 5

Name _____

Plot

- A **plot** includes the important events that happen in a story.

- A plot usually has a conflict or problem, rising action, a climax, and the resolution, or outcome.

Directions: Reread "The Brahman and the Banker." Then identify each important part of the plot in the story map.

Climax: When is the Brahman's problem solved?

4. _____

_____

_____

_____

Rising Action: What actions does the Brahman do to try to solve his problem?

3. _____

_____

_____

_____

Resolution: What is explained at the end of the story?

2. _____

5. _____

_____

_____

_____

_____

_____

_____

_____

_____

_____

Conflict: What problem does the Brahman have with the banker?

1. _____

_____

_____

_____

Notes for Home: Your child identified the important events in a story. *Home Activity:* Read a story to your child, or watch one together on TV. Have your child outline the plot by identifying a character's conflict or problem, the story's rising action, the climax, and the resolution.

© Scott Foresman 5

Vocabulary

Directions: Choose the word from the box that has the same or nearly the same meaning as each word or words below. Write the word on the line.

_____ 1. scoundrels

_____ 2. rarely

_____ 3. plentiful

_____ 4. enchanted

_____ 5. silliness

Check the Words You Know
__ fascinated
__ foolishness
__ generous
__ rascals
__ seldom

Directions: Choose the word from the box that best matches each clue. Write the word in the puzzle.

Down

6. mischievous persons
7. large; plentiful

Across

8. highly interested
9. not often
10. behavior that shows lack of judgment

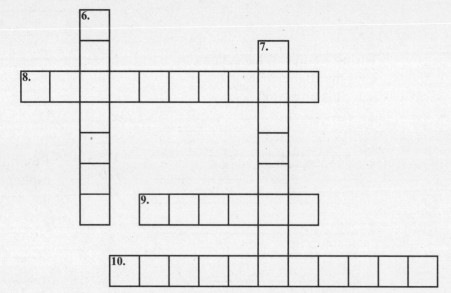

Write an Epilogue

Ever wonder what happens to the characters *after* a story ends? Pick a story you like very much. On a separate sheet of paper, tell what happens after the end of the story. You may set your epilogue weeks, months, or years in the future! Use as many vocabulary words as you can.

Notes for Home: Your child identified and used vocabulary words from "In the Days of King Adobe." *Home Activity:* Work with your child to make a puzzle that uses all these vocabulary words. The puzzle can be a word search or crossword, for example.

© Scott Foresman 5

Name _____

Plot

- A story's **plot** is the important events that happen in a story. These parts include the conflict or problem, the rising action, the climax, and the resolution, or outcome.

Directions: Read the plot summary of "In the Days of King Adobe." Then answer the questions below.

There once was a poor but thrifty old woman who had a fine ham. One evening two young men on a journey came to her door. She gave them lodging and ham for dinner. When they saw the ham, they decided to steal it.

That night, thinking the old woman was asleep, they took the ham and put it in their traveling bag. But the old woman, suspecting them, had watched them. After they were asleep, she took out the ham and put an adobe brick in its place.

The next day at breakfast the two young rascals told her a made-up dream about Hambone the First, king of a land called Travelibag. She responded with her own dream, in which King Hambone was usurped by Adobe the Great.

The young men went on their way. Later, upon opening the bag, they saw that the old woman had fooled them. The two hungry thieves never tricked another old woman.

1. Who are the main characters in the story?

_____

_____

2. What is the problem in this story?

_____

_____

3. Describe the rising action of the story where the problem leads to other events.

_____

_____

4. What is the climax, or high point, of the story?

_____

_____

5. What is the resolution, or outcome, of the story? Write your answer on a separate piece of paper.

Notes for Home: Your child read a story summary and identified different elements of the story's plot. **Home Activity:** Watch a television show or movie with your child. Discuss the important parts of the story, the main problem characters face, and how it is resolved.

© Scott Foresman 5

Name _____

1.	Ⓐ	Ⓑ	Ⓒ	Ⓓ
2.	Ⓕ	Ⓖ	Ⓗ	Ⓙ
3.	Ⓐ	Ⓑ	Ⓒ	Ⓓ
4.	Ⓕ	Ⓖ	Ⓗ	Ⓙ
5.	Ⓐ	Ⓑ	Ⓒ	Ⓓ
6.	Ⓕ	Ⓖ	Ⓗ	Ⓙ
7.	Ⓐ	Ⓑ	Ⓒ	Ⓓ
8.	Ⓕ	Ⓖ	Ⓗ	Ⓙ
9.	Ⓐ	Ⓑ	Ⓒ	Ⓓ
10.	Ⓕ	Ⓖ	Ⓗ	Ⓙ
11.	Ⓐ	Ⓑ	Ⓒ	Ⓓ
12.	Ⓕ	Ⓖ	Ⓗ	Ⓙ
13.	Ⓐ	Ⓑ	Ⓒ	Ⓓ
14.	Ⓕ	Ⓖ	Ⓗ	Ⓙ
15.	Ⓐ	Ⓑ	Ⓒ	Ⓓ

© Scott Foresman 5

Name _____

Selection Test

Directions: Choose the best answer to each item. Mark the letter for the answer you have chosen.

Part 1: Vocabulary

Find the answer choice that means about the same as the underlined word in each sentence.

1. Kayla <u>seldom</u> asks questions in class.
   A. every day
   B. often
   C. never
   D. not often

2. Those boys are <u>rascals</u>.
   F. people who are related to each other
   G. persons who cause mischief
   H. people who work together
   J. hard-working persons

3. Throughout the play, Jonas looked <u>fascinated</u>.
   A. very interested
   B. upset
   C. very sleepy
   D. proud

4. Everyone commented on the <u>foolishness</u> of the plan.
   F. danger
   G. lack of sense
   H. success
   J. difficulty

5. My grandmother served a <u>generous</u> bowl of soup.
   A. steaming hot
   B. tasty
   C. large
   D. leftover

Part 2: Comprehension

Use what you know about the story to answer each item.

6. At the beginning of this story, we know only that the old woman was—
   F. very poor.
   G. living with her family.
   H. very rich.
   J. going on a journey.

7. Where does the old woman live?
   A. in the marketplace of a town
   B. in a hotel where she works as a servant
   C. in the middle of a wilderness
   D. at the edge of a village

8. The old woman gets the ham by—
   F. saving a penny a day.
   G. stealing it.
   H. selling bricks.
   J. tricking the young men.

9. What can you conclude about the old woman based on the way she acts when the young men first come to her house?
   A. She is lonely.
   B. She is very suspicious.
   C. She is lazy.
   D. She dislikes young people.

© Scott Foresman 5

GO ON

10. The main problem in this story is between the—
    F.   woman's wish to eat the ham and her wish to share it.
    G.   men wanting to steal the ham and their wish to respect the woman.
    H.   men's wish to travel and their wish to stay with the woman.
    J.   men wanting to steal the ham and the woman's wish to keep it.

11. Which of these events is part of the rising action in this story?
    A.   The old woman sells most of her vegetables in the market.
    B.   The young men decide not to trick the next person they stay with.
    C.   The old woman buys the ham.
    D.   The young man tells about his dream of King Hambone the First.

12. The old woman shows that she has a sense of humor when she—
    F.   describes her dream of King Adobe.
    G.   takes the ham from the traveling bag.
    H.   notices the rascally look in the men's eyes.
    J.   prepares the ham for supper.

13. The climax of this story occurs when the—
    A.   young men steal the ham.
    B.   men open the bag and find the brick.
    C.   woman puts the brick in place of the ham.
    D.   woman asks the men about their dreams.

14. Which fact makes it hardest to forgive the young men's behavior to the old woman?
    F.   She was very generous to them.
    G.   They were very hungry.
    H.   She tricked them too.
    J.   They had a long way to travel.

15. The author's main purpose in this story is to—
    A.   explain how to cook a ham.
    B.   describe the travels of two young men.
    C.   teach a lesson.
    D.   convince readers to help travelers in need.

STOP

© Scott Foresman 5

Context Clues

Directions: Read the story. Then read each question about the story. Choose the best answer to each question. Mark the letter for the answer you have chosen.

Now You See It, Now You Don't

Rudy is a master of <u>legerdemain</u>. He can make scarves fly from his ears and mouth. He can make birds vanish and pull rabbits out of hats. He can make nickels and dimes appear out of his assistant's nose and ears. Children gasp to see these acts. Adults shake their heads in wonder.

Rudy's hands are so <u>nimble</u> that no matter how carefully you watch, you cannot tell how he does it. He rarely rests, either—his act continues for hours without a <u>hiatus</u>. The only time he pauses in his act is when the audience applauds. Rudy is so good that the audience always applauds long and enthusiastically as Rudy bows and smiles.

There is another way in which Rudy is amazing. He is a <u>stellar</u> student, ranking first in his class despite the fact that he needs so much time to prepare for his tricks. How he finds the time to study and practice his magic is a mystery to everyone. It seems to be just one more way in which Rudy can seem to perform magic.

Today, Rudy wants to work out a new trick for the upcoming school talent show. He's starting with some <u>ersatz</u> gold—it looks real, but it isn't. Then he adds a pile of feathers and sets to work. It's the most difficult trick Rudy has attempted. He's having a hard time making it work the way he wants. You can bet that Rudy will be practicing his new trick long into the night. This, of course, will be after he has finished his school work.

1. In this story, the word <u>legerdemain</u> means—
   A. sewing.
   B. thievery.
   C. magic tricks.
   D. silliness.

2. In this story, the word <u>nimble</u> means—
   F. invisible.
   G. quick.
   H. strong.
   J. dirty.

3. In this story, the word <u>hiatus</u> means—
   A. break.
   B. mistake.
   C. blunder.
   D. accident.

4. In this story, the word <u>stellar</u> means—
   F. pointed.
   G. good.
   H. dull.
   J. outstanding.

5. The best synonym for <u>ersatz</u> is—
   A. artificial.
   B. real.
   C. expensive.
   D. fancy.

Notes for Home: Your child used context clues to figure out the meaning of unfamiliar words. *Home Activity:* Encourage your child to make a list of unfamiliar words he or she finds while reading. Discuss how context clues can be used to figure out a word's meaning.

© Scott Foresman 5

Name _____

Phonics: *r*-Controlled Vowels

Directions: Read the words in the box. Listen for the vowel sounds heard in **star, for, deer,** and **dirt.** Sort the words according to their vowel sounds. Write each word in the correct column.

beard	cornmeal	guitar	peer	serious	worked
burn	farthest	large	purple	steer	world
circle	fear	morning	series	tortilla	worthy

Sounds like *star*

1. _____

2. _____

3. _____

Sounds like *for*

10. _____

11. _____

12. _____

Sounds like *deer*

4. _____

5. _____

6. _____

7. _____

8. _____

9. _____

Sounds like *dirt*

13. _____

14. _____

15. _____

16. _____

17. _____

18. _____

Directions: Read each sentence below. Listen for words that have the vowel sound in **dirt.** The sound may be spelled **or, ir,** or **ur.** Write each word on the line.

_____ 19. The large dinner left them bursting at the seams.

_____ 20. Their bellies were so full that their shirt buttons nearly popped!

_____ 21. It was the first good meal they had had in days.

_____ 22. To thank their hostess, they promised to do work in payment for the meal.

_____ 23. They felt a little labor was worth the good meal.

_____ 24. It also wouldn't hurt them to do some physical activity.

_____ 25. But the hostess assured them that there was no reason for them to leave their chairs.

Notes for Home: Your child identified words with vowels combined with the letter *r,* such as *star, for, deer,* and *dirt.* **Home Activity:** Read a story with your child. Help your child listen and look for words with these sounds. Say the words together to hear the sounds.

© Scott Foresman 5

Name _____

Questions for Inquiry

A good way to begin a research project is by **asking yourself questions** about your topic. These questions will help guide you as you research information to find answers for your questions. As you research and read, revise your questions as needed.

Directions: Suppose you are doing research on tricksters. Many cultures have folk tales about tricksters—characters who use tricks to show a special trait. Some are animals and some are people. Sometimes the tricks are to teach a hard lesson, and sometimes they are just pranks. Choose one of the tricksters described below as a topic for a research report. Then answer the questions on the next page.

Coyote is a clever and sometimes naughty character in Native American folk tales. He sometimes doesn't play fair, but there is always a point to his antics.

Reynard the Fox is sly. He knows the weaknesses of those he plays tricks on. Often his tricks let people know that they need to think more of others than of themselves.

Till Eulenspiegel is a German character. He uses his abilities as a trickster to help the townsfolk and sometimes the whole country.

Anansi is a spider in African and Caribbean folk tales. He often shows his cleverness by getting the better of the larger animals and teaching them that size isn't everything.

© Scott Foresman 5

Name _____

1. Which trickster will your report be about? _____

2. What would you like to know about your topic? Think of at least three questions that you could use to guide you as you start your research.

   _____

   _____

   _____

   _____

Directions: Which of the following resources do you think might be helpful in finding answers to your questions? Explain why.

3. *The Times of London World Atlas* _____

   _____

4. *Famous Folk Tales from Around the World* _____

   _____

5. *Encyclopedia of Myth and Folklore* _____

   _____

6. *A Celebration of African Folk Tales* _____

   _____

7. "Why Germans Love Till Eulenspiegel" (article) _____

   _____

8. *The Illustrated Guide to Native American Mythology* _____

   _____

9. "Fox Meets Coyote: A Comparison of Two Popular Folk Tale Characters" (article)

   _____

10. Why might you revise your questions during the research process? _____

   _____

   _____

   _____

   _____

Notes for Home: Your child formed questions for research and considered how to find the answers. *Home Activity:* Together with your child, write two or three questions about a topic you would like to know more about. Discuss how to find the answers.

© Scott Foresman 5

Making Judgments

- **Making judgments** means forming opinions about someone or something.

- Characters make judgments about situations and other characters. Authors make judgments on the subject of their writing. Readers make judgments about characters, authors, and ideas. A reader's judgment should be supported by evidence in the story or article.

Directions: Reread "Can You Change Your School Lunch?" Then complete the table. Give supporting evidence for each judgment. Then make your own judgment about the author's ideas.

Judgments (Opinions)	Supporting Evidence
Justin's opinion: The school lunches needed to be improved.	1.
Justin's opinion: The school lunches did improve.	2.
Author's opinion: You can change your own school's lunches.	3.
Your opinion of the author's ideas: 4.	5.

Notes for Home: Your child identified supporting evidence for opinions in the article and made judgments about the author's ideas. *Home Activity:* Help your child write a letter about something he or she thinks should be changed.

© Scott Foresman 5

Name _____

Vocabulary

Directions: Choose the word from the box that best completes each sentence. Write the word on the matching numbered line to the right.

★★★★★★★★★★★★★★★★★★★★

A SURE FIRE HIT

"My New **1.** _____" is a moving story about a fearless young woman's job search. Jean is a warm-hearted but extremely **2.** _____ person. She gets her dream job because she is an **3.** _____ worker, but then she gets fired for arguing with her boss. The conflict is **4.** _____ when Jean learns to accept people. People then learn to accept her. In my **5.** _____, this film has "Oscar" written all over it.

Check the Words You Know

__ career

__ critical

__ efficient

__ maneuvered

__ opinion

__ resolved

__ shattered

__ survey

1. _____

2. _____

3. _____

4. _____

5. _____

Directions: Choose the word from the box that best matches each clue. Write the word on the line.

_____ **6.** It's what the chess champion did.

_____ **7.** A college degree will help you start this.

_____ **8.** It's what surveyors do.

_____ **9.** You have a right to yours.

_____ **10.** It's what the china plate did after falling.

Write a List

What *really* bothers you—barking dogs, smelly feet, annoying siblings? On a separate sheet of paper, list ten things that bother you a lot. Next to each entry, explain why it annoys you. Use as many vocabulary words as you can in your list.

Notes for Home: Your child identified and used vocabulary words from "Just Telling the Truth." *Home Activity:* With your child, write a review of a book, television show, or movie like the one shown above. Guide your child to use as many vocabulary words as possible.

© Scott Foresman 5

Name _____

Making Judgments

- **Making judgments** means forming opinions about someone or something. Characters, authors, and readers all make judgments.

Directions: Reread what happens in "Just Telling the Truth" when Felicia tells her mother she doesn't know why her friends were mad at her. Then answer the questions below.

> Her mother looked at her for a long time. "Are you sure," she said finally, "you don't know why? You haven't even got an idea?"
>
> "Well," Felicia hesitated, "I told the truth. Maybe they didn't like that."
>
> "Felicia," her mother said gently, "there's a difference between truth and opinion. The truth is facts. Opinion is what you think. You told them what you thought."
>
> "And they didn't like that. Shouldn't I say what I think?"
>
> Her mother frowned. "Look, if you have a great idea for something and someone comes along and says, 'Boy, what a dumb idea, this is wrong and this is wrong,' wouldn't you feel bad?"

Copyright © 1973 by Ellen Conford. From FELICIA THE CRITIC published by Little, Brown and Company. Reprinted by permission of McIntosh and Otis, Inc.

1. Do you agree that "the truth is facts"? Why or why not?

_____

_____

2. How would you answer Felicia when she says, "Shouldn't I say what I think?"

_____

_____

3. What point is Felicia's mother trying to make?

_____

_____

4. What is your opinion of Felicia's mother? Explain.

_____

_____

5. What lesson does Felicia learn in "Just Telling the Truth"? On a separate sheet of paper, tell what Felicia learned and whether you think it was a worthwhile lesson for people to learn.

Notes for Home: Your child read a story and made judgments about its characters and ideas. *Home Activity:* Read a newspaper editorial with your child. Ask him or her to make judgments about the ideas expressed.

© Scott Foresman 5

Name _____

1.	Ⓐ	Ⓑ	Ⓒ	Ⓓ
2.	Ⓕ	Ⓖ	Ⓗ	Ⓙ
3.	Ⓐ	Ⓑ	Ⓒ	Ⓓ
4.	Ⓕ	Ⓖ	Ⓗ	Ⓙ
5.	Ⓐ	Ⓑ	Ⓒ	Ⓓ
6.	Ⓕ	Ⓖ	Ⓗ	Ⓙ
7.	Ⓐ	Ⓑ	Ⓒ	Ⓓ
8.	Ⓕ	Ⓖ	Ⓗ	Ⓙ
9.	Ⓐ	Ⓑ	Ⓒ	Ⓓ
10.	Ⓕ	Ⓖ	Ⓗ	Ⓙ
11.	Ⓐ	Ⓑ	Ⓒ	Ⓓ
12.	Ⓕ	Ⓖ	Ⓗ	Ⓙ
13.	Ⓐ	Ⓑ	Ⓒ	Ⓓ
14.	Ⓕ	Ⓖ	Ⓗ	Ⓙ
15.	Ⓐ	Ⓑ	Ⓒ	Ⓓ

© Scott Foresman 5

Selection Test

Directions: Choose the best answer to each item. Mark the letter for the answer you have chosen.

Part 1: Vocabulary

Find the answer choice that means about the same as the underlined word in each sentence.

1. Aunt Jessie told us about her new career.
   - A. job or occupation
   - B. apartment
   - C. hobby or activity
   - D. goal

2. Mr. Marlow maneuvered the car.
   - F. bought
   - G. fixed quickly
   - H. started
   - J. moved skillfully

3. My brother explained his opinion.
   - A. dream
   - B. what one believes
   - C. experience
   - D. what one plans

4. Why is Laura so critical?
   - F. forgetful
   - G. often sad
   - H. tending to be shy
   - J. quick to find fault

5. The vase was shattered.
   - A. painted
   - B. washed
   - C. broken
   - D. put away

6. Try to develop more efficient habits.
   - F. thoughtful of othefs
   - G. working in an effective way
   - H. tending to save money
   - J. careful

7. Nell told us what she had resolved.
   - A. completed
   - B. ruined
   - C. heard
   - D. decided

8. Mom came in to survey the damage.
   - F. look at
   - G. repair
   - H. blame someone for
   - J. clean up

Part 2: Comprehension

Use what you know about the story to answer each item.

9. Felicia's friends don't like her attitude about—
   - A. what a club should be.
   - B. walking to school alone.
   - C. Cheryl's mother.
   - D. her sister Marilyn.

10. When Felicia first comes home from school, she—
   - F. paints her nails.
   - G. makes a snack.
   - H. cleans the floor.
   - J. starts a building project.

11. Marilyn is partly responsible for the broken jar because she—
   - A. was the first to use the peanut butter.
   - B. left it on the table.
   - C. startled Felicia, causing Felicia's arm to hit it.
   - D. screamed when Felicia was picking up the jar.

12. You can tell from Felicia's problems at school that she—
   - F. tries to be cruel to others.
   - G. does not have any friends.
   - H. doesn't care what other people think.
   - J. doesn't understand the effect she has on others.

GO ON

© Scott Foresman 5

13. Felicia decides to change the broom closet because she wants to—
   A. keep her mother from becoming angry about the broken jar.
   B. get more attention from Marilyn.
   C. practice being constructive.
   D. put off doing her homework.

14. Telling Felicia to become a constructive critic is good advice because it—
   F. fools Felicia into thinking everyone likes her.
   G. gives Felicia a way to go out and get a job right away.
   H. makes Felicia see that there's nothing wrong with how she acts.
   J. gives Felicia a way to get along with others while still being herself.

15. How does Felicia show that she has understood her mother's advice about becoming a constructive critic?
   A. She interrupts her mother when her mother is trying to cook.
   B. She doesn't understand why her mother won't return the roast.
   C. She asks her mother if she would mind hearing suggestions about the broom closet.
   D. She yells at Marilyn to come look at what she has done with the closet.

STOP

© Scott Foresman 5

Character

Directions: Read the story. Then read each question about the story. Choose the best answer to each question. Mark the letter for the answer you have chosen.

The Lonely Critic

Anne and Teresa smiled and laughed as they left the movie theater. Joe walked close behind them. He had a serious expression as he rushed to keep up with Anne, Teresa, and their other friends.

"I really liked it," said Anne to the others as they walked outside.

"So did I," added Teresa. "It was so funny and entertaining."

"Didn't you love it when the dog got into the driver's seat?" commented another friend. One or two others in the group nodded their heads in agreement.

"Well," Joe said loudly, "I can't believe any of you liked it. The script was an absolute embarrassment. The acting was awful. The camera work was terrible, and the director doesn't know the first thing about filmmaking."

The others looked at each other and rolled their eyes.

"Joe thinks he knows everything," Anne whispered to Teresa.

"I'll say," Teresa whispered back.

"Who wants to grab some pizza and talk about the movie?" Joe asked. "There are a lot more things I could tell you about filmmaking."

"No thanks, we've got to get home," said Anne and Teresa at the same time. "It's getting late." One by one the others said they had to be up early in the morning.

Joe shrugged. "Suit yourselves," he said.

1. From what he says, Joe seems to—
   A. value his own opinion highly.
   B. value his friends' opinions.
   C. want to learn about movies.
   D. want to talk about himself.

2. You can tell from what Anne and Teresa say about Joe that he is—
   F. well liked.
   G. a film expert.
   H. good company.
   J. a know-it-all.

3. Which is **not** a clue to Joe's character?
   A. His friends roll their eyes.
   B. His friends turn down his invitation.
   C. His friends liked the movie.
   D. His friends whisper about him.

4. Joe might best be described as—
   F. good-natured.
   G. critical.
   H. emotional.
   J. kind.

5. What is missing from the story that would help you know more about Joe?
   A. his actions.
   B. his friends' actions.
   C. his thoughts.
   D. his words.

© Scott Foresman 5

Notes for Home: Your child read a story and drew conclusions about the characters. **Home Activity:** Take turns describing people you know by what they say and do, as well as by what others say about them. Then, take turns trying to guess who is being described.

Phonics: Complex Spelling Patterns

Directions: Looking at spelling patterns can help you figure out how to pronounce a word. Some words have simple spelling patterns such as **cat** or **lake.** These spelling patterns can be written as **CVC (consonant-vowel-consonant)** or **CVCe (consonant-vowel-consonant-*e*).** But many words have more complex spelling patterns. Carefully read each word in the box. Sort the words according to their spelling patterns by following the instructions below.

accident	curiously	gorgeous
actually	definite	grumbling
appreciated	disinterest	hesitated
constructive	dubiously	maneuvered
criticism	efficient	uncertainly

Write the words that have three vowels in a row—**VVV.**

1. _____   2. _____   3. _____

Write the words that have three consonants in a row—**CCC.**

4. _____   5. _____

Write the word that has four consonants in a row—**CCCC.**

6. _____

Write the words that start with the pattern **VCCV.**

7. _____   8. _____   9. _____

Write the words that alternate consonants and vowels.

10. _____   11. _____

Write the words that don't seem to follow a pattern.

Notes for Home: Your child recognized words with complex spelling patterns, such as *efficient* and *gorgeous.* **Home Activity:** Read a newspaper article with your child. Have your child look for consonant and vowel patterns in longer words.

© Scott Foresman 5

Name _____

Textbook/Trade Book

A **textbook** is a book you use in school to learn about a subject. You can use the chapters, headings, subheadings, captions, and index to locate information in a textbook. A **trade book** is any book that is not a textbook, a periodical, or a reference book.

Directions: Use the sample pages from a textbook and a trade book below to answer the questions on the next page.

Chapter 4: American Artists of 19th and 20th Centuries

Artists in the United States used many painting styles. In this chapter you will read about women and men who created their own styles as well as adapted the styles of other painters.

Lesson 1

Mary Cassatt (1844–1926)

Mary Cassatt was born in the United States but lived and painted in France for much of her life.

Many of her best known oil paintings are of mothers and children. She became **associated** with the art school known as **Impressionism.**

Check Your Understanding

1. With what style of art did Mary Cassatt become linked?
2. Where did Mary Cassatt live most of her life?

associated connected (with)
Impressionism (See glossary and Chapter 2.)

Mary Cassatt, a Woman for Her Time and Ours

This American artist, associated with the French Impressionist movement, was born in Pittsburgh, Pennsylvania, in 1844. We often think of her paintings as sincere renderings of the power of the bond between mothers and children.

In 1866, after completing her study at the Pennsylvania Academy of Fine Arts with Thomas Eakins, Mary Cassatt moved to France. She spent the rest of her life in France, where she died in 1926.

In France, Mary Cassatt had the good fortune to become a close friend of Edgar Degas and other Impressionist painters of the time. Her style adds a welcome sensitivity, which many of her contemporaries did not attain.

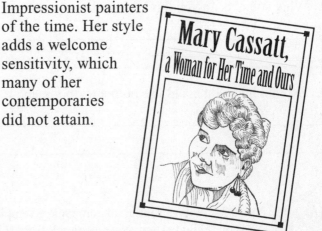

Mary Cassatt, a Woman for Her Time and Ours

© Scott Foresman 5

Name _____

1. What chapter is shown in the textbook? What is the title of the chapter? _____

_____

2. For what kind of class might you use this textbook? Explain. _____

_____

3. What is the title of trade book? What do you think this book would be about?

_____

_____

4. Why might someone want to read this trade book? _____

_____

5. How are the textbook and trade book sample pages alike? How are they different?

_____

_____

_____

_____

6. Which book would contain detailed information about the artist's childhood? Explain.

_____

_____

7. Why are the words *associated* and *Impressionism* boldfaced in the textbook?

_____

8. Why do you think the textbook includes questions? _____

_____

_____

9. What subjects do you think Mary Cassatt painted most often? Explain.

_____

_____

10. Explain how you could use both a textbook and trade books for a research report.

_____

_____

 Notes for Home: Your child compared a sample textbook and trade book. *Home Activity:* Ask your child to show you a textbook from school and explain to you how it is organized and what kind of information it has. Then do the same with a trade book from home or the library.

© Scott Foresman 5

Visualizing

- **Visualizing** is creating a picture in your mind as you read.

- Pay attention to description, imagery, and sensory words that help you imagine what you are reading. Also think about what you already know about the places, people, and things being described.

Directions: Reread "Mrs. Middlesome-Merry's Art Studio." Then complete the table. Tell what story details you used to help you visualize different parts of the story.

I Visualized	Using These Story Details
Mrs. Middlesome-Merry	1.
Mrs. Middlesome-Merry's apron	2.
Mrs. Middlesome-Merry's apron pocket	3.
Mrs. Middlesome-Merry's stairs	4.
Mrs. Middlesome-Merry's studio	5.

Notes for Home: Your child read a story and identified vivid images that helped him or her visualize the details. *Home Activity:* Describe a place, such as your kitchen. Give clues about things a person might see, hear, feel, taste, or smell there. Have your child guess the place.

© Scott Foresman 5

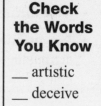
Vocabulary

Directions: Choose the word from the box that best completes each statement. Write the word on the line to the left.

_____ 1. *Literature* is to *literary* as *art* is to _____.

_____ 2. *Depend* is to *trust* as *mislead* is to _____.

_____ 3. *Paint* is to *painting* as *stone* is to _____.

_____ 4. *False* is to *real* as *fake* is to _____.

_____ 5. *Food* is to *taster* as *picture* is to _____.

Directions: Choose the word from the box that best completes each sentence. Write the word on the line to the left.

Check the Words You Know
__ artistic
__ deceive
__ realistic
__ represent
__ sculpture
__ style
__ viewer

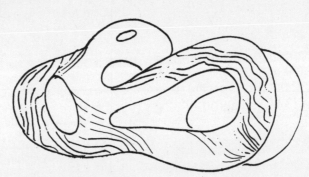

_____ 6. The paintings we saw at the museum were as _____ as photographs.

_____ 7. We also visited the _____ exhibit and saw many different statues carved out of marble.

_____ 8. The statues _____ the artists' ideas.

_____ 9. Some were done in a very modern _____.

_____ 10. One _____ sat for a long time just staring at an especially interesting piece.

Write an Essay

On a separate sheet of paper, write an essay about an art style or art work you especially like. Look at the paintings and sculpture in an art book for ideas. Use as many vocabulary words as you can in your essay.

Notes for Home: Your child identified and used vocabulary words from "Is It Real?" *Home Activity:* Have your child make an art project and then describe the process on an index card. Encourage your child to use as many vocabulary words as possible in the description.

© Scott Foresman 5

Visualizing

- **Visualizing** is creating a picture in your mind as you read.

- Authors may help you visualize by using imagery. These are words that give you a strong mental picture, or image.

- Another way an author may help you visualize is through sensory details. These are words that describe how something looks, sounds, smells, tastes, or feels.

Directions: Reread the passage below from "Is It Real?" about the time when Marilyn Levine had difficulty finishing her sculpture on time. Then answer the questions below.

Worried that the teacher would think she was too slow, she quickly molded two disks like the rubber tips on a pair of crutches. She placed these on both sides of her single ceramic shoe, so it looked like someone with an injured foot had hobbled to the party on crutches. The teacher was as impressed with Marilyn's quick-thinking as he was by her skill in creating a realistic shoe.

Later, a friend gave Levine a pair of worn-out work boots. Scuffed, scratched, and battered, the boots had a strange appeal. They told a story.

From ARTISTIC TRICKERY: THE TRADITION OF TROMPE L'OEIL by Michael Capek. Copyright © 1995 Lerner Publications. Reprinted by permission.

1. To which of the five senses does the phrase "molded two disks" appeal: touch, taste, sight, smell, hearing?

_____

2. What image does the author use to help you visualize the sculpture?

_____

_____

3. What do you see when you visualize Marilyn's finished sculpture?

_____

_____

4. What words help you visualize the work boots in the second paragraph?

_____

_____

5. Close your eyes and visualize Marilyn Levine's *Black Gloves*. Then, on a separate sheet of paper, describe what you see in your own words.

Notes for Home: Your child read an article and visualized images from it. ***Home Activity:*** Close your eyes while your child describes an object or a room in your home. Guess what is being described by the details your child uses.

© Scott Foresman 5

Name _____

1.	Ⓐ	Ⓑ	Ⓒ	Ⓓ
2.	Ⓕ	Ⓖ	Ⓗ	Ⓙ
3.	Ⓐ	Ⓑ	Ⓒ	Ⓓ
4.	Ⓕ	Ⓖ	Ⓗ	Ⓙ
5.	Ⓐ	Ⓑ	Ⓒ	Ⓓ
6.	Ⓕ	Ⓖ	Ⓗ	Ⓙ
7.	Ⓐ	Ⓑ	Ⓒ	Ⓓ
8.	Ⓕ	Ⓖ	Ⓗ	Ⓙ
9.	Ⓐ	Ⓑ	Ⓒ	Ⓓ
10.	Ⓕ	Ⓖ	Ⓗ	Ⓙ
11.	Ⓐ	Ⓑ	Ⓒ	Ⓓ
12.	Ⓕ	Ⓖ	Ⓗ	Ⓙ
13.	Ⓐ	Ⓑ	Ⓒ	Ⓓ
14.	Ⓕ	Ⓖ	Ⓗ	Ⓙ
15.	Ⓐ	Ⓑ	Ⓒ	Ⓓ

© Scott Foresman 5

Selection Test

Directions: Choose the best answer to each item. Mark the letter for the answer you have chosen.

Part 1: Vocabulary

Find the answer choice that means about the same as the underlined word in each sentence.

1. Max likes to <u>deceive</u> people.
   A. ignore
   B. refuse to help
   C. fool
   D. steal from

2. He has an interesting <u>style</u> of painting.
   F. place to work
   G. manner
   H. name
   J. amount of work

3. The <u>viewer</u> enjoyed the movie.
   A. actor
   B. someone who looks at something
   C. owner
   D. someone who makes something

4. What was she trying to <u>represent</u> in her picture?
   F. show
   G. explain
   H. buy
   J. fix

5. That painting is so <u>realistic</u>.
   A. like the actual thing
   B. expensive
   C. dark and ugly
   D. looking as if done by a child

6. We bought a <u>sculpture</u> for the garden.
   F. fountain
   G. art object that is usually carved or molded
   H. small bush
   J. tall wooden frame for vines to grow on

7. She has so many <u>artistic</u> interests.
   A. painted
   B. of money
   C. different
   D. related to art

Part 2: Comprehension

Use what you know about the story to answer each item.

8. In "trompe l'oeil," the artist tries mainly to—
   F. fool the eye.
   G. ask a riddle.
   H. show life as it should be.
   J. make people laugh.

9. Trompe l'oeil is an art form that—
   A. was recently invented.
   B. involves only one or two artistic techniques.
   C. is very hard to produce successfully.
   D. has been around for centuries.

10. Marilyn Levine's *Black Gloves* shows—
    F. a painting of the gloves.
    G. a life-size figure of a man wearing the gloves.
    H. leather gloves that look like ceramic.
    J. ceramic gloves that look like leather.

11. Which of these stories from the selection best proves how trompe l'oeil can fool people?
    A. Duane Hanson's *Traveler* portrays a person who looks tired.
    B. Some artists make floors look as if they are covered with litter.
    C. People said they smelled peanuts while looking at *Fresh Roasted*.
    D. The Greeks appreciated trompe l'oeil before the Romans did.

© Scott Foresman 5

GO ON

12. Which would be another good title for this selection?
   F. "Why Audrey Flack Painted *Strawberry Tart Supreme*"
   G. "When *Fresh Roasted* Was Painted"
   H. "How Artists Trick the Viewer"
   J. "Where to See Trompe l'oeil"

13. Which sentence best helps the reader visualize what is being discussed?
   A. ". . . looking like they were sliced just minutes ago, the apples and oranges seem to spill right out of the picture."
   B. "And the more familiar you become with the game, the more fun it is."
   C. "Throughout history, dozens of artistic movements and fads have come and gone."
   D. "Many different artistic styles and techniques have been used to create trompe l'oeil."

14. Which would be the best evidence that trompe l'oeil can fool people?
   F. A woman admires a mural on a bathroom wall.
   G. A child laughs at a painting of a clown.
   H. A man tries to open the door on a mural of a house.
   J. A teacher studies a painting of a pair of shoes.

15. Which of these best fits the definition of trompe l'oeil art?
   A. a ceramic frog made to look like a real frog that sits in a real pond
   B. a drawing of a historical figure wearing the clothes of that time
   C. a painting of flowers in which each blossom is a blot of color
   D. a life-size photograph of a real person

STOP

© Scott Foresman 5

Fact and Opinion

Directions: Read the passage. Then read each question about the passage. Choose the best answer to each question. Mark the letter for the answer you have chosen.

The Eyes Have It

The use of optical illusions in art has a long history. The ancient Greeks used trompe l'oeil techniques thousands of years ago. The painter Zeuxis, for example, reportedly painted such realistic grapes that the birds tried to eat them! Much later, the Italian painter Caravaggio painted insects in his pictures of fruit bowls to make them look more real.

I like optical illusion in art. It's fun to feel that your eyes are telling you one thing while your brain tells you something else.

In real life, however, it is always unpleasant when our eyes get fooled. On a hot summer's day, you might think you see water on a hot highway—but it's an optical illusion. Mirages in the desert are another type of optical illusion. They can be even more upsetting, especially if you're thirsty.

Why are some optical illusions upsetting? It's a matter of survival. To function each day, we need our eyes and brains to work together. We're uncomfortable when they don't. In art, optical illusions are a kind of game. But life is never a game. Life is serious business.

1. Which of the following is **not** a statement of fact?
    A. The use of optical illusions in art has a long history.
    B. The ancient Greeks used trompe l'oeil techniques thousands of years ago.
    C. Later, the Italian painter Caravaggio painted insects in his pictures of fruit bowls to make them look more real.
    D. I like optical illusions in art.

2. "In real life, however, it is always unpleasant when our eyes get fooled" is—
    F. a statement of fact.
    G. a statement of opinion.
    H. a combination of fact and opinion.
    J. a question.

3. "Mirages in the desert are another type of optical illusion" is—
    A. a statement of fact.
    B. a statement of opinion.
    C. both a statement of fact and opinion.
    D. a question.

4. Which of the following is a statement of fact?
    F. To function each day, we need our eyes and brains to work together.
    G. We're always uncomfortable when they don't.
    H. But life is never a game.
    J. Life is serious business.

5. This passage contains—
    A. only facts.
    B. only opinions.
    C. a mixture of facts and opinions.
    D. only one opinion.

Notes for Home: Your child read a passage and identified statements of fact and opinion. *Home Activity:* Work with your child to list statements of fact and opinion about a favorite food, such as *Oranges contain Vitamin C. I think they taste great!*

© Scott Foresman 5

Name _____

Phonics: Word Building

Directions: Sometimes when you add a prefix or a suffix to a word, the sound of the base word doesn't change. For example, when **-ness** is added to **dark,** the result is **darkness.** The sound of **dark** does not change. Other times, when you add a prefix or a suffix to a word, the sound of the base word changes. Add a suffix to each base word to make a new word. Write the new word on the line. Then tell whether the sound of the base word changes.

Base Word		Suffix		New Word	Change or No Change?
1. art	+	-ist	=	_____	_____
2. remark	+	-able	=	_____	_____
3. locate	+	-ion	=	_____	_____
4. assign	+	-ment	=	_____	_____
5. sign	+	-al	=	_____	_____

Directions: Sometimes when you add a prefix or suffix, the stressed syllable changes. Read the word pairs below. Underline the stressed syllable in each word, for example: **imitate** and **imitation.**

6. artist	artistic

7. reality	realism

8. prefer	preference

9. exhibit	exhibition

10. represent	representation

11. normal	normality

12. economy	economical

13. history	historical

14. process	procession

15. edit	edition

Directions: Read the paragraph below. Five words with suffixes are underlined. Write the base word for each underlined word on the line.

The art underline(exhibition) was not a huge success. It had a strong representation of the modern art world, and the artistic level of the paintings was high. However, most images were too abstract. Viewers expressed a preference for realism, for pictures of the familiar, everyday world.

16. _____
17. _____
18. _____
19. _____
20. _____

Notes for Home: Your child examined how the sounds of words change when a suffix is added, such as *artist* and *artistic.* **Home Activity:** Point out words in a story that have suffixes. Have your child compare each word to its base word to see if the sounds change.

© Scott Foresman 5

Name _____

Technology: Pictures and Captions

Most CD-ROM encyclopedias include **pictures with captions.** If you use an online encyclopedia, it may provide a special search function just for pictures. The welcome screen for an online encyclopedia might look like this:

Welcome to the Encyclopedia

Choose a letter to browse the encyclopedia.
Or, type the key words to search. Use AND between key words.
A B C D E F G H I J K L M N O P Q R S T U V W X Y Z

Search the Encyclopedia for:

Search for:

☐ Articles

☐ Pictures, Flags, Maps, Charts, Sounds

☐ Web Sites

☐ All of the Above

If you need help, click here.

If you want both articles and pictures, then check the first two boxes. If you just want pictures, check only the second box.

Directions: Use the computer screen above to answer these questions.

1. Explain how to get just pictures of optical illusions. _____

_____

_____

_____

_____

2. Explain how to find both articles and pictures about American oil painters.

_____

_____

_____

_____

© Scott Foresman 5

Online reference sources and web pages often include pictures with captions. You can usually click on either the picture or the caption to get more information. For example, a page about optical illusions might look like the one below. To get more information, you can click on any of the three pictures, any of the three underlined captions, or any of the four underlined links at the bottom of the page.

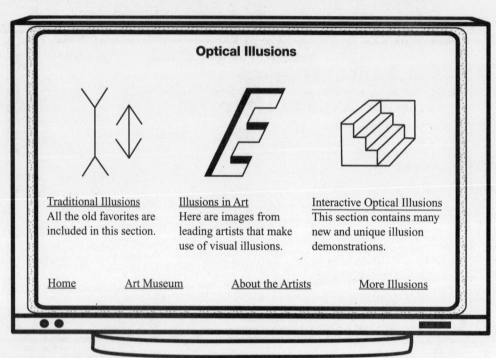

Directions: Use the web page above to answer these questions.

3. Where could you click to find a demonstration of an interactive optical illusion?

_____

_____

4. Where could you click to find a biography of the artist Scott Kim? _____

_____

_____

5. How are captions in an online encyclopedia similar to captions in a print encyclopedia? How are they different?

_____

_____

_____

_____

Notes for Home: Your child learned how to access and interpret pictures and captions that might be found on a CD-ROM or web page. *Home Activity:* Use a book, magazine, or newspaper to discuss with your child the information shown in a picture and its caption.

© Scott Foresman 5